D0008395

William Burroughs
El Hombre Invisible

Barry Miles

This revised and updated edition first published in 2002 by
Virgin Books Ltd
Thames Wharf Studios
Rainville Road
London
W6 9HA

First published in paperback in 1993 by Virgin Publishing Ltd

First published in Great Britain in 1992 by Virgin Publishing Ltd

Copyright © Barry Miles 1992, 2002

The right of Barry Miles to be identified as the Author of this Work has been
asserted by him in accordance with the Copyright, Designs and Patents Act, 1988.

*This book is sold subject to the condition that it shall not, by way of trade or
otherwise, be lent, resold, hired out or otherwise circulated without the publisher's
prior written consent in any form of binding or cover other than that in which it is
published and without a similar condition including this condition being imposed
on the subsequent purchaser.*

A catalogue record for this book is available from the British Library.

ISBN 0 7535 0707 2

Typeset by TW Typesetting, Plymouth, Devon

Printed in Great Britain by
Mackays of Chatham PLC, Chatham, Kent

Contents

Also by Barry Miles:

ALLEN GINSBERG: A BIOGRAPHY

JACK KEROUAC: KING OF THE BEATS

THE BEAT HOTEL: GINSBERG, BURROUGHS & CORSO
  IN PARIS, 1957–1963

PAUL McCARTNEY: MANY YEARS FROM NOW

WILLIAM S BURROUGHS: A BIBLIOGRAPHY, 1953–1973
(with Joe Maynard)

List of Illustrations

Acknowledgements

Thanks to William Burroughs, my favourite writer, whom I was privileged to know for 32 years. I first corresponded with Bill back in 1964, when he was living in Tangier, and first met him in 1965, introduced by my friend Ian Sommerville, who also introduced me to Brion Gysin that same year. Between June and November 1972, I catalogued the Burroughs archive, working with Bill, often on a daily basis, at his flat in Duke Street, St James's. I made occasional journal notes after dinner or after conversations with him, many of which have been used here in my descriptions of his job as an exterminator, his childhood, Scientology, life in London et cetera. Brion Gysin lived in the same building and I kept similar notes of the talks we had, some of which I have also used. Bill allowed me to interview him in both London and in Lawrence, Kansas, and also read through an early draft of the manuscript, making a number of helpful comments. I also extend thanks to my friend James Grauerholz, Bill's secretary, who read the manuscript and made many useful suggestions – most of which I acted upon. James also made available archive material and information to which I would not otherwise have had access. I would like to thank him for his unstinting hospitality when I was in Kansas, along with Steven Lowe and the late Michael Emerton. My ideas on Burroughs' literary output were most influenced by Oliver Harris' superb unpublished thesis, *The Last Words of William Burroughs*. Harris is the editor of Burroughs' selected letters for Viking Penguin. Alan Ansen's essay *William Burroughs*, published by Water Row Books in 1986, remains for me the most insightful American analysis of his work. I was helped enormously by conversations with two old friends: Allen Ginsberg, who first recognised Bill's genius, and Victor Bockris, author of

With William Burroughs. Thanks also to Michael Horovitz, Peter Wollen and Paul McCartney for sharing memories with me about Bill's sojourn in London. Thanks to Ken Lohf and his staff at the Rare Books and Manuscript department of the Butler Library of Columbia University, New York City. To Andrew Wylie, Jeff Posternak and Rose Gaete at the Wylie Agency and to Kirstie Addis at Virgin for giving me an opportunity to update the text and correct some of the more glaring errors. For this updated version I must thank Jim McCrary of William Burroughs Communications, Wayne Propst, Andrew Sclanders of Beatbooks.com, and Marilyn Wurzburger and her staff at the Special Collections department of the Hayden Library, Arizona State University at Tempe. Love and thanks to Rosemary Bailey for yet again acting as my 'in-house' editor, and for her suggestions and support.

1 Cultural Icon

William Seward Burroughs II: *el hombre invisible*, Old Bull Lee, Inspector Lee of the Nova Police, the God-father of punk, the Heavy Metal Kid himself; described by JG Ballard as 'The most important writer to emerge since the Second World War', and by Norman Mailer as 'The only living American novelist who may conceivably be possessed by genius.' When questioned, Samuel Beckett grunted, 'Well, he's a writer' (praise indeed from that source). It was a heavy image load to live up to.

William Burroughs probably had more influence on popular culture than upon literature. His ideas, images and language reached the general population largely by non-literary means: through films, videos, records, tapes or through art works by the many artists who were influenced by him. His ideas reached people who never read his books, and who thought of him only as a celebrity.

His work had considerable influence on the more literate end of rock and roll, and his imagery filtered into the modern cinema. There was something about Burroughs which acted as a catalyst, making things happen, inspiring people to do things, even though the man himself liked to live a quiet life with a severely restricted circle of friends. It was the *idea* of Burroughs that appealed, not the man; the popular Burroughs, the cult icon, reached them via printed and electronic media. This Burroughs was the man who saw the abyss and came back to report on it – Burroughs *el hombre invisible*.

Even before he began writing, William Burroughs was the epitome of cool. His drugs, his sardonic manner and interest in

1

fringe knowledge made him a modern-day Coleridge to Columbia College students such as Jack Kerouac and Allen Ginsberg, who were all attracted to him as a teacher back in the mid-40s. He introduced them to Hart Crane and Céline, Spengler and Count Korzybski.

It was that small circle of friends who later became known as the Beat Generation. The original group first met in New York in 1944 and all shared an apartment in the Upper West Side in 1945–6, but it was many years before they published anything, and it was not until the late 50s that they and their circles received the 'Beat Generation' sobriquet. The group was more of a fraternity of spirit and attitude than a literary movement, and their writings have little in common with each other; what they did have in common was an adverse reaction to the ongoing carnage of World War II, the dropping of A-bombs on civilian targets, and the puritan small-mindedness that still characterised American life. They shared an interest in widening the area of consciousness, by whatever means available.

The three original 'founders' of the group who had shared the apartment were all to produce works which are now regarded as classics of their time: Allen Ginsberg's *Howl* was published in 1955; Jack Kerouac's *On The Road* came out in 1957; and Burroughs' *The Naked Lunch* was first published in 1959.

Though Burroughs' first book, *Junkie*, appeared in 1953, it was *The Naked Lunch* that initially attracted a cognoscenti of the avant-garde and hipster to his work. They discovered a picaresque, Swiftian satire, a savage and devastating attack on the hypocrisies of politics, science and big business, filled with pot-head humour and some of the most memorable characters in modern literature: Dr Benway, Dr 'Fingers' Schafer 'the lobotomy kid', AJ and of course William Lee himself, the author's alter-ego. It was the book that made Burroughs' reputation. It was banned in Boston and scraped through only on appeal in a censorship trial that established the obscenity standards in America for the following decades. Of course, a censorship trial is very good for sales, and it gave the book a high profile, although Burroughs himself decided not to attend the proceedings. Now *The Naked Lunch* is in print in seventeen languages.

The trial established Burroughs' literary reputation in the USA but in the public mind he remained in the same category as Henry Miller, a serious writer whose work was supposedly pornographic. Since Burroughs lived abroad he was rarely interviewed, and before the mid-70s he was known mainly as an associate of Kerouac and Ginsberg: a shadowy Beat Generation figure who had rejected the United States in favour of Europe and North Africa. The notion of Burroughs as a cult personality was a more recent development.

Throughout the 60s and early 70s, his social life revolved around a small group of old friends, and most of his periodical appearances were in small mimeo literary magazines or else in underground newspapers. He was legendary in certain circles associated with the avant-garde and the underground press, but it was not until the 70s that he became a national celebrity. When Burroughs returned to the United States in 1974 after a 25-year voluntary exile, a great many people were surprised to find that he was still alive. His books were well known, but over the years he had himself become invisible.

When *The Naked Lunch* was first published, its early readers were delighted to learn that Burroughs the man was as extraordinary as his book: a homosexual who had shot his wife and lived in self-imposed exile in Europe and North Africa. In the early 60s, the great American corporations were the epitome of respectability, so the fact that Burroughs was the grandson of the inventor of the adding machine, and founder of the massive Burroughs Corporation, was seized upon with glee.

In the 50s, when drugs were sinister and evil, Burroughs spoke openly and with authority about his heroin addiction and his many experiments with both hallucinogenic and addictive drugs. In fact Burroughs' first appearance in a periodical was in the January 1957 issue of the scholarly medical journal *The British Journal of Addiction* which contained an extraordinary unromantic and intelligent article entitled 'Letter from a Master Addict to Dangerous Drugs'. The autobiographical volume *Junkie* had been published earlier, in 1953, but under the pseudonym of William Lee. (Throughout this book I use Burroughs' preferred spelling of *Junky* unless referring to the Ace edition, *Junkie*.) He used the same pseudonym for the first magazine extract from *The Naked Lunch* which appeared in *Black Mountain Review* in 1957. Later sections, published in the *Chicago Review* in 1958, were under his own name. (The Olympia edition – the only edition that Burroughs himself edited – was called *The Naked Lunch*, and I have retained this title throughout, even though the American edition dropped the article.)

Photographs from the 50s reveal a thin, middle-aged, aristocratic man with a bony visage, wearing a three-piece business suit and tie, often topped by a Chesterfield with velvet lapels and a hat. He quickly became the most famous junkie writer alive.

Then there was the voice: the flat mid-west accent of TS Eliot or Ezra Pound, dry as paper, the clipped syllables of a 1920s newscaster reporting the Great Crash, sometimes affecting a campy edge. When the spoken-word album *Call Me Burroughs* came out in 1965, it quickly became required listening for everyone with any pretensions to being at all hip. Many people have said they didn't really understand Burroughs until they heard *that voice* – the voice of a banker saying all those outrageous things.

This was the man whom the Spanish boys called *el hombre invisible* as he slipped quietly through the narrow alleys of Tangier, looking for a fix:

> I had not taken a bath in a year nor changed my clothes or removed them except to stick a needle every hour in the fibrous grey wooden flesh of terminal addiction . . . I did absolutely nothing. I could look at the end of my shoe for eight hours. [*The Naked Lunch*]

In the late 50s most people thought that drugs were confined to jazz musicians and their circles. For the scion of an old St Louis family to be doing this stuff seemed pretty outrageous, and the more that the disgruntled establishment, led by *Time* magazine, expressed their aversion and contempt, the more young people, naturally, wanted to know.

Burroughs was living at the Beat Hotel in Paris when *The Naked Lunch* was published, and the young American and British hipsters who also lived there, or were a part of the

Olympia Press circle, were quick to pick up on and promote the work.

After the initial flurry of interest in the Beat Generation, each Beat had his own decade. In the United States, the 50s was the decade of Jack Kerouac, and of the up-market soft-core porn magazines he wrote for, such as *Escapade*, *Swank*, *Nugget*; it was the decade of the hip, urbane bachelor who planned his wardrobe from Hugh Hefner's *Playboy*, liked cool white jazz (Brubeck, Baker, Mulligan) and maybe smoked a little reefer at weekends. Kerouac was his man, with his fantasy of freedom from responsibility – on the road, where the chicks were available and undemanding, and where the wine flowed freely.

Allen Ginsberg had the 60s. He achieved a certain notoriety and fame during the obscenity trial of *Howl* in 1957, but disappeared to Europe and India, only returning in 1963 to take up the mantle that Kerouac had drunkenly dropped. Ginsberg was the harbinger of the flower children and the hippie movement, a movement in which he invested huge amounts of time and energy. He advocated the use of LSD and marijuana to expand consciousness and promote spiritual awareness. His poetry is an extraordinary chronicle of the period, even if many of the kids with a poster of Ginsberg on their wall had never actually read his work.

It wasn't until the New Wave punk avant-garde of late 70s New York that Bill Burroughs finally came into his own as a media celebrity. Returning to America in the early 70s as the prodigal son, he was fêted, honoured and toasted by his fellow writers and hangers-on. Punk singer Patti Smith proclaimed him as 'up there with the Pope'. Frank Zappa read the talking asshole routine from *The Naked Lunch* live onstage, and in December 1981, Lauren Hutton introduced him on *Saturday Night Live*, then the hippest TV show on Earth, as 'in my opinion the greatest living American writer'.

The reasons for awarding him such adulation were not so clear: as with Ginsberg before him, many of his fans had not actually read much of his work; they simply liked his image: the deadpan expressionless businessman, neatly attired in short hair and suit, who took all manner of drugs and had ideas which made their parents froth at the mouth. It was a complex image, and one about which Burroughs himself was ambivalent, as he told poet Gerard Malanga in 1974:

> Often they have a picture, an image, that they have projected on me which may have nothing at all to do with me, at all ... I feel that for a writer to be a novelist, he doesn't have by nature of his profession a clear-cut image of himself or a clear-cut image in general. And if he cultivates his image too much his work will suffer. For example, a perfect case in point is Hemingway ... Finally ... there's nothing there but the image, Papa Hemingway ... I think it was disastrous to his work, that's what finally killed him: his own image ... I think that any writer is to some extent naturally typecast by his choice of subject matter. Like Genet is typecast as the saintly convict. And Graham Greene, of course, it's the old whiskey priest. Uh, of course, I'm no longer a drug addict.

This, however, was how many of his fans saw him: Old Bull Lee or Bill Hubbard from Kerouac's books, Inspector Lee of the Nova Police from his own, a man dedicated to saving the planet, albeit in his own highly individual way.

It was Ginsberg who first drew attention to *The Naked Lunch* by including it in his dedication to *Howl* in 1955: 'William Seward Burroughs, author of *Naked Lunch*, an endless novel which will drive everybody mad.' Bill's own autobiographical first novel, *Junkie*, was at that time still published under the pseudonym of William Lee, though it later came to be the main source of the image of Bill as a distant, ice-cold junkie in an anonymous suit.

Rock musicians were among the first to pick up on Burroughs, attracted by his outrageous imagery and the drug references – popular music, jazz or rock, has always been informed by drug culture. In the early 60s in Paris, London and New York, there was considerable crossover between poets, artists and musicians; the arts community in all these cities was relatively small and most people knew or knew of each other. The early 60s folk revival merged with rock and roll to create a mature new musical form which many young musicians and poets saw as the most appropriate vehicle for what they wanted to do.

One example was Cass Elliot and Dennis Doherty, both later of the Mamas and Papas, who, in 1963, joined with Zal Yanovsky and John Sebastian, both later of the Lovin' Spoonful, to form the Mugwumps. They made a single and an album then split up. It is easy to imagine them all sitting round, smoking pot, trying to come up with a name for a group. Someone reaches for a copy of *The Naked Lunch*: 'A Near East Mugwump sits naked on a bar stool covered in pink silk . . .'

In Paris, the Australian poet Daevid Allen was part of the Left Bank scene, centred around the Beat Hotel. He could be seen at the Domaine Poetique, with his strange thick steel-rimmed glasses, reading alongside Brion Gysin. He knew Burroughs and the Olympia Press crowd, and it was not surprising that, when he moved to London in 1966 to start a rock and roll group, he took the name the Soft Machine, from the title of Burroughs' third novel. Some years later Robert Wyatt, the original drummer with the band, started his own group. He called it Matching Mole, after the French edition of *The Soft Machine*: *La Machine Molle*.

One of the earliest, and perhaps the most enduring, proofs of Burroughs' prestige in rock circles is his presence on the front sleeve of *Sergeant Pepper's Lonely Hearts Club Band* which shows the Beatles standing before life-size cut-out photographs of people that they personally liked and admired. Burroughs was chosen by Paul McCartney. After being given the Beatles' imprimatur, Burroughs could no longer be regarded as obscure. His presence on the *Sergeant Pepper* sleeve undoubtedly introduced his work to many people who would not otherwise have read it. (A key to identifying the people on the sleeve appeared in many fan magazines and books.)

Another borrowing from *The Naked Lunch* was the term 'heavy metal'. The phrase 'heavy metal thunder' was first used in a lyric by Steppenwolf in their 1968 hard rock anthem 'Born To Be Wild', and was further popularised when the track was featured in the cult film *Easy Rider*. And in 1972, when Donald Fagen and Walter Becker were searching for a name for their new band, they wanted something hip and amusing; naturally they turned to William Burroughs, and found the perfect name: Steely Dan – the name of a dildo in *The Naked Lunch*. It even had the advantage of having a hidden meaning that the fans could boast about knowing:

> Mary is strapping on a rubber penis. 'Steely Dan III from Yokohama,' she says, caressing the shaft. Milk spurts across the room.
> Be sure that milk is pasteurised. Don't go giving me some kinda awful cow disease like anthrax or glanders or aftosa . . .

I got into William Burroughs through jazz [said Becker in 1974]. There always used to be a Beatnik corner in the bookshop – Ginsberg, Corso, Snyder and so on, and that's where I first came across *Naked Lunch*. Naming ourselves from something in the book shouldn't be taken too literally, though – for us the name has other associations, such as the fact that our band has a pedal steel guitar – but we have certainly picked up on some of his world view. I admire Burroughs a lot. I think certain of his ideas are valid. His ideas about control for instance. Not just in the drug sense but control by laws, by media, by newspapers, and so on. It's an extreme idea but I think valid.

'Yes. I've heard them,' said Burroughs of the band. He heard the track 'East St. Louis Toodle-Oo' on *Pretzel Logic* and said he liked it. It is a Duke Ellington title, but Burroughs used it in *The Naked Lunch*: 'Panorama of the City of Interzone. Opening bars of "East St. Louis Toodle-Oo" . . . at times loud and clear, then faint and intermittent like music down a windy street . . .'

It was ironic that despite his great popularity among rock musicians, Burroughs knew little or nothing about rock music and never listened to it for pleasure. *The Naked Lunch*, which once had the working title of *Word Horde*, became a treasure trove of words and phrases for rock groups, but the traffic was very much one-way.

In an interview in the early 70s, Burroughs revealed, 'I have heard The Insect Trust' [another band named after one of his lines]. 'That's very fancy music, a bit like the Pink Floyd. My relation with rock has been more peripheral. I have known people and written things, but I'm not knowledgeable on it.' In rock terms, Insect Trust was high art; one track on their album *Hoboken Saturday Night* took its lyrics from Thomas Pynchon's *V*. The band was fronted by Robert Palmer (not the British singer), one of the best *Rolling Stone* magazine journalists, whom Burroughs probably knew of through Brion Gysin. One of Palmer's early articles was on Gysin and the Joujouka musicians of Morocco, so Burroughs' influence on the name of the band came from within the cognoscenti. Insect Trust came together in the late 60s and made two albums before disbanding.

David Bowie, in Alan Yentob's BBC television documentary, *The Cracked Actor*, demonstrated how he wrote the words for his 1974 album *Diamond Dogs*: 'I use Burroughs' cut-up technique,' he explained. The camera focused in to show Bowie tearing sheets of lyrics down the middle and moving the torn edges against each other to find new lines created by the juxtaposition. Bowie was very involved in the Arts Laboratory movement in the 60s, and even started one of his own, where he was the main performer. Burroughs was a strong, though invisible, presence at the London Arts Lab; his films *Towers Open Fire* and *Cut Ups* were constantly screened at the UFO and other London underground clubs, so Bowie would have been very familiar with his work long before he made *Diamond Dogs*.

Earlier that year Bowie did an interview with Bill for *Rolling Stone* magazine:

Bowie: How do you take the picture that people paint of you?
WSB: They try to categorise you. They want to see their picture of you and if they don't see their picture of you they're very upset.

Bowie arrived at the Bunker, Burroughs' New York apartment, in the late 70s, carrying a four-foot-high vase of flowers, which he set at Bill's feet. He also had with him a Polaroid of a painting of Burroughs that he was working on. He had painted everything except the face, which was blank. The background to the portrait was a burning red sky. Burroughs was working on *Cities of the Red Night* at the time, though Bowie could not have known that, and found the coincidence very pleasing. He posed, giving his forced grin, while Bowie took Polaroids of his face.

One reason that the 60s groups were aware of Burroughs, and appreciated him, was because he was very active in the underground press at that time, giving interviews, writing articles and reviews. Most of the so-called 'progressive' bands had their origins in the underground clubs and depended heavily on the underground press for reviews and promotion. Even ten years after it was first published, *The Naked Lunch* was still a cult book, the sort of book groups took with them to their secluded cottage in Wales when they were 'getting their thing together'.

In the late 70s, it was the turn of the punks to discover his work and a fresh bunch of bands raided his books for names. Among those who got as far as releasing albums were Dead Fingers Talk and Naked Lunch. The punks felt very alienated from society and Burroughs was one of the few authors whose work they could relate to; *Trouser Press* magazine called him 'The Greatgodfather of Punk' and *New Musical Express* described him as the 'Godfather of Beat'. Burroughs himself felt far removed from all this:

I am not a punk and I don't know why anybody would consider me the godfather of punk. How do you define punk? The only definition of the word is that it might refer to a young person who is simply called a punk because he is young, or some kind of petty criminal. In that sense some of my characters may be considered punks, but the word simply did not exist in the 50s. I suppose you could say James Dean epitomised it in *Rebel Without A Cause* but still, what is it?

I think the so-called punk movement is indeed a media creation. I have, however, sent a letter of support to the Sex Pistols in England because I've always said that the country doesn't stand a chance until you have 20,000 people saying 'Bugger The Queen!' And I support the Sex Pistols because this is a constructive, necessary criticism of a country which is bankrupt.

Burroughs didn't ever want to associate with famous rock stars, but they came to find him, more often than not with Burroughs' friends arranging the introduction. At his seventieth birthday party in New York in 1984 he spoke briefly with Sting and Andy Summers from the Police, then one of the biggest bands in the world, and had his photograph taken with them for the *New York Post*. Later Bill warned some of his other guests who might have been carrying drugs, 'I don't know whether you're holding, but someone told me that those guys were cops.'

The tendency for the gossip columnists to regard him as a celebrity left Burroughs slightly bemused: 'It isn't true that I spend my time going to parties with Andy Warhol. I hate parties. I hardly know Mick Jagger, I don't know those pop people.'

Burroughs did see Warhol a number of times in New York during the 70s and early 80s, and Warhol was interested enough to plan a portrait of Bill. Burroughs visited the Factory one day and Warhol took 20 or 30 Polaroids of him in different poses. The photograph Bill liked the best was one of him with his hand up to his face – 'It makes me look like a French intellectual,' he said. Unfortunately Warhol never executed a portrait unless he was commissioned first, and since Burroughs was not about to come up with the money, the painting never happened.

In the 80s, there was a fusion between punk, avant-garde music, and what has been called 'modern classical'. The most prominent of these groups, Sonic Youth, a cross between the Velvet Underground and noise-music, played on Burroughs' 1990 CD *Dead City Radio*. Other performers on the same CD included ex-Velvet Underground John Cale, ex-Steely Dan Donald Fagen, and ex-Blondie Chris Stein. Bill delivered a memorable performance of 'Falling In Love Again' – in the original German. It was one of his most effective forays into recording.

On a less pronounced level, Burroughs also made his mark on the movies. His imagery has filtered into the modern cinema – the space bar in *Star Wars*, for instance, owes much to Hassan's Rumpus Room in *The Naked Lunch*, and the *Mad Max* movies are like *The Wild Boys* come to life. The distinct Burroughs influence on the science-fiction and cyberpunk end of Hollywood is not always as direct as in *Star Wars*, and often appears filtered through other sources. However, in the case of Alex Cox's cult movie *Repo Man*, the debt is acknowledged by having Dr Benway paged over the Tannoy in a hospital scene. And David Cronenberg's 1991 film based on *The Naked Lunch* saw William Lee and the Mugwumps finally making the big screen, though Burroughs had no hand in the script.

Despite not going to the cinema, Bill appeared in a considerable number of films, many of which subsequently become cult classics. These include Conrad Rooks' 1966 film *Chappaqua*, where he played the doctor who turned into Opium Jones, the personification of junk and a character from Burroughs' own writing, and the 1989 *Drugstore Cowboy* by Gus van Sant. One of van Sant's first films was an award-winning student short of Burroughs' *The Discipline of D.E.*, and in 1990 he made a short film called *A Thanksgiving Prayer* taken from Bill's CD *Dead City Radio*. Van Sant also wrote and played guitar on a record called *William S Burroughs, The Elvis of Letters*, which consisted of four songs based on Burroughs texts. One of them, 'Millions of Images', was released as a single.

In *Drugstore Cowboy*, Bill acted out another favourite stereotype, the old junkie priest, the drugs *paterfamilias*. Starring alongside Matt Dillon, Bill was so convincing in his cameo role that many people saw him as the true star of the film. When Gus van Sant first approached Burroughs, the character was to be a middle-aged junkie called Bob Murphy. Burroughs and Gus van Sant met in a hotel room in Portland, where the movie was set, and Bill talked about being an old junkie and how he would have behaved in Murphy's circumstances. Bill and James Grauerholz jointly came up with the idea that the character should be the priest, from Burroughs' story 'The Priest They Called Him'. Van Sant loved the idea and took notes in order to rewrite the part for this new character, but his rewrite didn't really capture it, partly because he was so busy making the film. James Grauerholz then suggested that he try writing the scenes. 'I rewrote four scenes for William,' Grauerholz said, 'and then William put his own unique polish on it, his own imprimatur. So I'm pleased to say that I wrote the line, "Drugs have been systematically scapegoated and penalised in this country" and others like that.'

The film was set in Portland in 1971, with Dillon playing a swaggering dope fiend who organises raids on drugstores to get his dope supplies from the source, and he turned in a fine performance in what was his best and most challenging role in years. The film was very well received, and was praised for not toeing the Hollywood moral line on drugs. Both *Less Than Zero* and *Wired* had followed the Nancy Reagan dictum of 'Just Say No', whereas *Drugstore Cowboy* gives a very authentic and amusing glimpse of the life of a junkie without resorting to a moralistic tone. Van Sant said that the message of *Drugstore Cowboy* isn't so much 'Just Say No'; it's 'Decide For Yourself'.

Burroughs' other film roles included playing the mafia don in Jacob Burckhardt's *It Doesn't Pay To Be An Honest Citizen*, and the energy czar in Robert Frank's 1981 *Energy And How To Get It*, in which he starred alongside Dr John. The film combined documentary and fiction to tell the story of 'Lightnin' Bob', Robert Golka, an engineer who received money from the Carter administration to develop fusion as a cheap energy source, and whose career was destroyed by big-business interests. Bill, playing the Ugly American, snarled such lines as 'He knows too much, we'd better shut him down.' This was a character familiar to him from the stage roles he'd played in London in the late 60s and early 70s, when he acted in *The Chicago Conspiracy*, Charles Marowitz's adaptation of the court transcript of the trial of Abbie Hoffman, Jerry Rubin *et al.* for their antics at the 1968 Democratic Convention in Chicago. Burroughs played grumpy Judge Hoffman, constantly masticating non-existent cud. This was followed in 1971 by *Flash Gordon and the Angels*, by David Z Mairowitz, of which BA Young in *The Financial Times* wrote, '. . . surely no-one could fail to enjoy William S Burroughs's performance as the 38th President of the United States.' Critic Irving Wardle wrote:

'The contrast between Burroughs's reptilian mask and grating voice, and the assortment of two-eyed winks and half kisses with which parts of his face mutiny against the whole, is quite marvellous.' He had to drink a lot of whisky to get into the right mood of 'controlled vituperation'.

In *Decoder* by Klaus Maeck he appeared as a back-room technician, enthusiastically digging into a piece of electronic equipment with a screwdriver. (The footage was repeated in Maeck's 1991 documentary *William S Burroughs: Commissioner of Sewers*.)

For *Twister*, a 1990 black comedy by Michael Almereyda starring Harry Dean Stanton, Crispin Glover and Suzie Aimes, Bill played a good ol' country boy, shooting at targets in his barn. In Laurie Anderson's 1986 *Home of the Brave*, he made a brief but memorable appearance as her dancing partner. He told Allen Ginsberg: 'We moved in tango steps across the stage then turned and came back. I still don't know how to tango.' It was, however, a spirited attempt. The tune was 'Language Is a Virus', a track based on one of his own lines. Burroughs had done a cross-country reading tour with Laurie Anderson and John Giorno, and it is said that for the first five days on the road Burroughs thought that she was a boy.

He also performed 'Sharkey's Night' on Anderson's *Mr Heartbreak* album, synching to the rhythm track using headphones. Co-producing the session with Anderson was Bill Laswell who later, in 1989, produced an entire album based around Burroughs' description in *The Western Lands* of the seven souls of the ancient Egyptians. The album, *Seven Souls*, was performed by Laswell's jazz-fusion duo Material and featured Burroughs reading from the text as an integral part of the musical arrangement. He also appeared on Material's *Hallucination Engine* album and, after Bill's death, Laswell released a CD of remixes of the *Seven Souls* material called *The Road to the Western Lands*.

Despite all this, in a 1985 interview Burroughs maintained, 'I have very little contact with pop culture.'

Burroughs' very high profile in the late 70s was caused, to a great extent, by a book project undertaken by writer Victor Bockris, who arranged a succession of dinner parties in New

York from 1974–9 at which famous people would dine with Burroughs. These included Andy Warhol, Lou Reed, Joe Strummer, Susan Sontag, Christopher Isherwood, Tennessee Williams and Mick Jagger. Bockris taperecorded the conversations and collaged the transcripts into a book, *With William Burroughs: A Report From The Bunker*.

While working on the book, he published transcripts of the tapes in dozens of magazines, from sex sheets like *National Screw* and *Chic*, through mimeographed literary magazines to glossies such as the *New Review* in London. This encouraged gossip columnists to mention Burroughs: *People* magazine ran their first story in 1974, shortly after Burroughs returned to the States, and, as the 70s progressed, squibs and stories began appearing in magazines such as *Oui*, *High Times*, and Andy Warhol's *Interview*. It was a long time coming, but finally Burroughs was an all-American celebrity.

It was in Europe that Burroughs first gained a reputation; he lived there and was first published there. The Europeans had a high regard for experimental writing and saw his cut-ups and three-column experiments of 1959 and throughout the 60s as being in the long tradition of Artaud, Rimbaud, Jean Genet, Céline, Dadaism, Surrealism and particularly Lettrism. He acquired a number of followers, and a 'cut-up' school developed which focused very much on collaboration. His main collaborator was the painter Brion Gysin, who actually invented cut-ups, but Burroughs worked with a number of other writers, including Carl Weissner, Claude Pelieu, Sinclair Beiles and Jeff Nuttall. Also involved were Alfred Behrens, Jürgen Ploog, Gerhard Hanak, Walter Hartmann, Jörg Fauser and the American poets Harold Norse and Mary Beach.

At the same time, a number of European translators, many of whom were academics or intellectuals, began work on Burroughs' texts. The first French translations were made by Claude Pelieu and Mary Beach, who worked on all the major books and routines up until *The Wild Boys*, with the exception of *The Naked Lunch*, which was translated by Jack Kahane. They were followed by Henri and Jean Chopin, Gerard-Georges Lemaire and Philippe Mikriammos, a group of French intellectuals loosely associated with the magazine *Tel Quel*. It was from this group that Burroughs received his imprimatur in France as a serious avant-garde writer, a development which eventually led to the famous Colloque de Tanger, organised by Gerard-Georges Lemaire, which was held in Geneva from 24–28 September 1975. Many weighty papers on Burroughs' work were presented by a group of largely European contributors. The proceedings, which have not been translated, were published in two thick volumes by Christian Bourgois Editeur in Paris.

It is significant that the first full-length critical analysis of Burroughs' work appeared in French: critic Daniel Odier published a book-length interview with Burroughs in Editions Pierre Belfond's 'Entretiens' series in 1969 (this was later published in English, in a much revised form, as *The Job*). The first English-language survey came from Eric Mottram, professor of English and American studies at Kings College, London. His *Algebra of Need* first appeared in 1971, and was re-issued, revised and considerably expanded, in 1977. A second French study followed Mottram's, when Philippe Mikriammos published his *William S Burroughs: La Vie et l'Oeuvre* in 1975 (Paris, Editions Seghers). This was followed by *À la Recherche d'un Corps* by Serge Grunberg in 1979 (Paris, Editions du Seuil), and there have been other subsequent French studies. The first American criticism was not until 1985, when Jennie Skerl wrote a volume for the Twayne United States Authors Series, aimed at college students.

It was in the 80s that Burroughs' influence upon literature began to show. The development of the new genre of science fiction known as cyberpunk would simply not have been possible without him: William Gibson (*Neuromancer*), Pat Cadigan (*Synners*), John Shirley (the *Eclipse* trilogy), Bruce Sterling (*Schismatrix*), Richard Kadrey (*Metrophage*), Charles Platt (*The Gas*), Misha (*Red Spider*), Rudy Rucker (*Wet Ware*), and dozens more could not have written as they did without having first read and absorbed Burroughs.

The cyberpunks were influenced also by writers such as Norman Spinrad, Thomas Pynchon, Michael Moorcock and particularly by JG Ballard, but the core is always Burroughs. In the 60s the *New Worlds* group of writers, Michael Moorcock in particular, took the idea of non-linearity and in many ways prefigured Burroughs' own later work. Moorcock's Jerry Cornelius novels could easily be seen as influenced by the *Cities of the Red Night* trilogy, had they not been written two decades earlier. Interestingly, it is not necessarily *The Naked Lunch* that informs these writers: cyberpunk is in part defined by its fast-moving, dense imagery which owes more to the cut-up trilogy than *The Naked Lunch*. Work such as Mark Leyner's *My Cousin, My Gastroenterologist* (quoted below), for example, has a tremendous amount in common with Burroughs' *Ticket That Exploded*: 'Your club sandwiches are made of mulch and wind perfumed with newsprint. Your frilly toothpicks are the deciduous trees of school days. I was an infinitely hot and dense dot. So begins the autobiography of a feral child who was raised by huge and lurid puppets.'

In 'Cyberpunk 101: A Schematic Guide' by Richard Kadrey and Larry McCaffery, included in *Storming the Reality Studio, A Casebook of Cyberpunk and Postmodern Fiction* (Durham, NC, 1991) edited by McCaffery, the authors say of *The Naked Lunch*: 'The influence of this book is enormous. Without *Naked Lunch* there would probably be no cyberpunk.' It is no accident that the book's title is taken from *Nova Express*, and the collection itself opens with an epigram from Burroughs.

In a discussion about cyberpunk in *Mondo 2000*, the musician Glenn Branca said, 'To me, the person who has the key to this kind of writing is Burroughs. You can go back and re-read Burroughs and even though you understand his world, it's always a mystery . . . My hope is that cyberpunk is going to end up simply becoming Burroughs. I'm just looking for more Burroughs!'

Cyberpunk is not the only area of writing to show a distinct Burroughian influence: writers such as Dennis Cooper (*Try*), Will Self (*The Quantity Theory of Insanity*), Iain Sinclair (*White Chappell, Scarlet Tracings*), Ronald Sukenick (*Doggy Bag*) or David Wojnarowicz (*In the Shadow of the American Dream*) simply could not have written what they did without Burroughs leading the way. Like the Beatles in popular music, Burroughs sits, an enormous unavoidable presence in the history of avant-garde arts. As Glenn Branca said, 'To go beyond Burroughs – I can't even begin to imagine.'

2 Narrative: The Saint Louis Blues

The first literary effort by William Burroughs, written at the age of eight, was a ten-page novel inspired by Ernest Thompson Seton's children's book, *Biography of a Grizzly Bear*. 'My first literary essay was called *The Autobiography of a Wolf*,' Burroughs wrote. 'People laughed and said: "You mean the biography of a wolf." No, I meant the autobiography of a wolf and still do . . . because I felt myself to be the wolf. I was identifying myself with my wolf. It was about ten pages. There was a red-haired wolf: "He was saddened by the death of his mate, and weakened by hunger he was overtaken by a grizzly bear . . ." '

Burroughs' characters, no matter how disagreeable they may seem to some people, are always drawn with complete conviction. There is no artifice, and the characters are not contrived, but always spring fully-formed from his imagination. Nor is there any character development (a characteristic of writing by children). It is as if his characters were waiting in the wings for Bill to write them. Literature itself was often the inspiration for Burroughs' writing, and he sometimes found a character waiting in someone else's book; in later years he would appropriate characters and even entire passages from books he particularly liked. The identification with and belief in their characters which characterises writing by children was to remain with Burroughs. His childhood would also remain a continual source of characters, images and inspiration.

William Seward Burroughs II was born on 5 February 1914, in St Louis, Missouri. His parents, Mortimer and Laura Lee, were well off and enjoyed a life which today would be unthinkable for anyone but the very rich. They were attended by a butler, a cook, and a maid. There was a gardener and a yard man. Young Billy and his older brother Mortimer had a Welsh nanny, Mary Evans, to whom Billy was greatly attached, but she left under mysterious circumstances when Billy was four years old, greatly upsetting the little boy.

They lived at 4664 Pershing Avenue, which still exists, a large, unpretentious red brick three-storey house with a slate roof, set back on a quiet tree-lined street with a 50-foot lawn in front. It had Victorian-style leaded glass windows and a sleeping porch. A dressing room and bathroom led off the master bedroom and there were servants' bedrooms on the top floor. There was a sizable back garden filled with roses, peonies, irises and a fish pond which attracted frogs. The gardens were separated from each other by high wooden fences overgrown with morning glory and rose briars. At the end was an ash pit which acted as a septic tank – 'No-one from Sanitation sniffing around in those days.' Beyond the garden was the River des Peres. Burroughs wrote in *Cobble Stone Gardens*:

> At that time the River of the Fathers was one of the sights and smells of St Louis though not exactly a tourist attraction. The River des Peres was a vast open sewer that meandered through the city . . . I remember as a child with my young cousin standing on its grassy banks and watching as turds shot out into the yellow water from vents along the sides.
>
> 'Hey looky . . . someone just did it.'
>
> During the summer months the smell of shit and coal gas permeated the city, bubbling up from the river's murky depths to cover the oily iridescent surface with miasmal mists. I liked this smell myself, but there was talk of sealing it in and sullen mutters of revolt from the peasantry: 'My teenage daughters is cunt deep in shit. Is this the American way of life?'
>
> I thought so and I didn't want it changed. Personally I found it most charming drinking Whistle on the back porch, blue mist and gay light in the hot summer night . . . the smell of coal gas from the river which ran just at the bottom of our garden beyond the ash pit.

It was a very conventional, comfortable life. 'The food was delicious, and everyone that I knew had country places as well. We'd go out there on weekends.' These were the days before the gas-driven automobile and the streets were filled with horses and steam cars: the Stanley Steamer and the White Steamer. There were also electric cars, 'My aunt had one when I was a child, they were for old ladies. They had a very simple lever, that's about all. They'd only go about twenty miles an hour.' Each summer they would go to Harbor Beach, on Lake Huron, Michigan, where they had a little summer house, and Bill would spend his time fishing for rock bass and yellow perch off the end of the pier. His father owned a four-berth, fifty-foot cabin cruiser which they would take out on to the lake.

These were the nostalgic childhood images which would haunt Burroughs' writing throughout his life: snatches of music on a windy street, the smell of coal gas, distant railroad whistles ... a fascination with swamps, rivers and mud banks. TS Eliot, who was born in St Louis 26 years before Burroughs, wrote: 'I feel that there is something in having passed one's childhood beside the big river which is incommunicable to those who have not.'

Only 60 years before, St Louis still had something of the atmosphere of a frontier town; it was still part French and in camp sites on the outskirts lived Indians whom local children would taunt with war-whoops until, exasperated, they would finally give chase. At the same time, massive industrial development was growing up all along the banks of the Mississippi. St Louis was expanding rapidly as the railroads opened up the west and river traffic connected St Louis to the South. By the turn of the century parts of the city were already suffering urban decay, and pollution from factory smokestacks caused fog and grime. The industrialists and bankers formed a new mercantile class who felt it was their bounden duty to give moral guidance to the waves of new immigrants who were arriving from the eastern seaboard. They were the upholders of the traditional American values, of thrift and respect for authority and its institutions. Their values were nineteenth-century American values. It was this world that Burroughs was born into:

The St Louis bourgeois . . .

'Well, I had a fine dinner, enjoyed it' – (after three stiff whiskeys) – 'but I can't help feeling a twinge of conscience when I think of all the millions of people who don't have enough to eat.' (Discreet belch.) [*Last Words*]

Bill was his mother's favourite. He described her as:

a seemingly very timid person but she had great authority at times. She had an ephemeral special quality . . . My mother believed in psychic phenomena. She wasn't at all religious but she didn't have a closed mind about it. She was very psychic. I remember once my brother was out and she had this dream that Mort came to her with his face covered with blood and said, 'Mother, we've had an accident.' As a matter of fact my brother did have an accident that night and he received a cut and his face was indeed covered with blood but his injuries were very minor. My mother would have a *feel* about a person, as she described it, just like an animal.

Burroughs inherited his mother's belief in psychic phenomena: 'I've always been a believer in spirits, the supernatural, like my mother.' This was based on his own experiences as a young child. He remembered one occasion when he was about four years old:

My brother and I were out in Forest Park and he had a BB gun. It was in late afternoon, I looked into this grove of trees and there I saw a little green reindeer. And I said, 'Mort, come here and look!' and he wouldn't. I can see it quite clearly now. It was very delicate, with very thin legs in a sort of green shade. So I was subject to visions, hallucinations, whatever you want to call them. Mort said I was always talking about the little green reindeer that I had seen. He wouldn't believe me.

Once I woke up early in the morning, and I'd made a little house of blocks, and I saw a little man a few inches high, just playing in the blocks. He went away. The little people. So many people have had these experiences as a child ... I mentioned the green reindeer to my parents. They weren't critical at all, they just said, 'Oh yes.'

It was around this time, when Burroughs was about four, that he experienced a traumatic event which, despite years of psychoanalysis, he was never able to identify: 'One of my analysts, Dr Federn, was one of Freud's direct pupils. He said, "What is this that could have affected you your whole life long? What happened?" And I said "Well doctor, I just don't remember, I don't know. I don't know." But that's what sent me to these analysts.'

Bill was very fond of his nanny, Mary Evans, and was disconsolate if she was ever away. 'I formed this hysterical attachment to her so that I would throw these terrible tantrums, screaming "All I want is Nursy!" when she went out on Thursdays.' Thursday was her day off, and she would sometimes take him with her when she went out. On one of these outings, something unpleasant occurred. Evans had a girlfriend, and the girlfriend had a boyfriend, a veterinarian. Burroughs surmised that he was made to suck the boyfriend's cock, or that he witnessed one of the women doing it, but on another occasion, under psychoanalysis in Paris, he had something of a breakthrough and decided that he had probably witnessed a miscarried foetus being thrown into the furnace. Whatever it was, it affected him deeply:

They say there is obviously some terrific trauma there, a terrific block. Something awful happened, but I don't remember anything. I don't even remember the outing ... I remember my brother saying to me, 'Should we tell on Nursy?' He wasn't on this outing but he knew Nursy had done something that was reprehensible. Well we never did and shortly afterwards she went back to Wales and managed a pub ... At any rate, I feel that my mother and father were not the ones to blame for any early traumas, that these were inflicted by criminal servants.

At the age of eight, Burroughs began using guns. His father had a duck club and would take his two sons along:

I used to go out duck shooting with the old man and the president of the First National City Bank and the owner of the Saint Louis Post Dispatch. You have to get up real early, six o'clock to catch the ducks. All in hiding in this marshy ground and we would put out decoys and then as the ducks came in, all these fat old businessmen would stand up and blast away at them. We had retriever dogs to collect the ducks. I used to really enjoy it.

He also shot quail and did a lot of fishing – healthy outdoor pursuits which contrast oddly with the later urban image of his adulthood. It was a privileged life, ordered and secure: 'It was just a completely different life. If you want to get an idea of what it's like read Fitzgerald; there's a lot of it in Fitzgerald. He was born in St Paul, Minnesota, and I think the Midwestern towns, places like St Paul, Kansas City, Cincinnati and St Louis, were pretty much similar.'

Burroughs was named after his paternal grandfather, William Seward Burroughs, the inventor of the adding machine. Although some forms of adding machine already existed, none was very reliable, often giving different results depending on how quickly the handle was pulled. Bill's grandfather invented the gimmick which made it practical: a perforated cylinder filled with oil which acted as a hydraulic regulator on the handle, so that no matter how sharply or slowly the handle was pulled, the pressure exerted on the mechanism was always the same.

Bill's father remembered him as being remote and cold, and the children were not allowed to go near him when he was working. He died of tuberculosis at the age of 43 in Citronelle, Alabama, where he had gone to convalesce, not long before his namesake was born. He left four children: Horace, the eldest; Mortimer – Bill's father – who was born in Mobile, Alabama; Jenny and Helen, who each inherited stock with a value of about $100,000. The executors advised the family that the whole idea of an adding machine was impractical and they had better sell their stock. They all sold, but Laura Lee insisted that Mortimer hold on to a few of the shares. Bill's father was working for the company in Detroit at the time and used the money to buy a small plate glass company in St Louis, which he renamed the Burroughs Glass Company.

The Burroughs Adding Machine Corporation grew and became one of the great American companies; the stock value soared. In 1929 they sold the remainder of their shares. 'My father sold the stock that my mother insisted upon his keeping a month before the Depression, and got about $200,000. That was the most money the family ever had at one time. That saw us through the Depression.' It was always a sore point with Burroughs that people regarded him as from a wealthy background. The myth was first put about by Jack Kerouac, who wrote a trust fund into existence in one of his novels, and it was further compounded by writers such as John Tytell in his 1975 book *Naked Angels* which caused Burroughs to fulminate:

> The point is *we were not rich*, and this circumstance alone would have excluded us from any elitist circles. With $200,000 in the bank, we were not accepted by old families with ten, twenty, fifty million. Of course we were invited to the *larger* parties. But when the WASP elite got together for dinners and lunches and drinks nobody wanted those ratty Burroughses about. My final inheritance on the death of my mother in 1970 was $10,000 and that doesn't make me a scion of anything.

Burroughs, writing about his childhood, said:

> The family was never *in*. This feeling I experienced from early childhood of living in a world where I was not accepted, caused me to develop a number of displeasing characteristics. I was shy and awkward and at the same time furtive and purposeful. An old St Louis aristocrat with cold blue eyes chews his pipe . . . 'I don't want that boy in the house again. He looks like a sheep-killing dog.' And a St Louis matron said, 'He is a walking corpse.' No, I was not escaping my elitist upbringing through crime; I was searching for an identity denied me by the WASP elite, who have frequently let me know where I stand.

Bill's father next went into the landscape gardening business and eventually opened a gift and art shop called Cobblestone Gardens, a name later used by his son for one of his books.

Burroughs was always quite sure that he wanted to be a writer, and from the age of eight the nascent author turned his hand to a wide range of subjects: western, Gothic horror, gangster stories and tales of exploration and adventure. 'There was something called *Carl Cranbury in Egypt* that never got off the ground . . . Carl Cranbury frozen back there on yellow lined paper, his hand an inch from his blue-steel automatic.'

When he was twelve the family moved to a large white frame house that Mortimer Burroughs built on a five-acre site at 200 South Price Road in Ladue, a western suburb of St Louis which is even now one of the four richest communities in the United States. The front door opened into a hall with the living room on the right and the dining room on the left. Behind the dining room were the kitchen and servants' quarters. The master bedroom was above the living room. Bill and Mort shared the back bedroom, which had windows on three sides. They each had a bed and a closet. There was a balcony opening onto the garden. The year before, in 1925, Burroughs had enrolled in the John Burroughs School (named after the great naturalist, no relation) which was now within easy walking distance.

Bill never fitted in at school. He was too much of a loner and was already regarded as a little bit odd by the wealthy young men of John Burroughs. However, it was there that he met Kells Elvins, who was to become a lifelong friend. Kells arrived at the school when Bill was twelve years old. He was a handsome, popular, athletic young man with brown eyes and curly hair. Burroughs idolised him. Bill already knew he was homosexual, but it was a taboo subject in the circles within which the two families moved. Burroughs: 'I was terribly attracted to him. He would take me on his lap and strum me like a banjo and I'd always get a hard-on.' His schoolmates could see what was happening and told Bill, 'You're his slave.' Kells also lived on Price Road and they would walk home together from school, Bill with his arm loosely draped over Kells' shoulder, the closest he could get to turning his fantasies into reality.

* * *

25

When he was thirteen, Burroughs discovered *You Can't Win* (Macmillan, 1926), the autobiography of Jack Black, a petty thief, drug addict and railroad hobo, who matter-of-factly described his experiences in and out of jail, bumming around the country, riding freight trains and trying to avoid the cops, during that forgotten era between the days of the Wild West and the development of the big metropolitan cities, the time between the death of Jesse James and the rise of Al Capone.

To the young Burroughs, stultified and confined by the rigid rules of behaviour in upper-middle-class 1920s St Louis society, where some things were 'done' and others 'not done', *You Can't Win* opened his eyes to another world: an underworld of seedy rooming houses, pool halls, whorehouses and opium dens, of cat burglars and hobo jungles, boxcars and the feared railroad cops. He read about the Johnson family, the good bums and thieves with a code of honourable conduct which made more sense to him than the hypocritical, arbitrary rules unthinkingly assumed by his peers. A Johnson paid his debts and kept his word. A Johnson minded his own business but would help out if he was needed and if help was asked for. A Johnson never held out on his colleagues or cheated his landlady. Thirty years later, Burroughs was to use characters from *You Can't Win* in his books, and quote sections from it, sometimes word for word. Salt Chunk Mary up and walked from *You Can't Win* straight into the pages of *The Naked Lunch* and was followed by the Sanctimonious Kid.

Burroughs saw the world divided into these types: 'A basic split between suits and Johnsons has emerged. I see the world as a stage on which different actors are assigned different roles. Of course, any Johnson does do shitty things at times. But he knows enough to regret such actions. It is very rare that a hard-core shit acts like a Johnson. He simply does not understand what it means to be a Johnson, and is irrevocably committed to a contrary viewpoint.'

Jack Black understood all too well. He dedicated his book to 'that dirty, drunken, crippled beggar Sticks Sullivan who picked the buckshot out of my back under a bridge at Baraboo, Wisconsin.' Sticks was a Johnson.

Inspired by *You Can't Win*, which he read and reread, Bill concentrated mostly on writing crime and gangster stories while he was at the John Burroughs School. 'I was fascinated by gangsters, and like most boys at the time I wanted to be one because I would feel so much safer with my loyal guns around me.' His stories frequently featured hangings, the method of capital punishment in use in Missouri at that time. Lurid descriptions and photographs of death by hanging filled the newspapers. When he came to write *The Naked Lunch* it was the hanging scenes in it which caused the obscenity trials: Burroughs used this ingrained imagery from his childhood as a potent symbol of barbarism.

As an adolescent, Bill had sinus trouble and the family consulted Dr Senseney, who had been a neighbour when they lived on Pershing Avenue. He recommended that fifteen-year-old Bill be sent to the Los Alamos Ranch School in New Mexico for a cure. It was Mrs Senseney who said that Burroughs looked like 'a walking corpse' – an anecdote recounted in several books. He was a thin youth and she told his schoolfriend David Kammerer, 'Listen, if you want to get ahead socially, get rid of him. It's a walking corpse!' Burroughs later commented, 'When I heard of her death, I said, "It isn't every corpse than can walk. Hers can't." Old bitch.'

The Los Alamos Ranch School occupied over 900 acres, high on the mesa overlooking the Rio Grande Valley, about 40 miles northwest of Santa Fe. It was self-sufficient, with its own water, an electricity generator, dairy, chickens and over 400 acres planted with crops. It was very expensive and rich boys were sent there to toughen up. Reading and other intellectual activity was discouraged, and horse riding and physical activities predominated. No matter how inclement the weather the boys were not allowed indoors between two-thirty and four-thirty in the afternoon and could frequently be found huddled in doorways, sheltering from the rain. In accordance with the school's general philosophy, the boys slept on an unheated porch and were only given a canvas blanket when snow actually blew through the wire mesh. There were no locks on the doors and the director, AJ Connell, liked to rush into the dorms to try to catch boys masturbating. His motto was, 'I know what is best for boys.'

Burroughs hated Los Alamos, and particularly disliked his horse, 'a sullen, spiteful, recalcitrant pony'. They had to ride twice a week and all day on Saturday; Bill rode bareback quite a lot of the time, just to avoid the nuisance of putting the saddle on. The school was not all bad. Bill enjoyed using the rifle range, where he developed his already considerable skill as a marksman. 'America has a gun culture, it was founded on the gun,' Burroughs said. 'When you are a child you get given your first air-rifle at a certain age, then a .22 repeater. And all the time you get revolvers and pistols. I used to be able to shoot the flame on a candle out from across the room!' While at Los Alamos Bill also became a proficient knife thrower, a skill he once demonstrated by killing one of the school's hens.

It was not long after Bill's sixteenth birthday that he conducted his first experiment with mind-altering drugs. During a visit to Santa Fe with his mother he gave her the slip and bought some chloral hydrate (knockout drops) at a drug store to experiment with; something he had learned about through his avid reading of gangster books. A few days later, he took an almost lethal dose which confined him to the school infirmary and caused consternation and embarrassment all round.

Bill sought refuge in the works of Anatole France, de Maupassant, Remy de Gourmont, and in Oscar Wilde's *The Picture of Dorian Gray*. However, his own writing remained fixed in the popular detective style of the period. During a visit to the Hotel La Fonda in Santa Fe, Burroughs conceived a story about four jolly murderers:

A middle aged couple very brash and jolly . . .
'Sure an' I'd kill my own grandmother just for a little kale.'
'We have regular rates of course . . .' the woman observed tartly.
A soft plump pearl gray man stands there with a sickly smile. He is flanked by a skull face Mexican also smiling.

It is the tough, pared-down detective style of Raymond Chandler, Dashiell Hammett and, of course, Jim Black. The characters inhabiting his juvenilia continued to live in Burroughs' imagination and the Mexican later became Tio Mate in *The Wild Boys*. The hard-boiled detective genre had a considerable influence on his later writing, enabling him to create a scene with a minimum of words, and convey character with a few carefully chosen words of dialogue.

Bill formed a romantic longing for one of the boys at Los Alamos and kept a diary of his adolescent fantasies which was to put him off writing for many years. During the Easter vacation of his second year he convinced his family that his feet (which were unusually long) were giving him pain, and managed to persuade them to let him stay home in St Louis. One of his school friends packed his things, including the incriminating diary, and sent them to him. 'I used to turn cold, thinking that maybe the boys are reading it aloud to each other. When the box finally arrived I pried it open and threw everything out until I found the diary and destroyed it forthwith without a glance at the appalling pages.'

He had deviated from his initial honesty in writing. 'The act of writing had become embarrassing, disgusting, and above all, *false*. It was not the sex in the diary that embarrassed me; it was the terrible falsity of the emotions expressed. The sight of my words on a page sickened me and this continued until 1938. I had written myself an eight-year sentence.' He had a painful passage through adolescence, caused mainly by the fact that homosexuality was so beyond the pale that there was no one at school he dared talk to about his emotions and anxieties.

The Los Alamos school was later taken over by the United States government for the Manhattan Project, and it was there that the atomic bomb was invented. 'It seemed so right, somehow,' Burroughs later commented.

Just as tradition dictated he go duck hunting with his father, in 1932 Bill went up, as expected, to Harvard. Everyone he knew went to college, that was what you did. He majored in English Literature, but did no creative writing there and did not particularly enjoy his time at the university. He was in the wrong house, was not invited to join any of the clubs, and did not mix with the right people. He did, however, develop a certain notoriety by keeping a ferret in his room along with a loaded gun.

I didn't like Harvard at all, I don't like Boston, I didn't like Cambridge. I didn't like the whole atmosphere. But I learned how to use a library. I think it's very valuable for a writer to do a lot of reading. You'll find that most writers at one time or another have done a great deal of reading. I'm not talking about research, I'm talking about reading; the English classics and the French. If you want to write you should know what's been done in your field. I think that's terribly important, to have some sort of background in English literature if you are going to be a writer.

He devoured Milton, Wordsworth and studied Chaucer. He took George Lyman Kittredge's famous Shakespeare course, during which he was required to memorise hundreds of lines of Shakespeare, most of which he retained and which peppered his speech throughout his life. He also studied Coleridge and De Quincey, who interested him very much, but in those days there were no drugs to be had in Harvard.

Burroughs later repudiated that whole period of his life: 'At Harvard I was just a completely beat down person with no idea of who he was or what he was. And I'd rather not think about it ever since then. It's too disgusting to think about ... I've never been back there ... What I'm trying to convey is [that] my whole past is something I have nothing to do with. I am now a completely different person. Anything in the past as far as I'm concerned is of no importance.'

As a graduation present his parents gave him an allowance of $200 a month from their gift shop and paid for him to go on a European tour. He had been to Europe several times with the family as a child. In 1933, he and David Kammerer spent the summer together in Paris and London, and the next year he travelled to Paris and Algiers with Rex Weisenberger, a friend from the John Burroughs School. On this occasion he travelled with Bob Miller, a friend from Harvard. They took in Paris, Vienna, Budapest and Dubrovnik. Instead of returning to the States, Bill decided to stay on in Europe and enrol in the University of Vienna Medical School. 'Vienna was the only medical school I could conceivably get into. I had no pre-med. But I decided after just one semester that it wasn't for me, I didn't want to clutter up my mind with all these facts.' There were other reasons as well: Bill was lonely and depressed. For six months Burroughs had lived in the Dianabad Hotel, brushing up his German but seeing very few people. He was recovering from the syphilis he had contracted in a brothel when he was at Harvard, and each week he had to have a painful intravenous arsenic injection, the only cure in those days. There were Nazis everywhere and the press was filled with hysterical articles denouncing the Jews. Then in the spring of 1937 he came down with appendicitis and had to have an emergency operation.

When Burroughs was first in Dubrovnik with Bob Miller, Bill had with him an introduction to Ilse Klapper, a German Jew who had fled Hamburg with the rise of the Nazis. They became friendly and, on his return to Dubrovnik to recuperate, he naturally saw her again. He found her in desperate straits. She was unable to renew her Yugoslav visa because she was Jewish, and saw her salvation in this naive, lonely twenty-three-year-old American boy, fifteen years her junior. If they were married she could get into the United States. She put tremendous pressure on Bill and, surprisingly, he agreed. He was fond of her and wanted to help, and it was understood from the beginning that it would be a marriage of convenience only. Needless to say his family were horrified, but Bill was determined to stand by his decision.

They were married in Athens, where Bill had an introduction to the American consul, who did the necessary paperwork. Directly afterwards Bill returned to Missouri and his worried parents. It had not been a wasted trip: he had probably saved Ilse's life, and he had equipped himself with the scientific basis needed for his later studies of addiction and virus control.

Bill arrived home in St Louis in 1938 with no plans. The Depression was well entrenched, there were 25 million people unemployed and no jobs to be had, but Bill had his monthly allowance and he was not desperate. Kells Elvins, his old friend from the John Burroughs School, had gone through a hasty marriage and divorce and was now taking a graduate course in psychology at Harvard. For lack of anything better to do, and to get away from St Louis, Burroughs joined him there and did graduate work in anthropology, studying Mayan archeology, a subject which became a lifetime interest.

For about a year he and Kells, together with another school friend, Alan Calvert, shared a wooden frame house on a quiet tree-lined back street in Cambridge near the Commodore Hotel, where they lived like young aristocrats, complete with a black manservant to cook and look after them. They frequently discussed writing and started a detective story in the popular pulp style. They took as their inspiration the sinking of the *Morro Castle* and the *Titanic*. In 1935, the *Morro Castle* had gone down off the Jersey coast with the loss of 200 lives; the first mate was in the first lifeboat to leave the sinking ship. One of the survivors in a lifeboat from the *Titanic* was found to be a man dressed in women's clothes. Burroughs and Elvins researched the subject in the Widener Library and read *The Left-handed Passenger*, based on the *Morro Castle* disaster. On the screened porch of their house, they started work on a humorous sketch called 'Twilight's Last Gleamings'.

In order to write the piece they acted out the different roles, laughing uproariously as they did so. 'We did definitely act the thing out,' Burroughs said. 'We decided that was the way to write. Now here's this guy, what does he say, what does he do? Dr Benway sort of emerged quite spontaneously while we were composing this piece.' Dr Benway, who became one of Burroughs' best-loved characters, was based on a real doctor that Elvins once knew. This was his first appearance:

> Dr Benway, ship's doctor, drunkenly added two inches to a four-inch incision with one stroke of his scalpel.
>   'There was a little scar, Doctor,' said the nurse, who was peering over his shoulder. 'Perhaps the appendix is already out.'
>   'The appendix out!' the doctor shouted. 'I'm taking the appendix out! What do you think I'm doing here?'
>   'Perhaps the appendix is on the left side,' said the nurse. 'That happens sometimes, you know.'

'We acted out every scene and often got on laughing jags,' Burroughs wrote. 'I hadn't laughed like that since my first tea high at eighteen when I rolled around on the floor and pissed all over myself.' They sent the story to *Esquire* magazine, who rejected it, saying, 'Too screwy, and not effectively so for us.'

'I see now that the curse of the diary was broken temporarily by the act of collaboration,' Burroughs wrote in 1972. 'Twilight's Last Gleamings' contains the genesis of much of Burroughs' future work. Twenty-four years later Burroughs used it, in a shortened and somewhat changed form, as 'Gave Proof Through The Night' in *Nova Express* and the original draft was finally printed in *Interzone* in 1989.

Collaboration was to become the key to writing for Burroughs. A collaborator is usually used for ideas, to give new metaphors or direction. Burroughs, however, needed someone to act as a catalyst, someone to encourage him, to get the flow going. The person didn't even have to be present, but there had to be an audience, if only by mail, and it helped considerably if this person were also someone with whom he had, or had once had, a romantic attachment. Elvins moved to Huntsville, Texas, where he had been offered a job as prison psychologist, and the Cambridge household broke up.

Bill moved to New York and attended to the formalities of getting his wife, Ilse Klapper, an American visa. Ilse landed in New York shortly afterwards. They remained friends, and Bill took her frequently for lunch, but always lived apart. 'She never asked me for one cent,' Burroughs said. After the war, in 1945, Ilse returned to Europe and was last heard of living outside Zurich. Bill later obtained a divorce in Mexico.

Burroughs had been intrigued by Alfred Korzybski's book *Science and Sanity*, and enrolled in Korzybski's seminar on General Semantics which was held in Chicago in August 1939. The week of lectures impressed Bill enormously. Korzybski railed against the Aristotelian notion of either/or, explaining how such a division was impossible: you can't make total divisions between subjective/objective, intellectual/instinctive, when elements of both are always present. Korzybski stressed the idea that 'a word is not the thing it stands for. Words mean what you make them mean. A chair is a chair, but the word "chair" is just a word.' When a word is too general, like 'fascist', 'communist', 'humanist', 'moralist', it has little or no meaning, he insisted.

Burroughs never used such words again and his non-judgemental stance became one of his most attractive characteristics.

Bill returned to New York, and shortly afterwards he met a male hustler called Jack Anderson in Tony's, a gay bar on 52nd Street. Bill was in a curious state of mind, very detached from reality, and felt a huge attraction towards this unprepossessing young man. Burroughs: 'We were sort of making it sporadically. He was like a beautiful face and very mediocre body and a sort of a chorus girl, shop girl mentality. Cheap. Essentially cheap.' All Anderson wanted was money, most of which he lost at the race track. He had an office job, and hustled on the side. He lived in an old red brick rooming house on Jane Street in the West Village.

Burroughs was then living in the Taft Hotel at Seventh Avenue and 50th Street, which in 1939 was expensive, at $2.50 a night. Burroughs:

He and I were making it there one night and some guy went through who checks the rooms to see if the door's open. For some reason we left the door unlocked. Ten minutes later the house detective and the manager burst in, and here we are both stark naked. So I said, 'What's going on here?' They said, 'Well, we want to know what's going on here!' We were completely outfaced. And the house detective said, 'You're the wisest prick I ever walked in on.' Quite a compliment. He said, 'Didn't anyone ever kick the shit out of you?' Well anyway, we were thrown out of the hotel in the middle of the night. They even gave us a refund.

They went downtown to Anderson's room and the next day Bill took a room next to Jack in the same building.

This was a mistake because the walls were thin, and every time Anderson brought home a client, or the occasional girlfriend, Bill could hear them and was driven to distraction by jealousy. Bill began a course of psychoanalysis with Doctor Wiggers, the first of Bill's many analysts. He was a classic Freudian and progress was slow, but it helped to have someone to talk to about his problems with Anderson. Determined to become the centre of Anderson's attention, Bill conceived of a dramatic gesture. He bought a pair of poultry shears and, holding his breath and staring at himself in the mirror as he did it, chopped off the last third of the little finger of his left hand. He had an appointment with Wiggers that day and presented him with the evidence of what he'd done. Wiggers was terrified and managed to talk Burroughs into going to Bellevue, where he was diagnosed as a paranoid schizophrenic. His father flew to New York and had him transferred to the Payne-Whitney, an expensive private mental hospital where he stayed for a month. His father didn't ask why he had done it, and Bill didn't tell him. According to Burroughs, 'Wiggers thought that I was going to have a complete psychotic episode which I didn't at all. He came to see me once in Payne-Whitney and I said "What are you so scared of? You think I was going crazy or something?" He was a fool.'

When he got out, Bill returned to his parents and spent most of 1940 in St Louis, working for their gift shop as a delivery boy. He hated it there and became withdrawn and moody. He tried to get away by enlisting in the Navy, but failed the physical. He tried the American Field Service but the elitist recruiter disapproved of Bill's house at Harvard and was horrified to find that he had not joined any of the clubs there. Bill did not get in.

Bill's father knew that Colonel Donovan was setting up an American spy organisation, the OSS – forerunner of the CIA – and Bill applied as a field agent, using a well-connected uncle as his contact. The interview with Donovan went well until he brought in his director of research and analysis, who turned out to be Bill's former house master at Harvard, James Phinney Baxter, who had objected to his keeping a ferret in his room. Bill knew there was no chance. Baxter disliked him intensely, and the class system in 1941 America was as bad as anything in Britain as far as commissioned officers was concerned.

The family wanted to see Bill doing something constructive and it was now Bill's father's turn to pull strings. Soon Bill found himself employed by the Van Dolan, Givaurdon and Massek advertising agency in New York where he was paid $30 a week to work the accounts that no one else wanted, such as

EndoCreme, which made women look younger – it contained a now-banned female sex hormone. Bill waxed lyrical on the subject of Cascade, a high colonic irrigation administered as an enema: 'Well done thou true and faithful servant – that is how many people feel about their Cascade. Immeasurable relief sweeps over them. The waste matter that has accumulated for years is swept away without a trace. You feel as if reborn.'

It was a relatively happy period for him. He got back together with Anderson, and they lived together on one of the most attractive brownstone blocks in Manhattan, on West 11th Street, between Fifth and Sixth Avenues; the only real problem was Anderson's jealous girlfriend. Then on 7 December 1941, America finally joined the war and Bill was drafted.

Bill was aggrieved to be in the St Louis Jefferson Barracks. It seemed wrong to him that they had found him unfit when he had volunteered to serve his country, yet now they were happy to register him A-1. This time it was his mother's turn to pull strings. As Burroughs had spent a brief period in Bellevue and Payne-Whitney she was able to get him a civilian disability discharge on the grounds of mental instability; he should never have been drafted in the first place. It took four or five months for the application for discharge to be processed and, in the meantime, Bill lounged around in the barracks reading the complete works of Marcel Proust. Each evening at six o'clock, his parents drove up with a packed dinner.

In the summer of 1942 Bill moved to Chicago, where he heard that it was easy to find work. He was still receiving his $200 a month, but needed more to live well. Here he finally made contact with the milieu of Jack Black's *You Can't Win* to which he had been so attracted. He lived in Mrs Murphy's Rooming House on the North Side, where the El ran past the back windows. It was a run-down neighbourhood of petty thieves, failed gamblers and short-change artists. He liked the company. Bill went to the race track and took part in the Sunday afternoon crap games. He had been rejected by the members of his own class at Harvard and in the military, but here he found unquestioning acceptance.

There was plenty of work in Chicago because so many men were away in the forces. He worked briefly for Merritt

Incorporated, a detective agency which specialised in catching store employees with their hand in the till, then took a job with an exterminator service run by a Mister AJ Cohen, whose initials Burroughs later used as the name for one of his characters. Each day he would set out in his own black Ford V-8 with his equipment: bellows and bulbs, phosphorous paste for water bugs, kerosene spray for bedbugs, arsenic for rats and pyrethrum powder and fluoride for cockroaches. He made $50 a week plus what he could make on the side working out of company hours. He had to get ten signatures a day.

I used to bang on the door real loud, 'You got any bugs, lady?' hoping to attract the neighbours so she might lie and say she didn't have any, and she would sign my book and I would get through my list early.

'Ssh! Ssh! Come in, come in.' The old Jewish woman would try and pull me in the door real fast and there it would be, her bedroom with the covers all pulled back.

'Can't spray beds, lady. Board of Health regulations.'

'Oh, you vant some more wine? It wasn't enough before?' and she'd pour me another glass of horrible sweet wine. So I'd hold out and eventually she'd hand me a crumpled dollar bill.

Of course, in the negro district it was different. I didn't come the Board of Health regulations there. I used to carry a gun. You never knew what might happen if one of those spade pimps woke up off the nod: 'Hey, what's this white boy doing in the apartment?'

'Shaddup, he's the exterminator!'

I can go into an apartment and I know where *all* the roaches are. I also know where *all* the bedbugs are. I used to have a spray gun and I could adjust it from a fine spray to a stream and go in a room and get a bug, 'Phatt!' from across the room, just like that. With sulphur or cyanide you have to be careful to seal the room because there have been dozens of deaths from cyanide seeping through into other neighbouring apartments. And if you have to enter the room, it's no good taking a deep breath and running in to open the windows because that stuff will attack your eyes and blind you before you even get there. You have to wear a gasmask or else open the door and let it escape some first. I never have any roaches. I just go in there to a new apartment and give them a spray with pyrethrum powder and they all rush out and die instantly on the floor. You have to get a broom to sweep them up. It's a great sight!

Bill liked the work and managed to hold down the job for eight months. Many of his experiences later turned up in his books, two of which were actually called *Exterminator*: the first, a collection of early cut-ups, the second, *Exterminator!* with an exclamation mark, a collection of short stories.

William Burroughs as exterminator is a potent image. An exterminator can take many forms: a straight-talker who cuts through hypocrisy, a deconstructionist ripping through text, a cut-up writer, an assassin. The word has automatic low-life associations since bug-ridden apartments are in the run-down part of town, and the exterminator's clients are usually the poverty-stricken inhabitants of rooming houses, ghettos and rotting tenements. Bill in his 40s Trilby hat and trenchcoat making his rounds, ringing doorbells, yelling 'Exterminator!' like something out of Raymond Chandler is a significant component of the later image.

Bill had not been in Chicago long when David Kammerer and Lucien Carr, two friends from St Louis, arrived in town. Carr was a freshman at the University of Chicago, and Kammerer, who was obsessed with Carr, had followed him there. Kammerer was one of Bill's best friends. He was tall and red-haired and often wore a beard. He and Bill got on because both were outcasts from respectable St Louis society and homosexual – they had explored the rue de Lappe *apaches* neighbourhood of Paris together in 1933. Carr was a handsome seventeen-year-old with blond hair and slanted grey eyes; Kammerer had been his supervisor in a pre-high school play group and had been fixated on him ever since. As a teenage boy, Carr had studied at Washington University, and gone to Andover, Bowdoin School and the University of Chicago. Everywhere he went he was followed by Kammerer. It was a one-way sexual attraction.

Though Carr felt flattered by the older man's attention, and enjoyed Kammerer's eccentric humour and friendship, he was not homosexual.

Kammerer and Carr always fooled around a lot together and Bill was thrown out of Mrs Murphy's Rooming House because they tore up the Gideon Bible and pissed out of the window. But they were fun to be around and Bill saw a lot of them.

In the summer of 1943, Lucien made yet another move to get away from Kammerer and transferred to Columbia University in New York as a second-term freshman. But Kammerer followed shortly afterwards and, since he was now bored with Chicago, and as he enjoyed the company of Kammerer and Carr, Bill went with him.

3 Junky

Once in New York, Bill got himself an apartment at 69 Bedford Street, overlooking a tree-filled backyard. David Kammerer had a small, white-washed room at 48 Morton Street, around the corner, where he lived rent-free in return for acting as janitor of the building. They were in the oldest part of the Village, which in those days was not yet gentrified and was still home to many artists and writers. They ate at nearby Chumley's, which had been a speakeasy fifteen years before, and at the Minetta Tavern and the San Remo Bar, bohemian Village places which would later go down in Beat Generation history.

Meanwhile Lucien Carr was a hundred blocks away, living at the Union Theological Seminary, which had been taken over for student dorms in wartime by Columbia University, because their own buildings were filled with V-12 naval cadets doing the requisite 90 days of college to become officers. Though Carr had moved to New York to escape Kammerer, he often took the subway down to see him and Burroughs; it would have been ridiculous not to visit the only people he knew in the city.

Just before Christmas of 1943, Lucien arrived at Bill's apartment with a fellow student from Columbia, a skinny seventeen-year-old with thick-rimmed spectacles and carefully brushed hair. This was Allen Ginsberg, on his first-ever visit to Greenwich Village. Ginsberg and Burroughs had little in common at the time; Burroughs was twelve years older, ancient in the eyes of the teenage student. 'To me anyone over 21 was superannuated,' Ginsberg said, 'and Burroughs already seemed to have the "ashen grey of an age-old cheek."'

Ginsberg was impressed, however, because Burroughs was the first person he had ever met who quoted Shakespeare to make a point. Lucien told Burroughs about a fight that he and Kammerer had instigated in the studio of a Greenwich Village artist during which Lucien had bitten off part of the unfortunate artist's ear. Bill tut-tutted and remarked: ' 'Tis too starved a subject for my sword.'

Through Lucien, Burroughs and Kammerer got to know a whole circle of Columbia students who hung out at the West End bar on Broadway across from the Columbia campus, Jack Kerouac and his girlfriend Edie Parker among them. Kerouac had recently left Columbia under something of a cloud and was working as a merchant seaman. Bill was interested in getting seaman's papers himself and first met Kerouac by tagging along with Kammerer on a visit to Edie's apartment. Kerouac was a few years older than Ginsberg and Carr, and quickly formed a friendship with Bill, despite their very different backgrounds. Of French Canadian parentage, Jack had not spoken English until he was six years old. He had been at Columbia on a football scholarship and, though very much the all-American boy, he appreciated Bill's off-beat humour and his learning. Bill, for his part, was impressed by the seriousness of purpose in Kerouac, who already saw himself as a writer, and knew that he was not the average college jock, even though he looked like one, with his brooding frown and stocky peasant body.

Lucien Carr had had a girlfriend in Chicago, but on arrival in New York he began a steady relationship with Celine Young, a beautiful half-French undergraduate at Barnard. They went everywhere together, holding hands and kissing, and driving Kammerer crazy with jealousy. Carr and Celine could never go anywhere alone without Kammerer hounding them. No matter how secret their arrangements, he always seemed to find them, climbing into parties up the fire-escapes and once breaking into Carr's room through an open window to stand and watch over him all night. Whenever he found Lucien by himself, he put heavy pressure on him to have sex, even threatening to harm Celine. Bill tried to reason with Kammerer, pointing out the hopelessness of the situation and insisting: 'What you're trying to accomplish is not at all to his advantage.'

Eventually disaster struck. On the night of 13 August 1944, Kammerer and Carr were drinking at the West End. When the bar closed they took a bottle across to Riverside Park, overlooking the Hudson; the night was too hot and humid to sleep. In the course of a long drunken exchange, Kammerer threatened to kill Lucien and then himself if he couldn't have him. He lunged at Lucien, who fought back. Kammerer was a much heavier, stronger man, but Lucien pulled out his boy-scout knife and stabbed Kammerer twice through the heart, killing him.

Lucien panicked and attempted to get rid of the body by weighting it with stones and rolling it into the Hudson. He went straight downtown to Burroughs' room and told him what had happened. 'I just killed the old man,' he said, and Burroughs knew at once what he had done.

Lucien spent two days walking around town with Jack Kerouac, seeing movies and going to bars, before he was able to work up the courage to tell his family and turn himself in. But when he arrived at the station house with his lawyers, the police at first refused to believe him. Then the Coastguard found Kammerer's body floating off 108th Street and changed their minds. Lucien was taken to the Tombs.

Both Burroughs and Kerouac were arrested as material witnesses for not reporting a homicide. Kerouac's father was outraged that his son should be mixed up in a murder and refused to have anything to do with him. Jack's girlfriend, Edie, eventually posted bail, but her parents would allow her to do so only after she and Jack had married in jail. Bill's father flew to New York to post his $2,500 bail. The killing made front-page news and Burroughs' indirect involvement was reported in the St Louis newspapers as a long-running story, much to the chagrin of his family. This was not the first time Mortimer Burroughs had had to bail his son out of trouble, but the family seem to have resigned themselves to their pampered younger son being a misfit.

Lucien was sent to prison for two years for what the newspapers dubbed an 'honour slaying'. Bill and Jack were not brought to court and decided to write a mystery thriller together, based on the incident. They called it *And The Hippos*

Were Boiled In Their Tanks, a title Bill took from a news report about a fire in a travelling circus. When he had collaborated with Elvins in 1938, they had worked up dialogue by acting it out or they had alternated, writing a paragraph each. Working with Kerouac, Bill would write a chapter and then Jack would write one, though Kerouac later complained that Burroughs would never comment on Kerouac's material. When pressed for an opinion, Burroughs would grunt, 'It's OK.' Burroughs needed the encouragement and support of a collaborator to make him write, but was not all that interested in collaboration as such.

The resulting book was sent around to various publishers, but no one was interested and it remained unpublished. Looking back, Burroughs was not surprised: 'It isn't very good, it isn't worth publishing.'

In New York, Bill gave his *nostalgie de la boue* full rein and began a half-serious anthropological study of the Times Square area, in the course of which he met a wide range of petty thieves, hustlers and marginal hoodlums. He remained fascinated by the low life as described by Jack Black, and found some traces of the old camaraderie remaining. Certainly the characters were just as interesting as he had expected them to be. He ingratiated himself with them, sometimes acting as an accessory or receiver of stolen goods.

Once he tried to unload a stolen submachine gun and a gross of morphine syrettes to an acquaintance called Bob Brandenberg, who worked in a coffee shop near the Columbia campus. Brandenberg took him to his apartment on Henry Street under the Manhattan Bridge and introduced him to his room-mates: a street-wise young thief known as Phil 'The Sailor' White, and a ravaged-looking Times Square hustler called Herbert Huncke.

In *The Town and the City*, Jack Kerouac described Huncke as 'a small, dark, Arabic-looking man with an oval face and huge blue eyes that were lidded wearily always, with the huge lids of a mask. He moved about with the noiseless glide of an Arab, his expression always weary, indifferent, yet somehow astonished too, aware of everything. He had the look of a man who is sincerely miserable in the world.' Huncke was utterly amoral, there was no one he wouldn't rob; even the cops on

Times Square were disgusted by him. They nicknamed him 'The Creep' and sometimes banned him from the area.

Bill had not tried hard drugs before, but was interested in all aspects of the life and asked Phil White how it was done. Phil and Huncke were only too pleased to demonstrate, since they were both junkies and were so low on funds that they were unable to fill a doctor's prescription for junk which they had just obtained.

After a couple of months hanging around with Phil, Bill developed a small habit and Phil showed him how to persuade doctors to write scripts for morphine – 'making the croaker', they called it. (Morphine, like heroin, was of course illegal.) For Bill it was a chance to join a milieu in which he was completely accepted. It was *You Can't Win* come to life, a childhood dream fulfilled. Though he did not realise it, Bill was also gathering material for his future books, in particular *Junky*, which is an autobiographical account of this period.

It was during this time that Allen Ginsberg and Jack Kerouac introduced Bill to Joan Vollmer, a student at Columbia University School of Journalism. She had been away during the summer of 1944 giving birth to a baby, Julie, at her parents' home in Albany, NY, in September, and so missed the excitement surrounding the Kammerer affair. She had just split up with her husband, Paul Adams, a writer, who was away in the Forces. She returned to New York with her daughter and took a large apartment on 115th Street, near Columbia. Kerouac and Edie moved in; Hal Chase, another Columbia student, took one of the rooms, and when Allen Ginsberg was kicked out of Columbia University in the spring of 1945, he joined them, sharing a room with Chase. Bill got along very well with Joan, and eventually took the remaining spare room.

Jack and Allen had quite consciously acted as matchmakers when they introduced Bill to Joan. 'Jack and I decided that Joan and Bill would make a great couple,' Ginsberg said. 'They were a match for each other, fit for each other, equally tuned and equally witty and funny and intelligent and equally well read, equally refined.' Not long after Bill moved in they became lovers. It was his first, and only, serious relationship with a woman.

Though Burroughs said he always knew that homosexuality was his inclination, in Howard Brookner's documentary on Burroughs' life Lucien Carr remembered him as something of a womaniser and Bill concurred:

> Lucien Carr: 'I was just thinking of Willie in the old days when Willie was more robust of figure and used to speak of a thunder in his chest as he chased skirts around St Louis.'
> WSB: 'Yes, I used to be quite a woman chaser.'
> Allen Ginsberg: 'You were?!'
> LC: 'Oh, Willie the lover, I'll tell you. There was a line that always got 'em. He tore open his shirt screaming, "There's a thunder in my breast" and they all fell flat on their backs!'
> WSB: 'Every time!'

Now the trio who composed the original Beat Generation – Burroughs, Ginsberg and Kerouac – were all living together in one apartment, though by the time Bill moved in, Kerouac's marriage had broken up, Edie had moved out and Jack was spending much of his time at his parents' home in Ozone Park where his father, Leo, was dying of cancer and needed constant care. However, Jack frequently came to the city and would always stay over at 115th Street with his friends.

Bill continued his experiments with drugs, joined by Allen, Jack and Joan. Joan developed a liking for benzedrine, which was easily available in nasal inhalers, and she quickly became addicted. Jack took so much that his health suffered; he became very run down and developed phlebitis in his legs. Ginsberg found that it made him write 'stanzas of gibberish' and used it much less than the others.

Burroughs had always been interested in psychoanalysis, and read a great deal about it, which probably interfered with his treatment. Most recently he had been seeing Dr Paul Federn, an early pupil of Freud, who appears to have impressed him. Federn now referred him to Dr Wolberg, a hypnoanalyst. (Burroughs was to later try Jungian, Reichian, narcoanalysis and Karen Horney's method with varying degrees of success.)

Bill attempted to psychoanalyse both Allen and Jack and they also conducted experiments with telepathy; although the three men were in many ways very different, they shared a passionate desire to 'widen the area of consciousness'. One of the more important activities at 115th Street was the acting out of 'routines', a term which Burroughs credits Ginsberg with inventing. These were like charades, often based around the various character types revealed by Wolberg's hypnoanalysis.

Hypnoanalysis had supposedly revealed many layers to Bill's character: beneath the Harvard-educated scion of an old Southern family was a simpering English governess, always shrieking and giggling. Further down came Old Luke, a good ol' boy with the personality of a psychotic Southern sheriff who liked to sit on his porch with his shotgun over his knees and watch the catfish come up the river; and underlying them all was a bald-skulled silent Chinaman, absolutely alone in the world, starving by the banks of the Yangtze.

It was the lesbian governess character that they acted out at 115th Street, in much the same way as Bill and Kells Elvins had acted out the characters in their sketch of 1938. Allen Ginsberg would assume the personality of the 'well-groomed Hungarian' and, speaking with a thick *mitteleuropaisch* accent, try to sell phoney family heirlooms and paintings to the naive Americans, played convincingly by Jack Kerouac and Hal Chase. Jack wore his father's straw boater for the occasion. Bill's role was to act as Allen's shill, an Edith Sitwell character, vaguely lesbian, the go-between. In order to do this, Bill had to dress up in drag in one of Joan's dresses and invite everyone to tea.

The development of these routines – situations extended and exploited to their most surreal and humorous ends – is absolutely key to Burroughs' writing style, where situations are developed almost to breaking point, and sometimes repeated in another variation, resulting in a variety of different, usually hilarious, resolutions. Material came to him from a wide range of sources – psychoanalysis, dreams, overheard conversations – and would be processed by whatever means necessary to make it usable. At the time, of course, Burroughs did not regard himself as a writer. The acting out of the findings of his hypnoanalyst was a part of the exploration in consciousness they were all engaged in, rather than literary experiment. Routines were, in fact, to be the key which unlocked Burroughs' abilities as a writer.

The favourite routine of literary scholars, the one usually chosen for literary analysis, is the 'talking asshole' sketch from *The Naked Lunch*, where a character's asshole takes on a life of its own and eventually controls him completely, sealing up his mouth with undifferentiated tissue. It is a classic example of a simple idea taken to a wild extreme. Routines were to become Bill's method of communication; they were the engine driving his literary production and it was through them that he conducted his love affairs – using them to amuse and attract lovers.

After *And The Hippos Were Boiled In Their Tanks*, which Bill wrote under the name of Will Dennison, Kerouac kept nagging him to write more, but the failure to sell the book had discouraged Bill and he was more interested in his experiments with narcotics:

> In the 1940s it was Kerouac who kept telling me I should write. I had never written anything after high school and did not think of myself as a writer and I told him so. 'I got no talent for writing . . .' I had tried a few times, a page maybe. Reading it over always gave me a feeling of fatigue and disgust and aversion toward this form of activity, such as a laboratory rat must experience when he chooses the wrong path and gets a sharp reprimand from a needle in his displeasure centres. Jack insisted quietly that I did have talent for writing and that I should write a book called *The Naked Lunch*. To which I replied, 'I don't want to hear anything literary.'

It was very much to Kerouac's credit that he persisted: 'During all the years I knew Kerouac, I can't remember ever seeing him really angry or hostile. It was the sort of smile he gave in reply to my demurs, in a way you get from a priest who knows you will come to Jesus sooner or later – "You can't walk out on the Shakespeare squad, Bill." '

The name, *The Naked Lunch*, which dates back to this period, was discovered by Kerouac one day when Ginsberg was reading aloud from one of Bill's chapters from *And The Hippos Were Boiled In Their Tanks*. Allen misread Bill's sloppy handwriting and instead of 'naked lust' read 'naked lunch', which Kerouac immediately recognised as a good title for a book.

The situation at the 115th Street apartment slowly deteriorated after Bill moved in. Joan took so much benzedrine that she began having hallucinations. She had very acute hearing, and some evenings she could hear the old couple in the apartment below discussing them, calling her a whore and wondering if they were all drug fiends. Often she heard them quarrelling and one evening they had a terrible argument; the man threatened to kill his wife and Joan insisted that Allen and Jack go downstairs and intervene to save the woman's life. They rushed down and banged on the door loudly. There was no one home. Joan had been imagining all the conversations and arguments for weeks.

Bill's friend Huncke took to using the 115th Street apartment as a place for storing stolen goods, once even leaving a stolen car parked outside. Bill was shooting up quite openly in front of everyone and Hal Chase decided it was time to leave. He liked the idea of bohemia, but did not want to mix with petty thieves and drug addicts.

All the time Bill lived at 115th Street, he also maintained a crummy little single room on Henry Street, not far from Huncke and Phil White's old place, to use when he was downtown. When Huncke had to make a rapid exit from Phil's place he naturally moved right into Bill's room. Then someone split on Huncke and the police arrested him for drugs in Bill's apartment. It did not take them long to find Bill; using his own name, he had forged a signature on a prescription for drugs on script from a stolen pad, and his misspelling of 'dillaudid' had attracted the attention of an inspector. One day in April 1946, two detectives, Shein and O'Grady, arrived at 115th Street with a warrant under the Public Health Act for obtaining narcotics through the use of fraud. He described them in *Last Words*: '(When you see a Jew can an Irishman be far behind?) Just cops. Trying to be as nice as they aren't. No push. No slap. Just a few snarls from Shein.' Years later, two detectives, Hauser and O'Brien, were to feature in *The Naked Lunch*.

Bill's analyst, Dr Wolberg, was informed and he notified Bill's parents. Once more, Mortimer Burroughs flew into town with the bail money. Bill was released on bail but still needed to pay for his habit; his $200 a month from his parents, which in 1946 was plenty to live on, was not enough to feed his habit. Bill began helping Phil White roll drunks on the subway – 'the hole' in the local argot.

In his book *The Evening Sun Turned Crimson*, Herbert Huncke recalled what happened.

They informed me they were making the hole together as partners with Bill learning to act as a shill and cover-up man for Phil – helping him to pick pockets by standing near, holding a newspaper open, spread wide – Phil reaching behind Bill, fingers feeling the inside breast pocket of the mark's suit jacket or perhaps the overcoat pockets searching for the wallet – or poke, as Phil referred to it. Somehow there was something ludicrous about a man of Bill's obvious educational background becoming a business partner with knock-around, knock-down, hard hustling Phil.

(Even this eventually found its way into Burroughs' work. The revised editions of his third book, *The Soft Machine*, open with the line, 'I was working the hole with the sailor . . .'

But this wasn't enough. Bill also teamed up with Bill Garver, someone Huncke had met during his latest spell in Riker's Island prison. Together Bill and Garver pushed heroin to Garver's contacts in the Village.

Bill's case came up in June and, since it was his first offence, the judge gave him a four-month suspended sentence and sent him home to St Louis for four months in the care of his father. Bill was 32.

With Chase gone, and Bill away, Joan had trouble making the rent. Huncke moved in, and introduced her to a friend of his known as Whitey, because of his blond hair. It was not long before Whitey moved in himself, and he and Joan began what she described as 'a light affair'. The apartment grew ever more full of stolen goods and, after an unfortunate matter involving a stolen valise, Huncke was soon back in jail, this time the Bronx County Jail at 153rd Street, leaving Joan, Julie, Whitey and Allen in the apartment.

Joan was lonely without Bill, and countered her unhappiness by taking more and more benzedrine, until she finally cracked and was taken to Bellevue Hospital suffering from acute amphetamine psychosis. It was the first female case they had ever had, and they kept her in the ward for ten days for detoxification. Julie was sent to stay with a relative. Since Joan was about to be evicted for non-payment of rent, Ginsberg closed down the apartment and moved to a furnished room.

Allen was very concerned at Joan's predicament and wrote to Bill in St Louis to tell him what had happened. Bill left at once for New York to rescue her. He and Joan stayed in a hotel on Times Square, visiting museums and art galleries as if on vacation, and it was here that William Burroughs III was conceived. Bill devised a plan to get Joan out of New York.

His enforced stay in St Louis had not been as bad as Bill had feared. Kells Elvins was in town, now deaf in one ear from a Japanese shell, and he had a proposition to make. He had bought 100 acres of cotton plantation and ten acres of citrus groves in south Texas near the Mexican border. He suggested that Bill come in with him. Bill's parents approved of the idea and bought him 50 acres of cotton fields in the Rio Grande Valley. Late in June 1946, he and Kells went to Pharr, Texas, about 60 miles from the Gulf coast. They rented a house and settled in. 'We had some land, and we were in the cotton raising business for a while, did pretty well. It wasn't a job and it wasn't anything that interested me at all, either of us, no, we'd gotten this land and it was fairly profitable.'

Each day he and Kells would go and look at the cotton. They knew nothing whatsoever about the crop, which was being picked by illegal Mexican labourers. Then at exactly 5.00 p.m., drinks would be served. Kells would take a tin pail out front and bang it and all the neighbours would come running.

Back in New York, Bill asked Joan to move to Texas with him and she agreed. The idea was to find a secluded place where people would leave them in peace. Here they would live the healthy country life and grow a cash crop of marijuana while Kells managed Bill's cotton plantation for him. They found the ideal place near New Waverly, about 40 miles north of Houston, set in 97 acres at the end of a logging road. There was a weathered cabin without running water or electricity and a few tumbledown barns and sheds surrounded by wild berry thickets. Next to the house Bill built a 700-gallon cistern on a stand to collect precious rainwater from the corrugated iron roof. The land sloped away to a bayou filled with semi-tropical undergrowth and swampland. There were tics and chiggers, armadillos and scorpions.

Joan was pregnant, and it seemed a good idea to have another person around to help out. By then Herbert Huncke was out of jail again, and Bill paid for him to come and stay. He was sent to Houston to buy pot seeds and find a source of benzedrine inhalers for Joan, and was also kept busy around the farm: fencing land, carrying water and screening the front porch. The pot seeds were planted among moss-draped oak and persimmon, with a cover crop of tomatoes to screen them.

Each morning Bill would appear in his usual suit and tie, and drive into town and collect the mail and local papers. Then he would sit on the porch, remarking on local events. Years later, when he was making newspaper-style manuscripts, he named one the *Coldspring News*, after a small community to the east of New Waverly. Many later texts draw on his impressions from this period: 'Old sow got caught in the fence last week. Man, are we ever in hicksville.'

In the evenings Bill and Joan would sit out on the porch by the light of kerosene lamps while Huncke grilled the steaks and four-year-old Julie played. It was also Huncke's job to wind up the old phonograph and change the records: 'Low Flame' by Coleman Hawkins or the Viennese waltzes that Bill liked.

In March 1947, Huncke wrote to Allen Ginsberg, 'Bill is a good friend. He is exceedingly interested in guns. He has allowed me to shoot and I find them much less awe inspiring. Bill is quite a guy.' There was so much gunfire in the woods, in fact, that the locals first thought that gangsters had bought the old place. Far from living in anonymity, they stuck out like a neon sign; strangers in a small rural community in which everyone knew everyone else's business.

At 3 a.m. on 21 July, Joan knocked on Bill's door. 'I think it's time,' she said. Bill got up, dressed and drove her to Conroe, the nearest town. They had made no arrangements at all concerning her pregnancy, but fortunately the birth went well and the next day she was back home with the baby, William Seward Burroughs III.

At the time Joan was using two benzedrine inhalers a day and had to bottle feed the unfortunate child because her own milk was shot through with amphetamine. She had made no effort to kick her habit during her pregnancy. Billy Jr was addicted at birth and went into immediate withdrawal. Not surprisingly, he was a difficult child and cried all the time. Bill spent hours each day carrying him in his arms, trying to calm him.

Allen Ginsberg and his friend Neal Cassady arrived, hitch-hiking in from Denver; Cassady was later immortalised by Kerouac as Dean Moriarty in *On the Road*. Ginsberg had been trying all summer, with insignificant results, to get Cassady to have sex. Huncke, realising the situation, had attempted to make a bed for Allen and Neal but he was not the most practical of men: 'I conceived of getting these sideboards together in some kind of bed situation,' he said. 'The only place to work was in front of the cabin, everybody could see me working with that fucking bed ...' Ginsberg had arrived expecting to finally achieve some kind of homosexual bliss with the fickle Cassady, only to find there was no bed for them to sleep in. 'I was absolutely outraged at Burroughs for not having the sense to get a decent bed or make provision,' Ginsberg said. He and Cassady were in the final days of their torturous relationship and Ginsberg only stayed a few days before shipping out on a freighter to West Africa from Houston.

Cassady stayed on to help harvest the pot and at the end of September Burroughs put Joan and the children on the train to New York, packed the back of the Jeep with mason jars filled with pot and set out to drive to the city. They covered the 1,900 miles in three days, non-stop, with Neal doing most of the driving. The normally garrulous Cassady remained silent for most of the trip.

The effort was hardly worth it: there was no market for green, uncured pot in New York, and Bill finally let it go for

$100, just to get rid of it. His parents arrived in town and installed Bill and Joan in a resort hotel in Atlantic Beach, thinking it would be good for the children. But no sooner had they arrived in New York than Bill's old friend Garver managed to get Bill back on junk. (In January 1948 Bill had made a determined effort to kick and had committed himself to the Federal Narcotics Farm in Lexington, Kentucky, after which he returned to the farm in New Waverly more or less straight. This was a pattern which was to repeat itself for many years.)

After taking a loss on the pot, Bill decided to sell the farm and move to a city, choosing New Orleans as his new base. He bought a house at 509 Wagner Street in Algiers, just across the Mississippi from New Orleans. It was large, comfortable and surrounded by a large plot of land. It took no time at all for Bill to sniff out the New Orleans junk neighbourhood. Each day he went over on the ferry to score. There was plenty around but it cost two dollars a cap; soon Bill was using three caps a day and needed to do a little pushing on the side to help pay for his habit.

One day he woke up sick and went across the river to see his connection. When he returned he tried to recapture on paper the painful over-sensitivity of junk sickness, 'the oil slick on the river, the hastily parked car'. These texts are lost but Burroughs has often mentioned the fact that a mild junk sickness causes acute nostalgia, and he embodied this in *Junky*, which he began writing the next year.

One morning in April, I woke up a little sick. I lay there looking at shadows on the white plaster ceiling. I remembered a long time ago when I lay in bed beside my mother, watching lights from the street move across the ceiling and down the walls. I felt the sharp nostalgia of train whistles, piano music down a city street, burning leaves.

A mild degree of junk sickness always brought me the magic of childhood.

The stay in Algiers was brief. Bill got on badly with his Italian neighbours and was finally busted for possession of heroin. The police seized his car and searched his house without a warrant, finding a small quantity of heroin, a jar of marijuana and a variety of firearms. Fortunately Joan was able to find him a good lawyer and Bill was immediately transferred to a private sanatorium where he kicked his habit. He was very lucky to avoid jail. There was a mandatory two to five years in Angola State prison in the State of Louisiana for possession of narcotics and Bill was very fortunate that the police searched his house illegally; the Federal DA would not touch the case. If he was caught again in Louisiana, he would go down for a mandatory seven years. Bill's lawyer hinted to him that it would be prudent to leave the country.

In May 1949, Bill took the family to stay with Kells Elvins on his farm near Pharr, Texas. Here he began reading Wilhelm Reich and he and Kells built themselves one of Reich's orgone accumulators: an experimental device to collect orgone energy, the natural life force which Reich believed circulated in the atmosphere and could be concentrated using a simple box made from layers of organic material and metal. They built a wooden box about eight feet high, lined with galvanised iron. Inside was an old ice-box, which in theory doubled the effect. The box was supposed to boost your orgone level, tone you up and get your sexuality flowing again, and Burroughs was convinced of its efficacy. 'The Orgone box does have a definite sexual effect,' Burroughs wrote later. He made a little portable one from a gasoline can wrapped in organic material. 'The orgones would stream out of the nozzle of the gas can. One day I got into the big accumulator and held the little one over my joint and came right off.'

Taking his lawyer's advice, in late 1949 Bill took Joan, and the two children, Billie and Julie, to Mexico City, where he enrolled in Mexico City College on the GI Bill, studying Mayan and Aztec history and Mayan language. The statute of limitations meant that his case in Louisiana would be cancelled in five years. In fact it was to be 25 years before Bill returned to the States, other than for brief visits.

Even in Mexico Bill still had trouble with his middle-class neighbours, who suspected that he was a dope fiend, and with the local children who screamed '*Vicioso*!' ('Junkie') at him in the street. They were right, of course: Bill was on junk again.

But life in Mexico for an American was very free, with none of the restrictions concerning drugs and homosexuality that had hampered him in the USA. It was during the reign of President Aleman and the 'Mordida' was king: 'A vast pyramid of bribes reached from the cop on the beat to the President.' The only real problem was that Joan was unable to get her benzedrine inhalers in Mexico and went through three weeks of painful withdrawal. She substituted tequila, which was 40 cents a quart, and told Allen Ginsberg that she was 'somewhat drunk from 8 a.m. on'.

Forty cents was also the cost of a boy. Joan did not seem to mind about Bill's homosexuality, or at least did not complain publicly. This did not stop Ginsberg writing to ask Bill whether it was fair on Joan for him to go with boys. Bill replied testily,

Now this business about Joan and myself is downright insane. I never made any pretensions of permanent hetero-sexual orientation. What lie are you talking about? Like I say, I never promised or even implied anything. How could I promise something that is not in my power to give? I am not responsible for Joan's sexual life, never was, never pretended to be. Nor are we in any particular mess. There is, of course, as there was from the beginning, an impasse, and cross-purposes that are, in all likelihood, not amenable to any solution.

Kells Elvins and his wife Marianne visited Mexico City and, with Kells' encouragement, Bill began writing. Elvins insisted that he should record his experiences as a junky, using straightforward narrative. Elvins had always been impressed by Bill's remarkable memory, his brilliant dry wit and ability to tell a story, and he gave Bill the self-confidence needed to make a beginning. Despite being on junk, Bill worked every day, writing his story in chronological order, as if writing a diary. He called it *Junk*. We first hear of it in a letter to Allen Ginsberg written on 1 May 1950, from the cotton plantation in Pharr, where Bill was visiting Kells. In it Burroughs said that he been working on a novel about junk which he had almost finished; however, he doubted if anyone would publish it because of the criticisms of the narcotics department it contained. By December 1950 Bill and his family had moved to a new address at 37 Cerrada de Medellin, Mexico City, and the first draft of the book was complete.

Junk dealt with Burroughs' experiences in New York as a junky through four increasingly traumatic attempts at withdrawal, and finished up in New Orleans. In April 1951, he decided to add another chapter on his further experiences in Mexico City. It was a *roman à clef*, a remarkable confessional document, completely honest, describing every indignity, each embarrassing incident and failing. The early draft, now lost, contained much theoretical discussion about drug addiction and the ideas of Wilhelm Reich, but Bill decided to cut them all out and concentrate entirely on straight narrative. There was so much that Bill wanted to say. He wrote to Lucien Carr: 'The connections between junk and sex are extensive, and definitely belong in the book. When I wrote the original MS I was on the junk. You might say there were two books to be writ, one written on the junk one off, or more accurately half the book written on and half off.'

Allen Ginsberg was working as a market researcher in New York and had taken on the role of literary agent for Burroughs, Kerouac and several of his other friends – it would be many years before Ginsberg himself was published. He found the editors at the big New York publishers less than sympathetic towards Bill's manuscript. Jason Epstein at Doubleday told him: 'The prose is not very good. This could only work if it were written by someone important like Winston Churchill.'

In June Bill moved his family to 210 Orizaba, Apartment 5, in the centre of Mexico City near to the university and the Bounty, a bar popular with American expatriates. His previous neighbours had turned him in to the police and it had cost $200 in bribes to keep from being arrested.

Three months later an event occurred which was to transform his life forever: Bill had been on an expedition to Ecuador with a new friend, Lewis Marker, in search of the hallucinatory drug yage. The trip was fraught with problems because Bill had amorous intentions regarding Marker, but Marker was not really gay – he had agreed to go on the journey only because

Bill was paying the costs, and had agreed in advance to restrict sex to only twice a week. They had a miserable time in the jungle and failed to find any yage; the story of the expedition is told in hilarious detail in Bill's book *Queer*. Bill and Marker returned to Mexico City at the beginning of September to their respective apartments, their relationship strained to breaking point.

A few days later, on 6 September 1951, Bill heard the whistle of a knife sharpener in the street and took down a knife he had bought in Ecuador to be sharpened. 'I was walking down the street and suddenly I found tears streaming down my face. So I said, "What the hell is the matter? What the hell is the matter with you?" ' He found it difficult to breathe and was filled with an enormous sense of depression. He returned to his apartment and began drinking heavily. He and Joan drank all through the afternoon.

Bill was low on money and had arranged to sell a gun, a Star .380 automatic. Bill's friend John Healy, co-owner of the Bounty, knew someone who was interested and had arranged for him to meet Bill at his place. At six o'clock Bill and Joan went to Healy's apartment over the Bounty to meet the buyer. The buyer had not arrived but there was a drinking party going on. 'Because I felt so terrible, I began throwing down one drink after the other. And then this thing occurred . . . I was very drunk.'

Bill opened his travel bag and pulled out the gun. 'I suddenly said, "It's about time for our William Tell act. Put a glass on your head." ' They had never performed a William Tell act but Joan, who was also very drunk, laughed and balanced a six-ounce water glass on her head. Bill fired. Joan slumped in her chair and the glass fell to the floor, undamaged. The bullet had entered Joan's brain through her forehead. She was pronounced dead on arrival at Red Cross Hospital.

Bill's lawyer, Bernabé Jurado, got him out of jail on bail in thirteen days, something of a record. Bill was charged and found guilty of *imprudencia criminal* and was released on bail until sentencing, which would occur one year later. Each Monday Bill had to report to Lecumbere Prison and sign in. Bill's son, Billy, went to live with Bill's parents in St Louis.

Joan's daughter, Julie, went to her grandparents in Albany. Bill was left alone in Mexico City, his wife dead, his family dispersed.

More than 30 years later, Bill wrote,

> I am forced to the appalling conclusion that I would never have become a writer but for Joan's death, and to a realisation of the extent to which this event has motivated and formulated my writing. I live with the constant threat of possession, and a constant need to escape from possession, from Control. So the death of Joan brought me in contact with the invader, the Ugly Spirit, and manoeuvred me into a lifelong struggle, in which I have had no choice except to write my way out.

Although Bill had already written the first draft of *Junk*, the evidence of the previous 37 years of his life suggested that he was unlikely to stick at it as a writer. The constant moves and the repetitive cycle of junk addiction and cure added up to a dilettante, unfocussed life, a talent wasted, perhaps to be remembered only as a bar-room raconteur.

Regrettably we do not have the early draft versions of *Junk* written before Joan's death, which would show the extent to which that event affected the form of his work. Lewis Marker and Eddie Woods, another friend of Bill's in Mexico City, left it in a restaurant in Jacksonville, Florida, where Marker's parents lived, and were too embarrassed to go back for it. It is possible that Burroughs might have continued to pursue the straight, hard-boiled narrative. But after this shattering experience he had to find a new method of expression – something less restrictive and much more flexible, which would be a suitable vehicle for his over-active imagination. He returned to the idea of the routine, first developed with Elvins, but now he perfected it. Not surprisingly there was a period of transition – the transitional work being his novel *Queer*.

4 Queer

Despite Ginsberg's efforts, no regular hardback publisher wanted *Junky*; then he had an idea. In 1949, after an incident involving Herbert Huncke and a stolen car, Ginsberg had been arrested even though he was only in the car for the ride. After various lawyers had done their work, Ginsberg finished up in the Columbia Psychiatric Institute rather than in jail. There he met a fellow patient, Carl Solomon, who later inspired his celebrated poem, *Howl for Carl Solomon*. Solomon was now out of the mental hospital and working for his uncle, AA Wyn, at Avon Paperbacks. Allen sold him the idea of publishing *Junk*, as it was then called, as a paperback original, an idea to which Bill responded enthusiastically.

The paperback revolution was sweeping America. Paperbacks were sold mostly from newsstands and railroad stations rather than through bookshops, but they had huge print runs and reached far more people than conventionally published hardbacks. They were never reviewed and tended to be downmarket novels: crime or westerns, or else cheap reprints of classics. It was not the practice in the 50s for a best-selling novel subsequently to appear in paperback.

By March of 1952, Bill was working on a new novel. He wrote to Allen, 'With Marker away and no one around I can talk to I have need of distraction. Novel could be part II of Junk (is, however, complete in itself). Dennison main character but I have shifted to 3rd person narrative. Relationship of Allerton and Dennison (Marker and myself though both Allerton and Dennison are to be regarded as derived from rather than copied from the originals) seems to be the central theme.'

He also told Jack Kerouac about his new book, 'This is a Queer novel using the same straight narrative method as I used in Junk.' Kerouac replied suggesting that *Queer* would be a good title for the book, an idea which Bill gladly took up because he had been baffled for a title. Bill recognised that *Queer* was really a continuation of *Junk*, but the shift from first to third person in the narrative seemed to abrogate the idea of joining the two together in one book. As Bill saw it, there was no satisfactory stylistic way around the problem, as he wrote to Ginsberg:

The 3rd person is really 1st person. That is, the story is told from the viewpoint of Lee. When someone walks out of the room where Lee is he is gone until Lee sees him again. There is nothing in the story Lee isn't there to see, you understand, exactly as in 1st person. The subject matter makes 3rd person convenient and at times mandatory. Take this passage for example. 'Lee has undressed preparatory to laying an Indian. Though he was near 40 he had the thin delicate body of an adolescent.' OK I do have the same physique I had at 18, which is uncommon and significant in delineating the character. But wouldn't I feel silly putting the above passage in the 1st person? I will however experiment with 1st person as I write. Now *Junk* is, of course, complete without this part I am writing, but the two sections do complement each other. I have some misgivings about the present work. Sex and love are difficult subjects. There is always impairment of the critical faculty, and what is interesting to me may not be of interest to others.

It is significant that, from the very first, Burroughs' novels run on, one from the other, as they continued to do throughout his career with the same characters and events reappearing from book to book.

There was another problem: Bill's mother had read Kerouac's *The Town and the City* and immediately recognised the thinly-disguised Burroughs. She had not approved. In *Junk*, Burroughs had planned to use the same name, 'Dennison', for himself, but was worried that it would be too obvious a clue for his mother to find and identify. He intended to publish the book under a pseudonym, since he did not want to antagonise his parents and jeopardise his allowance, and after many suggestions, Bill adopted the name of William Lee as a *nom de plume* – hardly a disguise at all since his mother's maiden name was Lee.

AA Wyn at Ace Books agreed to publish the book, but wanted to include some of the material from *Queer* in the second half. Bill was happy to go along with their demands, trusting that Allen would get him the best deal possible. Accordingly, at the beginning of April 1952, Ace agreed to publish *Junkie* (their preferred spelling) for an $800 advance. They expected it to be a commercial success because, ever since Nelson Algren's *The Man With The Golden Arm* in 1949, there had been a vogue for books about junkies. Ace thought that Bill might make as much as $8,000 from it in the end. Bill wrote Allen: 'You really are a sweetheart. I could kiss you on both cheeks . . .'

Ace now began clamouring to see *Queer*, which was only about one quarter finished, because they wanted the second half of the book within two months, and Bill began to regret agreeing to the inclusion of material from it. He wanted Ace to go ahead and publish *Junkie* so that he could take his time on the new novel. He planned to write about his trip to Ecuador with Marker, knowing that it was a potentially amusing, yet tragic, subject. However, he left it up to Allen to decide and Allen went along with Ace, probably because he thought they would not publish it otherwise.

Contrary to their original agreement, Ace now held up payment on the whole advance until Bill delivered the material from *Queer*, something which rankled with Burroughs and gave him his first taste of what a career in writing would be like. Time passed and still Wyn did not publish the book; in the meantime several other books on the same theme came out, including *Down All Your Streets* and *H Is For Heroin*. 'I think this is beginning of deluge,' Bill wrote Allen, 'NOW is the time to publish or we bring up rear and lose advantage of timeliness . . . Subject is hot now but won't be hot long.'

Bill completed 60 pages of *Queer*, under great pressure, but still Wyn sent no contract and no money. It was only when Bill flatly refused to write any more that Wyn gave in, but on condition that Burroughs write an additional 40 pages about his Mexican experiences which would be added to *Junkie*.

The contract with Ace was finally signed on Saturday 5 July 1952. Bill got the first of his payments, $180, and began work on the remaining 40 pages of *Junkie*. He was still aggrieved that he was now under pressure to complete the additional Mexican material and warned Allen, 'As it is I am rushed, there is going to be some sloppy work – I am also kicking, really kicking now, and it can't be helped. I will do the best I can.'

The new material consisted of 40 pages transposed from the first to third person taken from the opening section of *Queer* and reworked to fit. On 13 July, Bill sent the completed manuscript to Allen, noting, 'It is the best I could do on such short notice . . . I had to write more or less to order. I am not completely satisfied, especially not with that fucking preface.' The preface was a disclaimer from Ace who had panicked at the thought that the book might be somehow construed as condoning narcotic addiction.

With the book, as he thought, finally out of his hands, Bill replied to Allen's query, 'I don't see myself writing any sequel to *Queer* or writing anything more at all at this point. I wrote *Queer* for Marker. I guess he doesn't think much of it or of me.' Once again, Burroughs was in need of a collaborator or receiver for his routines; without this audience to encourage him, he was unable to get started.

Wyn continued to hold up publication, and in December 1952 came up with the idea of sandwiching Bill's book back to back with the memoirs of a narcotic agent as part of the Ace Double-Book series. Ace presumably thought that they could ride out any criticism by showing that they had balanced Burroughs' neutral text by appending an overwhelmingly anti-junk text to it. Bill was naturally appalled, but thought that any complaints would lead to even further delay.

In 1953, Bill left on an expedition to the South American jungles to make a further search for the drug yage, which was said to aid telepathy; Allen had researched the subject for him in New York the previous summer at the 42nd Street and Columbia University libraries. Unfortunately the garrulous Ginsberg told Wyn of Bill's plans and Wyn decided that he now wanted to see the new material about yage as well, and began pestering Bill for yet another section for the book. Bill agreed to write something on yage but complained to Allen, from Quayaquil: 'If they are holding up publication waiting on yage material they may wait a long time.' Wyn had clearly had second, and even third, thoughts about the book and really did not know what he wanted. He saw the book as autobiographical, and since Ginsberg told him that Burroughs was continually writing new material, he naturally wanted to see it all in case he could make a better selection.

Finally Wyn realised that things could not go on indefinitely and in May 1953, when Bill was in Lima searching for yage, *Junkie* was published in an edition of 100,000 copies. It contained about 40 pages from the opening of *Queer*, but most of the technical material about drugs was edited out, as was the material on yage. The memoirs of the narcotic agent, sandwiched with it, turned out to be an innocuous reprint of a book from 1941. 'Narcotic Agent not so bad as I expected it would be,' Bill wrote to Allen. 'He does not sound like an overly obnoxious character. How are sales?'

At the time, *Junkie* did not generate much excitement. There were no reviews since it was published for the newsstand trade, with a lurid cover of a man struggling with a woman in a red dress for possession of a hypodermic syringe. Bill himself regarded it primarily as a commercial venture. In the introduction to its companion volume, *Queer*, which was not published until 1986, 33 years after its composition, he wrote: 'The motivation for that [*Junkie*] was comparatively simple: to put down in the most accurate and simple terms my experience as an addict. I was hoping for publication, money, recognition. Kerouac had published *The Town and the City* at the time I started writing *Junky*. I remember writing in a letter to him, when his book was published, that money and fame were now assured. As you can see, I knew nothing about the writing business at the time.'

Like the Benway routine composed with Kells Elvins, *Junkie* was written in the hard-boiled gangster genre of Hammett and Chandler which Burroughs had now mastered completely:

> Three young hoodlums from Brooklyn drifted in, wooden-faced, hands-in-pockets, stylised as a ballet. They were looking for Jack. He had given them a short count on some deal. At least, that was the general idea. They conveyed their meaning less by words than by significant jerks of the head and by stalking around the apartment and leaning against the walls. At length, one of them walked to the door and jerked his head. They filed out.

Though *Junkie* is straight narrative, being autobiographical it lacks the kind of plot that readers might expect. Though billed as 'the confessions of an unredeemed drug addict', few people could have guessed that it actually was what it claimed to be. The action in the book is governed by the fact that junk (heroin and morphine) is illegal. Since Lee (Burroughs) is a heroin addict, the action consists of the search for drugs and the avoidance of arrest. It is an adventure story – Lee versus the law – episodic like the cliff-hangers at the Saturday morning children's movie matinees. In *Junkie* Lee goes through four progressively worse periods of withdrawal, and after surviving each one, embarks on further adventures. The book ends with him setting off in search of yage. The last line of the book reads, 'Maybe I will find in Yage what I was looking for in junk and weed and coke. Yage could be the final fix.'

The book opens in 1944 with Bill first taking possession of the stolen syrettes of morphine that he was to sell to Phil 'The Sailor' and Huncke. (Huncke becomes Herman in the book.) William Lee's life up until his first shot of junk is summarised in a brief prologue, which understandably changes some of the facts to provide anonymity, but for the most part the book sticks accurately to the real chronology and events of Burroughs' life. There are periodic expository passages in which Bill gives the reader factual information about drugs, Federal and State laws, the conditions in the Kentucky detox facility in Lexington and so on. The book works as a how-to-do-it manual, an encyclopaedic introduction to the junky world for the uninitiated reader, including facts such as how to cure pot, prepare paregoric, details of drug laws in the United States ('In 1937, weed was placed under the Harrison Narcotics Act'), and even what to do should you find yourself on an airplane without a hypodermic syringe: 'His pants were spotted with blood where he had been fixing on the plane with a safety pin. You make a hole with the pin, and put the dropper over (not in) the hole, and the solution goes right in. With this method you don't need a needle, but it takes an old time junkie to make it work.'

The confessional form is normally used as a vehicle to reveal the inner life of the author, the passage from innocence to experience, as a *Bildungsroman* or quest for self-knowledge. With Bill there is no mention of an inner life. William Lee, the narrator, appears to have no inner life at all. His only mention of a subjective state appears towards the very end when he opines that he is really in bad shape: 'I had deteriorated shockingly ... My emotions spilled out everywhere. I was uncontrollably sociable and would talk to anybody I could pin down. I forced distastefully intimate confidences on perfect strangers.'

Lee's wife is mentioned only in passing when he is arrested in Algiers, and there is no mention of his children. There is only one character, only one point of view: that of the cool, detached hipster. The reason for this detachment was of course the junk, as Bill explained in his introduction to *Queer*:

In my first novel, *Junky*, the protagonist 'Lee' comes across as integrated and self-contained, sure of himself and where he is going. In *Queer* he is disintegrated, desperately in need of contact, completely unsure of himself and of his purpose.

The difference of course is simple: Lee on junk is coveted, protected and also severely limited. Not only does junk short-circuit the sex drive, it also blunts emotional reactions to the vanishing point, depending on the dosage. Looking back over the action of *Queer*, that hallucinated month of acute withdrawal takes on a hellish glow of menace and evil drifting out of neon-lit cocktail bars, the ugly violence, the .45 always just under the surface. On junk I was insulated, didn't drink, didn't go out much, just shot up and waited for the next shot.

When the cover is removed, everything that has been held in check by junk spills out. The withdrawing addict is subject to the emotional excesses of a child or an adolescent, regardless of his actual age. And the sex drive returns full force. Men of 60 experience wet dreams and spontaneous orgasms . . . Unless the reader keeps this in mind, the metamorphosis of Lee's character (in *Queer*) will appear as inexplicable or psychotic.

Though narrow in its reference, *Junkie* contained much wry humour, and it is Burroughs' very specific mixture of hustler-junkie jargon with WASP articulation, the hip talk mixed with the formal language of Harvard, compounded by a light camp overtone, that gives his prose its particular, distinctive flavour and makes it very hard for his followers to duplicate. They can copy the street talk, but never the ease with which he enunciates such lines as 'obviously inept', 'fabricating preposterous lies', 'perform some unspeakable act upon his person'. In *Junkie* Burroughs found his voice. Though the elements of his style were not yet fully integrated he already had the ability to evoke a scene and an atmosphere in short, telling physical detail: 'There are no more junkies at 103rd and Broadway waiting for the connection. The connection has gone somewhere else. But the feel of junk is still there. It hits you at the corner, follows you along the block, then falls away like a discouraged panhandler as you walk on.'

Another aspect of Bill's humour comes from Bill the misanthrope: just because he had sex with boys, took drugs and smoked dope didn't mean that he tolerated or in any way supported the majority of junkies, homosexuals or pot-heads. Bill simply didn't like most people. Ever since school he had always been the outsider, the loner. He preferred to be left alone and for other people to mind their own business. His general dislike of mankind was transformed in his books into a surreal, Céline-esque panorama. Drawing on his ability for outrageous exaggeration, even the straight narrative of *Junkie* took on this aspect as Bill veered off into 'routine' territory, paving the way for *The Naked Lunch*:

> He has the mark of a certain trade or occupation that no longer exists. If junk were gone from the earth, there might still be junkies standing around in junk neighbourhoods feeling the lack, vague and persistent, a pale ghost of junk sickness.
>
> So this man walks around in the places he once exercised his obsolete and unthinkable trade. But he is unperturbed. His eyes are black with an insect's unseeing calm. He looks as if he nourished himself on honey and Levantine syrups that he sucks up through a sort of proboscis.
>
> What is his lost trade? Definitely of a servant class and something to do with the dead, though he is not an embalmer. Perhaps he stores something in his body – a substance to prolong life – of which he is periodically milked by his masters. He is as specialised as an insect, for the performance of some inconceivably vile function.

This was not the stuff of the normal tell-all, 'I was a depraved junkie' books of the period. It was already clear that fiction was Bill's natural home; fiction informed by his acute eye for detail and dialogue taken from the real world.

There was already a plan for another book. Bill's letters to Allen Ginsberg described his travels in hilarious detail, and the descriptive sections were always intended for publication. Despite his allowance, circumstances often conspired to cause him to run out of money and sell his typewriter, and during those times Bill's travel reports would be written by hand or typed up in stores which rented typewriters by the hour in Ecuador or Peru:

> Arriving in Manta a shabby man in a sweater started opening my bags. I thought he was a brazen thief and gave him a shove. Turns out he was customs inspector.
>
> The boat gave out with a broken propeller at Las Playas half way between Manta and Guayaquil. I rode ashore on

a balsa raft. Arrested on the beach suspect to have floated up from Peru on the Humboldt Current with a young boy and a toothbrush (I travel light, only the essentials) so we are hauled before an old dried up fuck, the withered face of cancerous control. The kid with me don't have paper one. The cops keep saying plaintively:

'But don't you have any papers at all?'

Ginsberg and Burroughs had evolved a loose plan for a book to be called *The Naked Lunch*, which would consist of three parts: 'Junk' (the more technical material missing from *Junkie*, including notes on cocaine); 'Queer' (except those parts already used in *Junkie*) and 'Yage'. The final part was to consist of the South American material that Wyn wanted to see for *Junkie*. In the event, *Queer* was not published until 1985 and sections of 'Yage' were published in 1963 by City Lights as *The Yage Letters*. The 'Interzone' and 'The Market' sections of the final published text of *The Naked Lunch* were originally part of 'Yage' but everything else was written later, mostly in Tangier.

The affair with Marker was over, or abandoned, and Mexico City held too many bad memories, as well as the possibility of prison. Bill decided to move to Tangier, where he had heard the living was cheap and drugs and boys plentiful. He arranged to spend a month en route with Allen Ginsberg in New York and arrived at Allen's tenement apartment at 206 East 7th Street, just off Tompkins Park, in the middle of August 1953. He and Allen had not seen each other for six years, not since Allen and Neal Cassady visited him in New Waverly, Texas, but they had been in correspondence ever since, particularly regarding the publication of *Junkie*, and were delighted to see each other.

Ginsberg felt Burroughs had changed. He wrote to Cassady:

He is really exciting to talk to, more so for me than ever. His new loquaciousness is something I never had the advantage of. I'm older now and the emotional relationship and conflict of will and mutual digging are very intense, continuous, exhausting and fertile. He creates small, usable, literary symbolic psychic fantasies daily. One of the deepest people I ever saw. He is staying with me. I come home from work at 4.45 and we talk until one a.m. or later. I hardly get enuf sleep, can't think about work seriously, am all hung up in great psychic marriage with him for the month – amazing also his outwardness and confidence, he is very personal now, and gives the impression of suffering terribly and continuously. I am persuading him to write a really great sincere novel. He is going to Tangiers ... The new impression of Bill that I get is that he is very great, greater than I ever realised, before even.

After Joan's death and the failure of his relationship with Marker, Bill had been using Allen as a receiver in order to continue writing. His routines were his main communication with the outside world, and whoever received them became the focus of his emotional as well as his literary life. It was usually a one-sided relationship but it sufficed, and now he returned to New York filled with thoughts of Allen.

There had not been an emotional relationship during the time they lived together in 1945–6, but Allen had a tremendous respect for Bill as a friend and was prepared to do anything he wanted. 'I thought he was my teacher, so I'd do what I could to amuse him,' he said. Allen recognised that, since Joan's death, Bill had no one to talk with on an intimate level, and no one to love him. Ginsberg recalled, 'Burroughs fell in love with me and we slept together and I saw a soft centre where he felt isolated, alone in the world and he needed ... a feeling of affection, and since I did love him and did have that respect and affection, he responded. I kinda felt privileged.'

Herbert Huncke commented on the effects of Joan's death:

Joan was dead and his changes had been many and varied – and I guessed at the time he felt his loneliness intensely, and much of the time was occupied attempting to forget at least most of those happenings which might have helped recall her to mind. Their relationship, from what I personally knew, had been of an extremely intimate nature insofar as Joan was concerned, at least ... She and Bill had something rare and certainly, from the standpoint of the observer, very fine and beautiful. Unquestionably the adjustments required of Bill to continue seeking meaning and purpose must have placed him under exhausting strain, and I couldn't help but wonder at his self-control.

The poet Gregory Corso was staying with Ginsberg when Bill arrived, but soon moved out. Bill wanted all Allen's attention and gave Gregory blood-curdling looks as he used his machete to slowly and methodically chop up the two suitcases of yage that he brought back from Peru.

It was a very productive period: Allen and Bill did a great deal of work on Bill's letters from South America, editing, shaping and tightening the anecdotes, routines and hilarious descriptions of his tribulations while searching for the yage vine. Many of the ideas that appeared later in *The Naked Lunch* were first thought of at East 7th Street. The futuristic vibrating city of Interzone was inspired by the fire escapes and washing lines in Allen's Lower East Side backyard. Bill looked out of the window and saw a woman reach out over the fire escape and start pulling in the laundry. Fire escapes faced each other across the backyard courtyards, with washing lines going from building to building; level upon level of apartment fire escapes and laundry lines all connected. Bill conceived of a futuristic city with its levels connected by a web of catwalks, boardwalks and fire-escapes; a great labyrinth of alleyways and hallways; a city so old that it had been rebuilt layer upon layer, one building upon another. As he described the idea to Ginsberg he developed it into the notion of a city with a vibrating soundless hum, of many larval entities waiting for a live one, as yet unborn – the essence of Burroughs' literary imagery.

Another idea to emerge that autumn was that of *schlupping*: the complete assimilation of another person (although it is alluded to in a less overt form in *Queer*). Burroughs' proposition was that he and Allen would become soulmates and somehow merge into one entity. Bill kept making up weird routines about the idea of parasitic symbiosis, like Bradley the Buyer in *The Naked Lunch* who schlupps up the District Supervisor in some unspeakable manner. Bill was hoping to amuse and please Allen with these routines, but in fact he was sending chills down his spine. 'Bill became more and more demanding that there be some kind of mental schlupp. It had gone beyond the point of being humorous and playful. It seemed that Bill was demanding it for real. Bill wanted a relationship where there were no holds barred; to achieve an ultimate telepathic union of souls.'

Allen saw the depth of Bill's intense loneliness and his genuine desire to be totally bonded to another person – and grew scared. Much as he loved and respected Bill, his own preference was for younger men, and he was also scared of being completely taken over by Bill. When Bill began talking of taking Allen to Tangier with him, Allen blurted out, 'But I don't want your ugly old cock.' Bill was devastated.

Ginsberg later said, 'It wounded him terribly because it was like complete physical rejection in a way I didn't mean. Like a heart blow that severed the trust, because I'd freaked out for that moment and regretted it ever since.' Bill left New York on 1 December 1953, on the TSS *Nea Hellas* bound for Rome.

Ginsberg was left to close up the apartment, since his own plan was to move to California via Chiapas. He packed his things and sold the furniture. All that was left was the orgone accumulator that Bill had built in the bedroom. An unpublished Ginsberg poem despaired over it:

And the great blue pool of bedspread running from my torso down the bed.
And the inaudible stupid snout of the unbelievable homemade orgone accumulator sticking over the foot of the bed
Empty valises over the door on shelves – but not to be used.

It was an unhappy parting for both of them.

5 Tangier

From New York Bill went first to Rome, where he had arranged to meet his friend Alan Ansen. He arrived there before Ansen and was very bored. There were no bars to speak of, and no boys. He hated looking at ruins and, when Ansen moved on to Venice, Bill continued his journey to Tangier which he had read about in the novels of Paul Bowles. It was to be his home for the next five years.

For the first six months of 1954, Ginsberg explored Mayan ruins and settled for a time in a coffee *finca* in the middle of the jungle. He wrote frequently to Bill, but none of the letters got through. At first Bill thought that Allen was ignoring him and wrote to Jack Kerouac: 'I have really been terribly upset and hurt that Allen doesn't write to me and I need someone to talk to. Amazing how few people can pick up on what I say. In short most people are plain bone stupid, and right now I am in need of routine receivers. Whenever I encounter the impasse of unrequited affection my only recourse is routines. Really meant for the loved one, to be sure, but in a pinch somebody else can be pressed into service.'

Months went by, and still Bill heard nothing. He told Kerouac,

Allen's neglect will drive me to some extravagance of behavior. I don't know what I will do but it will be the terror of the earth. You must remonstrate with him. I didn't expect him to act like this (not a line in four months) and I didn't expect I would feel so deeply hurt if he did. That is rather a confused sentence and I think contains some sort of contradiction. What I mean is, I did not think I was hooked on him like this. The withdrawal symptoms are worse than the Marker habit. One letter would fix me. So make it your business, if you are a real friend, to see that he writes me a fix. I am incapacitated. Can't write. Can't take an interest in anything.

PS No matter what Allen says I want to hear it understand? If he says something that you know would hurt me, please don't keep it from me. I want to know. Nothing is worse than waiting like this day after day for a letter that doesn't come. THIS IS SERIOUS JACK, DONT let me down.

When Bill found out that no one else had heard from Allen either, he began to panic, thinking that Allen had been murdered or arrested. He wrote frantically to Allen's father, to Neal Cassady, Lucien Carr and to Kerouac, anxiously demanding news. He told Kerouac: 'I don't know what I would do if anything happened to Allen. I guess you have seen the letters I wrote to him and have some idea of how much he means to me.'

Finally one of Allen's letters got through, and Bill calmed down; however, the intensity of Bill's feelings did concern Ginsberg, who wrote to Neal Cassady: 'He sure is lonely, or imagines himself such and I guess it drives him off the road at times . . . This kind of need, with which I cannot but sympathise & try to do something real about . . . will be a real problem. But of our friendship, so complicated now and in some ways difficult . . . I hardly know what to do and straighten out.'

Bill was clearly still in love with him and, once Allen reached California, continued to use Allen as the recipient for his routines and as his literary agent. Despite these problems, Ginsberg remained convinced that Burroughs was a brilliant writer, and over the years he did a huge amount of boosting on Bill's behalf, sending manuscripts to little magazines and trying to interest editors. Without Ginsberg's heroic efforts it is unlikely that Burroughs would have ever been published – indeed it is unlikely that he would have even written his early books without Ginsberg's constant encouragement.

In Tangier Bill was lonely, cut-off, and constantly haunted by the death of Joan. His letters to Allen show that he spent much of the next three years heavily addicted, usually to Eukodol, a chemical variation of codeine (dihydro-oxy-codeine) which could be bought over the counter. Bill found a room for 50 cents a day at Anthony Reitshorst's notorious male brothel at number 1 Calle de los Arcos, near the Socco Chico. The owner – Dutch Tony as he was known – always wore make-up and began each day by walking his five poodles. Living in a male brothel had its disadvantages, as Burroughs remarked, 'Understandably there was some neighbor trouble: "You like beeg one Meester?"' Also living at Dutch Tony's was an American journalist named David Woolman, who provided some companionship, and Bill began to meet some of the expatriates, but they seemed a sorry crowd. In February he found a boyfriend, an attractive gentle young Spanish boy called Kiki, who later nursed him through a particularly bad junk withdrawal. Tangier in the days of the International Zone had a big Spanish community which had little or no contact with the Arabs. Bill was fluent in Spanish from his many years in Mexico and South America, so it was only natural that he should move in the world of the Spanish boys; they were more familiar and he felt more at home among them.

Kiki was a companion, and though Bill liked him, it was not a close emotional relationship; nor was Kiki someone with whom he could discuss his writing. It was a pleasant interlude. Bill wrote to Allen: 'Kiki and I spent one of our delightful afternoons today, lying on the bed naked, dozing and making desultory love, smoking a little kif, and eating great, sweet grapes. What a tranquil, healthy young male he is. There doesn't seem to be a conflict in him ... As you say, he is a dream for which I will have nostalgia.'

Ginsberg remained the recipient of Bill's routines: 'He began sending me letters,' Ginsberg said. 'He began making up routines which reflected one of two moods: either situations of total vulnerability and parasitism, or total outrageous humorous raucous comedy. So on one side there's Dr Benway and on the other side there is the image of the man who is hung and comes involuntarily. That's an image of his own erotic fix. The involuntary orgasm when being screwed anally which he found a symbolic form of in the man being hung.'

The hanging routine, like the other routines, eventually went into *The Naked Lunch* (the 'Blue Movie' section): 'Routines like habit,' Burroughs wrote Ginsberg. 'Without routines my life is chronic nightmare, grey horror of Midwest suburb . . . I have to have receiver for routine. If there is no one there to receive it, routine turns back on me and tears me apart, grows more and more insane (literal growth like cancer) and impossible, and fragmentary like berserk pinball machine and I am screaming: "Stop it! Stop it!" '

Bill and Allen's collaboration was unique in literary history because it was essentially one-way. Ginsberg's role as receiver was to encourage, admire, preserve and eventually edit the material into book form. With Allen he knew that he could write absolutely anything – Ginsberg would not be shocked nor censorious no matter what the subject matter. He was the perfect receiver.

Despite his addiction (at one point he was shooting Eukodol every two hours), Bill worked hard on his writing. He wrote to Allen, 'Here is my latest attempt to write something saleable.' It turned out to be the famous 'talking asshole' routine: 'Did I ever tell you about the man who taught his asshole to talk? . . .' It was apparent that Bill's work was not destined for traditional commercial success. His humour was way too far out for the times. It was also becoming obvious that there was no difference between Bill's personal letters to Allen, and the extracts from his novel in progress which he enclosed with them. 'Maybe the real novel is letters to you,' he wrote.

He worked on this idea, and in June 1954 wrote to Allen, 'I've been thinking about routine as art form and what distinguishes it from other forms. One thing, it is not completely symbolic; that is, it is subject to shlup over into "real" action at any time. In a sense the whole Nazi movement was a great, humorless, evil routine on Hitler's part. Do you dig me? I am not sure I dig myself.'

The problem with routines was that they did not fit together easily; there was no continuous narrative, no recurring characters even; the results seemed to Bill like the notes for a novel rather than the novel itself. He never seems to have been tempted to revert to the pulp-detective narrative style of *Junkie*. Routines were his literary invention and he was determined to make them work, though the act of creation needed to unify this material seemed to be beyond his power. He felt discouraged and wrote to Kerouac: 'It's hopeless, Jack. I can't write in a popular vein.' By the end of 1954 he had sold even his typewriter to buy drugs, but he continued to write, filling page after page in longhand.

Then he found a unifying principle for the work; he decided to set the book in Tangier, which he called Interzone, and began to incorporate all of his scattered routines and notes within that framework. He told Allen: 'The fragmentary quality of my work is inherent in the method and will resolve itself so far as necessary.' The routines began to come thick and fast, and in January 1955 he wrote to Ginsberg, enclosing a routine and saying, 'Like I say, that's only a small fragment. I was throwing myself on the floor and generally carrying on, but I forgot it all. Routines are specially liable to be forgotten.'

His Spanish boyfriends aside, he had no close friends in Tangier and his literary correspondence was his only contact with the outside world. He was yet to become a friend of Paul Bowles and the other expatriate writers and members of the Tangier community. He reached terrible depths of despair in that first year, and was sustained only by his writing, as one of the early routines revealed:

At the present time writing appears to me as an absolute necessity, and at the same time I have a feeling that my talent is lost and I can accomplish nothing, a feeling like the body's knowledge of disease which the mind tries to evade and deny.

This feeling of horror is always with me now. I had the same feeling the day Joan died, and once when I was a child, I looked out into the hall, and such a feeling of fear and despair came over me for no outward reason, that I burst into tears.

I was looking into the future then. I recognise the feeling, and what I saw has not yet been realised. I can only wait for it to happen. Is it some ghastly occurrence, like Joan's death, or simply deterioration and failure and final loneliness, a dead-end set-up where there is no one I can contact? I am just a crazy old bore in a bar somewhere with my routines? I don't know but I feel trapped and doomed.

Writing was no longer a project, as *Junkie* had been, something he had to be encouraged to do. Now it had become an essential part of his being; Bill *had* to write. He had become a writer. Interzone was a perfect vehicle for such a book; it mirrored Tangier itself which, for the period 1945 until 1956, was essentially an independent country. The city with a little strip of land around it was ruled by a consortium of nine countries with equal privileges which they divided up between them: the French controlled the Customs and the British and the Belgians had the police force. The town was wide open to corruption and shady deals, and one boulevard in the newly built French section was reputed to have 600 banks in a 300-yard stretch. The nine per cent customs tax at the port paid all the taxes and smuggling was rife – which meant it was a very cheap place to live. For residents like Brion Gysin, who moved there in the summer of 1950 with Paul Bowles, Tangier was like heaven: 'It was paradise then, absolute paradise. Everything was free, everywhere, drugs, boys, everything. There'd be money floating up and down the street and the sun shone all day, and the sky was as blue as the sea . . .' But Bill did not move in the same Moroccan circles and he was there for a year before he connected properly with the expatriate community. His view of the city was not so rosy, though he appreciated the cheap boys, the availability of drugs and the low cost of living.

In January 1955 Bill wrote a mock jacket blurb for his novel-in-progress, which summed up the completed *The Naked Lunch* with uncanny accuracy:

The book grabs you by the throat (says L Marland, distinguished critic). It leaps in bed with you and performs unmentionable acts. Then it thrusts a long cold needle deep into your spine and gives you an injection of ice water. That is the only way I know to express the feeling of fear that reaches out of these pages. Behind the humor, the routines, the parody (some of it a bit heavy-handed to be sure), you glimpse a dead-end despair, a bleak landscape of rubble under the spreading black cloud of the final bomb.

Burroughs tried a succession of self-administered cures for his drug addiction. These usually involved making sure he couldn't go out and score by having Kiki take away his clothes and then administering a reduced shot each day until he was clean, but even when such methods worked, Bill was usually back on the Eukodol within a few weeks. All his money was going on drugs and it was beginning to affect his health. One incident made him check into the Jewish Benchimal Hospital for a cure, as he related to Ginsberg:

Some nights ago I got hold of some ampules each containing 1/6 grain of dolophine and 1/100 gr. of hyoscine. Now 1/100 gr. of that awful shit is already a lot, but I thought the dolophine would offset it and shot 6 ampules in the main line. The ex-captain found me sitting stark naked in the hall on the toilet seat (which I had wrenched from its moorings), playing in a bucket of water and singing 'Deep in the Heart of Texas', at the same time complaining in clearly enunciated tones, of the high cost of living – 'It all goes into razor blades.' And I attempted to go out in the street naked at 2 a.m. What a horrible nightmare if I had succeeded and came to myself wandering around the Native Quarter naked. I tore up my sheets and threw bottles all over the floor, looking for something, I did not say what. Naturally Dave and the Old Dutch Auntie who runs this whorehouse were alarmed, thinking my state was permanent. They were vastly relieved to see me the following morning fully dressed and in my right mind. I could only remember snatches of what had happened, but I do remember wondering why people were looking at me so strangely and talking in such tiresome, soothing voices. I concluded that they were crazy or drunk, and told Tony he was stinking drunk . . . I hope to enter the clinic in two days.

Later in 1955 Bill moved to the Hotel Villa Muniria, at 1 Calle Magallanes, in the old French quarter, which was then owned by a Belgian. Bill had a small whitewashed garden room with a view out over the harbour. Paul Lund, a gangster from Birmingham who had done three years in Dartmoor and was on the run from the British authorities, also lived there and they spent a great deal of time in each other's company. Bill loved his stories of British jails and the various hold-ups he had carried off, some of which wound up in *The Naked Lunch*. Later that year, Bill's friend Jim Wylie, an eccentric English painter who roamed the streets in a flowing cloak, rented him his house in the Kasbah. There he had four rooms for $20 a month: 'There was no neighbor trouble since I sat around all day shooting junk and once dripped blood all over Paul Bowles' first edition of *One Arm* by Tennessee Williams.'

The self-cures had never worked properly and even after the private sanatorium he was soon back on Eukodol. Bill realised that something more dramatic was needed. He borrowed $500 from his parents, settled his debts, and in February 1956 he moved to London to take the apomorphine cure pioneered by Dr Yerbury Dent. Apomorphine is a metabolic regulator and cures addiction by returning the body cells to their normal metabolic balance. The cellular need for the drug is removed, making the cure more successful. It worked, and Bill took his time exploring London, which he hated, visiting Alan Ansen in Venice and stopping off in Algeria before eventually returning to Tangier in September.

With Bill gone from his life, Kiki took up with the male leader of an all-girl orchestra, a Cuban who fell madly in love with him. Kiki went with him to Madrid, but was discovered in bed with one of the girls from the orchestra. The bandleader flew into a jealous rage and stabbed Kiki to death with a kitchen knife before killing himself. Kiki was twenty. He appears fleetingly in many of Burroughs' books, a presence – one of the people who affected Bill's life. There is a very sad sequence based on his death in *The Western Lands*. It was a death that clearly affected Burroughs very deeply, but it was one that time would heal, unlike that of Joan, which always remained with him.

On his return to Tangier, Bill moved back into the Villa Muniria, now owned by a Frenchwoman who had previously run a whorehouse in Saigon. 'You can be free here, you understand,' she said, digging Bill in the ribs. He was able to get his old room back, which was entered from a walled flower garden where the housekeeper's two cats sunned themselves and Bill grew pot plants to make his own majoun. The two other garden rooms were occupied by Bill's friends, David Woolman and Eric Gifford from Dutch Tony's. The rooms were separate from the rest of the hotel and very private. Bill covered one of the white plaster walls entirely with photographs, mostly from his 1953 jungle expedition in search of yage. Another wall, pitted with bullet holes, was used as his shooting gallery. He would stand matchboxes on end and take pot shots at them from his desk. He built an orgone accumulator in one corner of the room and would sit doubled up in it, smoking kif. He was very proud of his home-made majoun, or hashish candy, which he cooked up on a little spirit stove. It was made from finely chopped kif, honey, cinnamon, caraway seeds and ground nutmeg, and came out like sticky toffee. One tablespoon of it would see you through the night. All of this activity naturally gave Bill a certain reputation in town. The Spanish boys called him 'El Hombre Invisible', for the way he could slide inconspicuously from street to street, so anonymous-looking that he went undetected by the Arab boys on the lookout for foreigners to 'guide' round the city. He also had another name – Gerald Richardson, the CID chief, referred to him as 'Morphine Minnie', having observed his interest in Eukodol.

'For the first time in my life I began writing full time,' he wrote, 'and the material from which *The Naked Lunch* was later abstracted and a good deal of the material that went into *The Soft Machine* and *The Ticket That Exploded* was produced at this time. Often I would take a note book out to dinner with me and make notes while I ate. During this period I was taking majoun every day and certainly would not have achieved what I did achieve without it.'

The floor was littered with manuscript pages torn from the typewriter in haste and thrown over his shoulder. Sometimes a sea breeze came in through the open door and carried pages out into the garden. The new book now had the working title of *Word Hoard* Bill hunched over his typewriter, furiously pounding the keys, hair awry, chuckling to himself, sweating profusely in the heat, as he developed endless majoun-inspired routines about Interzone and its cast of characters.

'Routines are completely spontaneous and proceed from whatever fragmentary knowledge you have,' he wrote Allen. 'In fact a routine is by nature fragmentary, inaccurate. There is no such thing as an exhaustive routine, nor does the scholarly type mind run to routines . . . Glimpsed a new dimension of sex: Sex mixed with routines and laughter, the unmalicious, unrestrained, pure laughter that accompanies a good routine, laughter that gives a moment's freedom from the cautious, nagging, aging, frightened flesh.'

Bill remained off narcotics. He ate well, rowed Venetian-style (front-facing) in the harbour each day and attacked his writing with a new vigour. 'I'd usually take majoun every other day,' he said, 'and on the off days I would just have a bunch of big joints lined up on my desk and smoke them as I typed.' He had a succession of boys and even began to look favourably upon women. He wrote to Ginsberg, 'What are these strange feelings that come over me when I look at a cunt, little tits sticking out so cute? Could it be that?? No! No! He thrust the thought from him in horror.' Bill was finally enjoying himself: 'So many things give me pleasure, walking around town, sitting in a cafe,' he told Allen. 'I think I must be very happy.'

Six months later, Bill was still at work: 'Interzone is coming like dictation, I can't keep up with it. Read in any order. It makes no difference,' he wrote. In February 1957 he told Allen: 'This is almost automatic writing. I often sit high on hash for as long as six hours typing at top speed.'

By 1955 Burroughs had established a connection with Paul Bowles and through him began to meet the other members of the expatriate community. He became a known figure at the Parade Bar and one or two other watering holes. Bowles has described his early meetings with Burroughs when he was badly addicted: 'He was living down in the medina, in a brothel. He lay in bed all day, shot heroin, and practised sharpshooting with a pistol against the wall of his room. I saw the wall, all pockmarked with bullet holes. I said to him, "Why are you shooting your wall, Bill?" He said, "It's good practice." I didn't get to know him until '55, '56. He was writing *Naked Lunch*.'

Their initial meeting was not a success, but in 1957 they got to know each other and developed a friendship. Bowles described Burroughs' room in the Villa Muniria:

> There were hundreds of pages of yellow foolscap all over the floor, month after month, with heel prints on them, rat droppings, bits of old sandwiches, sardines. It was filthy. I said, 'What is all that, Bill?' He said, 'That's what I'm working on.' 'Do you have a copy of it?' I asked. 'No,' he said. I couldn't help myself from saying, 'Why don't you pick it up?' Candy bar in hand, he said, 'Oh, it'll get picked up someday.' As he finished a page, he'd just throw it on the floor.

Though things were finally going well for him in Tangier, Bill still had a great desire to see Allen and his other old friends from the States. In addition, his writing had reached a stage where he needed to work with Allen in person on the manuscript. He first requested Allen's assistance early in 1955, but Allen's success in San Francisco with *Howl* (written in 1955, published in 1956) and his subsequent acclaim had caused the trip to be postponed. Ginsberg had become a celebrity and even the *New York Times* had singled him out as being the most significant of the new generation of poets working on the coast. However, rather than bask in his new-found fame, Ginsberg thought it was now time to travel. He had never been to Europe and wanted very much to see Bill and work with him on assembling and editing the manuscript. He remained convinced that Bill was a great writer and was full of admiration for the new material Burroughs sent him weekly. Bill was delighted: 'I just got your letter so will expect you and entourage January,' he wrote. 'The place relaxes me so I am subject to dissolve. I can spend three hours looking at the bay with my mouth open like a Kentucky Mountain boy.'

Allen had suggested that he bring his boyfriend, Peter Orlovsky, and Jack Kerouac with him, the plan being that they would continue on from Tangier to Spain, Italy and finally France. This was fine with Bill, who replied in October 1956, 'By all means bring Jack and Peter. I assure you I will not be jealous . . . In fact jealousy is one of the emotions of which I am no longer capable. Self-pity is also impossible for me . . .'

Allen was not so sure, having detected desire and loneliness in Bill's letters, but he discussed it with Peter, who had never met Bill, and he was in favour. Ginsberg later described their visit: 'At this time Peter and I decided that since he was so lacklove, the two of us would take him on and do anything he wanted, satisfy him. So we went to Tangier to fuck him. To exhaust his desires, that was our idea. See if we could . . . So Peter and I decided we'd go there and satisfy him, satisfy his soul, put an end to his misery.'

Allen and Peter left San Francisco in December 1956 but were delayed, first in Mexico City, then in New York. As it worked out, Jack Kerouac was the first one to get to Tangier, having borrowed the boat fare from Allen. He landed in late February 1957 and moved into the Villa Muniria. He offered to help Bill by typing a fair copy of *Word Hoard* but Bill's powerful imagery soon began to have a disturbing effect on him. 'I had nightmares of great long baloneys coming out of my mouth,' he wrote. 'I had nightmares typing that manuscript.' In vain he tried to excuse himself but Bill insisted that he keep typing. Kerouac was a fast, accurate typist and, as a reward for completing the first two chapters, Bill bought him a small kerosene stove from the medina because Jack's rooftop room was cold at night.

Kerouac insisted on typing exactly what Bill had written since his theory of literature was that nothing should be changed once it had been written down; the 'spontaneous prose' system he used in his own books. Kerouac's title, *Naked Lunch*, used by Burroughs on a number of different manuscripts since the 40s, was now given to the work in progress.

Bill had developed certain habits and rituals; at 4 p.m., it was his habit to drink cognac with his neighbour Eric Gifford, an old Etonian who would entertain Bill with far-fetched descriptions of his experiences in the Far East. Afterwards Bill would often eat dinner at one of the good cheap French restaurants in the neighbourhood. Paul Bowles wrote that Bill always insisted on eating well and probably spent more money on food than most of the expats.

In March 1957, Bill's orderly ways were thrown into confusion by the arrival of Allen Ginsberg and Peter Orlovsky, who had finally shipped out of Manhattan on 8 March, on a freighter bound for Casablanca and Tangier. They wanted to do everything and see everything and for a short period Bill was overwhelmed by his old friends after so many years by himself. Shortly after Allen and Peter arrived, Kerouac departed for France so Allen and Peter took his rooftop room overlooking the flat roofs, the minarets and the old harbour. They quickly developed daily habits. Allen rose at dawn and put in five or six hours on Bill's manuscript, sitting at the typewriter at a table out on the red-tiled roof terrace. Then he and Peter would go to the market and later Allen would cook a meal for them all. While Bill sipped cocktails with his next door neighbours Eric and Dave, Allen wrestled with huge fish on Bill's little stove or made big pots of his famous spaghetti with clam sauce. After dinner they would take Bill's majoun and stay up half the night talking, or reading aloud from the manuscript pages now neatly piled on Bill's desk. Paul Bowles would often stop by to hear Bill read aloud. 'I took it all as an hallucination under heroin,' he reported. The discussions usually consisted of Bill lurching about the room, taking tokes on the many joints left burning in various ashtrays and stirring his drink with two fingers, goaded on by Ginsberg. Bowles told Michelle Green for her book on Tangier, 'It was always Bill who attacked the intellect from all sides, which I suspect was exactly what Allen wanted to hear.'

Alan Ansen, whom Bill visited in Venice, arrived to help type the manuscript, and between them the team cleaned up the text, inserted punctuation and paragraphs and produced a fair copy. Allen had brought all of Bill's letters with him from the States and they went through them all, pulling out all the routines and sections of narrative. By the end of May they had over 200 pages of material. Allen wrote to Lucien Carr: 'It's quite a piece of writing – all Bill's energy & prose, plus our organisation & cleanup & structure, so it's continuous and readable, decipherable.'

The manuscript was still unfinished, but a final form was now beginning to take shape in Bill's head. He envisioned the book as having four sections: South America, the States, Interzone (Tangier) and Freeland, Freeland being 'a place of the living dead', modelled on what he had heard about Scandinavia. After Allen and Peter left to spend the summer with Alan Ansen in Venice, Bill flew to Copenhagen to visit Kells Elvins, who was now married to a Danish actress, Mimi. The utter boredom he encountered in Denmark was even better than he had imagined, inspiring him to further develop the concept of Freeland. He wrote Allen, 'I made no mistake to come here. Only Scandinavia could have catalysed the Great Work, and no other place could be the background.'

He now decided that the theme of the novel was addiction. He hypothesised an addicting virus which was passed from one person to another in sexual contact. The virus only passed from man to man or woman to woman. 'Real theme of the novel, Desecration of the Human Image by the control addicts who are putting out the virus,' he wrote to Allen. In *The Naked Lunch* he presented the concept in a more oblique and poetic manner: 'Males who resign themselves up for passive intercourse to infected partners like weak and soon to be purple-assed baboons, may also nourish a little stranger.' It was an uncanny prophecy of the AIDS virus.

Bill returned to Tangier where he wrote the main 'Dr Benway' section and worked on the Scandinavian angle. Dr Benway, first invented by Burroughs and Kells Elvins for their 'Twilights Last Gleamings' routine in 1938, was to become Burroughs' most popular character:

NURSE: 'Adrenalin, doctor?'
DR BENWAY: 'The night porter shot it all up for kicks.'
He looks around and picks up one of those rubber vacuum cups at the end of a stick they use to unstop toilets . . . He advances on the patient . . . 'Make an incision Doctor Limpf,' he says to his appalled assistant . . . 'I'm going to massage the heart.'

There had been some talk with Allen about incorporating *Queer* and the *Yage Letters* in the book, which was still far from its final state, but in September 1957 Bill finally rejected the idea. He also rejected Allen's idea that the book should be given some sort of chronological order: 'It is not at all important how anybody gets from one place to another,' he told Allen. 'Entirely too much space is wasted in this transporting one's characters here and there which, with the aid of American Express, they are able to do for themselves.'

Allen had seen this as a way of connecting the disparate elements of the book, but Bill disagreed:

> The MS in present form does not hold together as a novel for the simple reason that it is not a novel. It is a number of connected – (by theme) – but separate short pieces. My feeling is that it will eventually grow into several novels all interlocking and taking place simultaneously in a majoun dream. But I do not see organisation as a problem . . . P.S. I don't see where there is any confusion in MS if regarded as separate pieces connected by interweaving of theme and characters.

He told Allen: 'The characters reoccur in different guises and it is all converging somewhere.' This is the key to Burroughs' writing: characters and fragments of plot flop over from one book to the next, unifying his entire output into one long 'map of consciousness'. Several books later, it comes as no surprise when Dr Benway makes an appearance in *Nova Express*.

Bill was also working on a 'General Theory of Addiction' essential to the understanding of the work which he now saw as an illustration of this theory. The final book would incorporate this theoretical text, and use the metaphor of the junkie throughout to illustrate the human condition: the 'algebra of need'.

In the fall of 1957, Ginsberg and Orlovsky arrived in Paris from Venice. Ginsberg's first move was to take a carbon copy of Bill's manuscript as it then stood to Maurice Girodias at Olympia Press.

The Olympia Press was the most interesting, and certainly the hippest, English-language publishing house in the 50s, and was famous for publishing pornography, much of it written under pseudonyms by writers such as Alexander Trocchi, Christopher Logue and Iris Owens, who needed the money in order to get on with writing their own, less commercial, work. The owner, Maurice Girodias, also published quality writing that was unlikely to get past the censor in Britain or America, and it was this combination of literature and pornography which made the press so unique. As well as translations of erotic work by Georges Bataille, Guillaume Apollinaire, Jean Genet, the Marquis de Sade and Dominique Aury (author of *The Story of O* under the pseudonym of Pauline Reage), Girodias published books by Aubrey Beardsley and Roger Casement, which, for various reasons, could not be published in Britain. He also published contemporary works which might be liable to censorship, such as Nabokov's *Lolita*, Donleavy's *The Ginger Man*, Durrell's *The Black Book*, Samuel Beckett's *Watt* and *Molloy*, and the works of Henry Miller: *Sexus*, *Plexus*, *Quiet Days in Clichy* and, of course, *Tropic of Cancer* and *Tropic of Capricorn*, which had both originally been published by Girodias' father, Jack Kahane, at the Obelisk Press. Burroughs would be in good company.

Girodias told writer Victor Bockris: 'Allen Ginsberg brought me the first manuscript of *Naked Lunch* in 1957. He was acting as Burroughs' friendly agent. It was such a mess that manuscript! You couldn't physically read the stuff, but whatever caught the eye was extraordinary and dazzling. So I returned it to Allen saying, "Listen, the whole thing has to be reshaped." The ends of the pages were all eaten away by the rats or something . . . The prose was transformed into verse, edited by the rats of the Paris sewers. And Allen was very angry at me.'

This version of the story is a typical Girodias exaggeration. The manuscript might have become a bit tatty, having been in Ginsberg's rucksack throughout his summer travels in Spain and Italy, but it was cleanly typed and presented. The reason that Girodias rejected the book was simply because he did not think it was commercial enough. It was only when extracts from *The Naked Lunch* caused a censorship row in the States that he showed interest.

This is certainly the version given by Terry Southern, who was living in Paris at the time. The cafe most frequented by the

Beats was the Café Saint-Germain des Près, opposite the Flore. One winter morning, Mason Hoffenberg (with whom Southern co-authored *Candy* for Girodias) and Southern were having their customary *grande tasse*, when Gregory Corso arrived at their table.

He plopped a manuscript down and said in his usual gross manner, 'Now dig this . . .'

It turned out that the MS was, of all things, *Naked Lunch*. It seems that Burroughs had given it to Allen Ginsberg and he had given it to Gregory. Mason and I set out to convince Gid that it was worthy of his distinguished imprimatur.

His first response was to leaf through it impatiently. 'There is no fucking in the book,' he said. 'No sex at all in the book.'

We pointed out something on page seventeen.

'Ah, yes!' he said triumphantly. 'All the way to page seventeen! And still it's only a blow job!'

He got up from his desk and turned to an old wooden filing cabinet. His offices had a Dickensian mustiness and clutter which he seemed to believe lent his operation a degree of respectability. He took out a couple of letters.

'Let me show you what our readership requires,' he said, bringing them over. If memory serves, they were from a couple of Indians in the British Army, and they pleaded for books that were 'brutally frank' and 'frankly explicit', phrases they had picked up from porn advertisements.

'Could we truly recommend such a work as this to these readers? And the title is no good. What does it mean, this "Naked Lunch"?'

I told him that Jack Kerouac had suggested the title, hoping that might impress him. But Mason had the right idea: he said that it was American slang for sex in the afternoon.

Gid brightened somewhat. 'Ah, comme notre cinq-à-sept!' he declared, referring to the cherished French tradition of having sex (with a mistress, of course) every day from five to seven p.m.

'No, this is more like an orgy,' he was told.

And eventually he came around.

I have read, God (certainly) knows, other accounts of how this great milestone book came into print, but the actual facts are those above. The scary thing about it is that Girodias could have as easily remained adamant. [*Grand Street*, 37, 1991]

In Paris Allen and Peter and Gregory Corso found a room at 9 rue Git le Coeur. It was a Class 13 hotel – which meant that it met the absolute minimum legal requirements for accommodation. The Beat Hotel, as Gregory Corso named it, had 42 rooms, which were in great demand with a long waiting list.

Once they had settled in, Allen immediately encouraged Bill to join them there. He finally arrived, six months later, in January 1958, when a room became free. Peter Orlovsky was leaving for New York the next day, and Allen was fearful that Bill was coming to claim him, now that Peter was out of the picture. There had been some jealousies when they first arrived in Tangier and it was obvious that Bill was still emotionally hung up on Ginsberg. Now in Paris he and Bill had sex for the sake of their old friendship, but it turned out that Bill really had changed. They had a heart-to-heart talk in which Allen confessed his doubts, and Bill told him what had been happening to him in Tangier.

Towards the end of 1957 Bill had finally kicked junk; he had stopped drinking and stopped writing. Each afternoon he sat on his bed and meditated, slowly and repeatedly analysing his thoughts. He accepted all the unpleasant or horrible fantasies that entered his head as a real part of himself, and instead of suppressing them with a shudder of revulsion, he concentrated on each one, developing and analysing it in more or less the same manner as he developed ideas to their absolute limits in his routines. Burroughs finally became aware of what he called 'a benevolent sentient center to the whole Creation'. He had, in his own way, the same vision of what Ginsberg called a 'big peaceful Lovebrain'. It was a revelation to him and had given him the courage to examine his whole life dispassionately, in particular his relationship with Allen. He told Allen that he had not come to Paris to claim him, but to visit, and also see a psychoanalyst to try and clear up the unconscious blocks that still remained after his self-analysis.

He stopped putting pressure on Allen for sex and Allen wrote to Peter: 'He no longer needs me like he used to, doesn't think of me as a permanent future intimate sex schlupp lover, thinks even he'll wind up maybe after difficulties with women.' Bill's new outlook extended to the poet Gregory Corso. Bill was now friendly towards him, and there was no sign of the marked animosity which existed between them when they first met at Ginsberg's East 7th Street apartment in New York in 1953. Gregory, for his part, had mellowed somewhat from the tough street kid of five years before and gave Bill a big leather coat he had acquired in Germany.

The rue Git le Coeur is a short medieval lane in the Latin Quarter running down to the Seine from the rue St Andre des Arts. Number 9 is a sixteenth-century building with sloping floors, noisy plumbing and no soundproofing. The rooms were heated by radiators and there was hot water on Thursday, Friday and Saturday; however, advance notice had to be given if a guest wanted a bath so that extra water could be heated, and there was naturally a surcharge for this service. The toilet facilities consisted of a Turkish hole-in-the-floor toilet on each stair landing. Residents were periodically plunged into darkness when someone overloaded the fragile electrical circuit. The proprietor, small, blue-haired Madame Rachou, could tell by consulting her electrical switchboard of dimly glowing bulbs, one for each room, if anyone had smuggled in an illicit hotplate or tape recorder.

Whores and petty criminals lived side by side with artists, poets and jazz musicians. Madame Rachou regarded them all as her children but, as Burroughs said, she 'was very mysterious and arbitrary about who she would let into the hotel'. Rooms were five francs a night or 120 francs a month, but Madame sometimes permitted residents to pay their rent with paintings or manuscripts, none of which she kept, not for a moment thinking they would ever be valuable.

At street level was a small bar with a traditional zinc counter where Madame Rachou dispensed coffee, beer and wine, cognac and calvados and would sit talking endlessly to her tenants over cups of watery espresso. Next to the bar was a dining area separated by a curtain, where she served large cheap lunches of cassoulet or rabbit stew. Madame gave occasional lunches for the local police inspectors with whom she maintained a very good relationship, and her tenants were therefore spared searches and harassment. When they did come on official business, she could sense their presence and was always able to head them off. She did not want them to close her down, nailing the doors and windows shut as they had done to so many of the small hotels in the quartier since the war.

Burroughs moved into room fifteen on the fifth floor. The room was sparsely furnished with a two-burner gas stove on the table in one corner, a wash-stand in the other, a wardrobe, two chairs, a bed, and a table on which stood his old Spanish portable. Four wire baskets hung on the wall over the table, ready to receive manuscripts. A single naked light bulb hung over the table. Bill's window looked out to a blank wall in the light well. The Beat Hotel became his home for many years to come. For a short period, three of the major Beat Generation writers, Ginsberg, Burroughs and Corso, lived and worked together in the same building for the first time since Ginsberg, Burroughs and Kerouac had shared an apartment in New York in 1945.

6 Naked Lunch

Burroughs' relationship with Ginsberg deepened. They were more relaxed around each other and, though Bill went to bed with Allen a few times, he thought that they would finish up with a non-sexual relationship because he didn't really need such intimacy any more.

They had long discussions about the means of extending 'Love bliss' to others – Ginsberg's phrase. Allen and Peter Orlovsky had attempted it in Tangier by bringing other people into their relationship, and their bed, but with little success. The problem was how to do it without sacrificing intimacy. Bill and Allen had long talks about the subject, concluding that it was possible. Ginsberg wrote to Orlovsky, 'We'll solve that problem before we're done.' It took them a few years, but by the mid-60s, the Beat ideas of love and peace, free open sexuality and the use of marijuana and other consciousness-expanding drugs had spread to hundreds of thousands of young people worldwide. The hippie movement, in this respect, had its roots directly in the Beat Generation.

Bill was pleased to find that paregoric, an elixir of opium, could be bought across the counter at any drugstore, and began to enjoy his life in Paris. He began to spend time at the Café Monaco where he met a bearded folk singer called Darryl Adams who wore a ring through his ear, an unusual adornment for a man back in in the 50s. Adams would visit Bill in the afternoons and they would sit in his room and talk. Bill had positive feelings about this new American generation and thought they would change things. In a way he was right because this was the generation that created Woodstock, out of which developed the ecology movement, the women's movement and many other social changes in the United States.

Bill discovered the medical library in the rue Dragon, and began to research the biology of schizophrenia, reading reports of experiments in which schizophrenic patients were given mescaline. He and Ginsberg sat around for days talking about the implications of the research, and bits of this material found their way into Bill's manuscripts, particularly the medical details of obscure and weird diseases he read about there.

His life settled into a routine; he got up at 1 p.m. and would eat a light breakfast of bread and tea, then he and Ginsberg would usually talk for an hour or so. In the late afternoon he would go out to buy his supply of paregoric and to see his analyst. Ginsberg shopped and cooked for them all in his room, usually a soup with a Bayonne ham bone, a lamb stew or spaghetti. They ate early, around 7 p.m., then walked over to Boulevard St Germain for coffee. Bill and Allen still made it occasionally but Bill wasn't much interested in sex any more. He sensed that something new was happening to him, probably caused by his analysis, and thought that maybe he would become celibate or take up women.

Ginsberg typed up a few chapters from the manuscript of *The Naked Lunch* and sent them out to little literary magazines in the USA and Britain while Bill spent his time revising the manuscript. Years later, in a recorded conversation with Maurice Girodias, he said, 'The manuscript which you saw in 1958 was not even approximately similar to the manuscript published in 1959 which was really fragmentary and confused.' Each day he added new material and gave the chapters more shape.

A wealthy young Frenchman appeared on the scene and befriended Bill. Jacques Stern was a Rothschild. He was 25 years old and had been crippled by polio, which left him with braces on his thin hips and only able to walk with the aid of an aluminium crutch. Like Bill, he had studied anthropology at Harvard and, also like Bill, he was being psychoanalysed. Ginsberg would carry him up the four flights of stairs to his room and Bill would visit with him there. Stern was very intelligent, very serious and enormously knowledgeable. Polio had kept him bedridden for many years and he had passed his time studying Roman history, anthropology, Spengler and Indian philosophy. Bill liked him for his intellect and the factual information he had on junk or the latest experiments with brainwashing. Stern knew Salvador Dali and Jean Cocteau and the fashionable side of Paris but was bored by it. He thought that Bill was a great teacher and often came over to the hotel to talk; sometimes he took them all out in his huge chauffeur-driven cream Cadillac convertible.

Stern had a friend called Harry Phipps, a 24-year-old, short, blond-haired, baby-faced, narcissistic American millionaire. Phipps brought over three of his old suits to the hotel, one each for Ginsberg, Corso and Burroughs. Bill received a black worsted Averell Harriman flannel suit that fitted him perfectly, making him look very distinguished with his greying temples. Bill and Allen sat at Allen's kitchen table, all dressed up, sniffing the cocaine which Phipps also gave them, pleased with this new turn of events. They walked with Phipps to his place on the Île St Louis and only then did they realise how rich he was. He lived in the town house where Chopin and Voltaire had once lived.

Phipps produced more cocaine and Ginsberg later recorded in his journal that he looked at Bill framed against the fireplace in the huge eighteenth-century drawing room, his body thin from the effects of the paregoric, hair thinning, making stiff-armed gestures as he explained a scientific theory of chess probability and horse-betting, and thought that Bill looked like 'a great sober, Palm Beach chess-player private genius'.

Ginsberg's stay at the Beat Hotel resulted in the place becoming like Grand Central Station as endless visitors surged in and out of his room bringing manuscripts, drugs and gossip. In 1958 Allen made two brief trips to England, leaving his room in Bill's care. Bill used it for typing. In a humorous letter to Allen in London, he described how he was dealing with Allen's friends: 'That kid Dick whatever was around trying to move into your room. "Nooooo" I brayed with inflexible authority. "Don't like you and don't know you. I need two rooms. When I get tired of sitting in one I go and sit in the other." Such crust. These Paris mooches would move right in and shove a man out of his own bed.' People took advantage of Allen but knew better than to confront Bill.

In 1958 Bill made a few trips to England. Allen Ginsberg had given him some names there, including Michael Horovitz and David Sladen who were about to publish a literary magazine called *New Departures* in Oxford; the first issue, published in 1959, contained two sections from *The Naked Lunch*. Bill took mescaline with Horovitz and Sladen, who had access to a supply through the university. Bill liked Oxford, and would sometimes show up with a rent boy to stay in a hotel, seeing no problem in introducing such a person to the Oxford intellectuals he knew. They were intrigued, because Bill obviously enjoyed the company of the boys and wasn't just using them for sex. Bill seemed to like one boy who was a rabid communist, and they joked around a lot together. But when the boy began talking about the revolution Bill froze and pretended the boy wasn't even there.

Ginsberg returned to New York in July 1958 but Burroughs and Corso stayed on at the Beat Hotel, helping to establish the legend of the Beat Generation on European soil. Burroughs' *Junkie* had been published in England by Digit Books as a cheap paperback but, as in the States, it was published under the name William Lee, and no one appeared to have seen it or made the connection between its author and the quiet American in the Beat Hotel. The UK edition of *Junkie* was pulped shortly after publication because the publisher finally realised what the book was about and got nervous.

The English poet Gael Turnbull arrived at the Beat Hotel shortly after Ginsberg left in 1958 and his journal gives an interesting account of Burroughs' life in the days before *The Naked Lunch* was published and his fame and notoriety assured:

July 31, 2:30 P.M. I knocked on the door of this other friend of Ginsberg's, called Bill Burroughs – he only just up, in pyjamas, looking like a man dying of cancer, thin, pale, unsteady, the curtains still drawn – he made some tea ... Burroughs dressed, an older man, about 40 I'd say, very slow speaker – two themes in his talk, a hatred of

America, the physical culture of it, and also an interest in all forms of drugs of all kinds – eventually monotonous, but despite this, a rather pathetic sort of sad stick, one couldn't help liking him.

August 1, 4 P.M. Went to see Burroughs, and had more tea with him, he must consume as much tea as Dr Johnson is said to have drunk . . .

August 2 . . . to Burroughs' room – but he is in a bad mood, I can tell because he has taken an extra dose of opium to deaden the pain in his heart, and his face is a mask, sunken, his speech maddeningly slow – he talks of his theory of addiction of a biological requirement – and of how there is no boredom under opium, one can't feel bored, because boredom arrives from undischarged tension, and then the tension is cut off and there is contentment – he says he sat looking at his shoe for several hours at a time, quite content.

While in Paris, Burroughs met a number of important artists and writers including Tristan Tzara, Man Ray, Marcel Duchamp, and on one occasion he and Allen Ginsberg visited Louis-Ferdinand Céline at his house in Meudon. Céline and Bill discussed the notion that you can tell the true state of a nation by examining the state of its prisons. They had both experienced incarceration, though Bill rather less of it than Céline. It was also in Paris that Bill finally connected with Brion Gysin, who was to become his greatest friend and biggest influence.

Gysin was an American painter, born in England of a Swiss father and a Canadian mother. He was solidly built with a Swiss mountaineer's ruddy face, blue eyes and thick hair. His looks were a constant disappointment to him; he always maintained that he was born in error:

I am a compromise, a compromise between the sexes in a dualistic universe. I am just passing through, waiting out my vital visa, my Easy Exit permit, I hope. Oh I know it's better to have a body than not to have a body but the minute I got here I screamed ungratefully: 'Wrong address! Wrong address! There's been a mistake in the mail. Send

me back. Wherever you got me, return me. Wrong time, wrong place, wrong colour!'
[Introduction to *Here to Go: Planet R101*]

Gysin was gay and for many years had lived in Tangier where he ran the celebrated 1001 Nights restaurant. Burroughs had eaten there from time to time when his monthly cheque came through, and had been introduced to Gysin by Paul Bowles, but it was not until a chance encounter in Paris that they became friends. Gysin had written a book on slavery, the story of Uncle Tom, called *To Master a Long Goodnight*, published in Canada in 1946, but saw himself primarily as an artist. His paintings were calligraphic, in the manner of Mark Tobey's 'Targets' or 'White Writing', and often suggested Saharan landscapes. Gysin was very much the product of an English public school (he went to Downside); he adored the aristocracy and loved to mix with famous people such as Alice B Toklas, who credited him in her famous cookbook with supplying the recipe for hash brownies (she neglected to say that you have to cook them). In Paris Gysin was staying with the Princess Ruspoli but had outlasted his welcome. At Burroughs' suggestion he moved into the Beat Hotel, and they began to see each other regularly.

This was to prove the beginning of a close friendship that continued until Gysin's death, in 1986, aged 70. Over the years they collaborated on a number of books and lived together in New York, London and Paris, though there was never a sexual relationship between them. Gysin influenced Burroughs' ideas and life more than any of his other collaborators or friends.

They had much in common, including a belief in the magical world: animal spirits, curses, trance states, and the power of suggestion. They conducted many experiments together and one time in a trance Brion saw something and wrote on a piece of paper: 'The Ugly Spirit shot Joan because . . .' That was as far as the message went; the reason was not revealed, and Brion was unable to complete the sentence when he came out of it. But he had given the thing a name, and from then on Burroughs knew what he was up against. It was the Ugly Spirit.

* * *

When he was in Paris, Ginsberg, in his editorial role, had submitted several chapters from *The Naked Lunch* to Irving Rosenthal, editor of the *Chicago Review*, who had published them in the spring and autumn 1958 issues of the magazine. Rosenthal was so enthusiastic about the work that he decided to print a ten-chapter section in his winter issue. Unfortunately a local gossip columnist had seen the Burroughs material in the previous issues and devoted one of his columns to an attack on the magazine and its editorial policy. The *Chicago Review* was published by the University of Chicago and the Dean immediately asked to see the contents for the next issue. He was appalled, not only by the Burroughs material, but by articles from Kerouac and Edward Dahlberg, and suppressed the entire contents. In a flurry of gossip column tidbits Rosenthal resigned and started his own magazine, *Big Table*, to publish the suppressed material. The affair was seized on joyfully by the press and it even made a full page in *Time* magazine. Allen Ginsberg and Gregory Corso, both now back in New York, rode into town like the Lone Ranger and Tonto to give a hugely publicised benefit reading for the new magazine, and all the society ladies vied with each other to invite the 'beatniks' to their living rooms.

When Maurice Girodias saw the ten chapters from *The Naked Lunch* in *Big Table* his opinion of the book was transformed; he now wanted to publish the book immediately in order to capitalise on the publicity surrounding the suppression of *Chicago Review*. He sent his assistant, Sinclair Beiles, over to say that Bill had two weeks to get the manuscript together. In fact, it took Bill, working with Beiles and Brion Gysin, ten days to prepare the book for the printers, and as Bill wrote to Allen, 'Pressure welded the whole book together into a real organic continuity which it never had before.' The great haste in assembling the material sometimes gave rise to material appearing twice, such as the ten line section beginning, 'I was travelling with Irene Kelly . . .' which was repeated again unintentionally and without change 170 pages later, and several other smaller repeats.

Bill had been concerned that putting the chapters into some kind of order would be a time-consuming job which would hold up publication, but when the printers, who could not read English, returned the galleys in the random order in which the sections had been typeset, Beiles read them through and said, 'Why don't you leave them like this?' Bill read them and agreed, but made one change, taking the 'Hauser and O'Brien' section and placing it at the end so that the book opened with 'I can feel the heat closing in', and ended (last but one page) with 'the heat was off me from here on out', making the detectives into a frame around the book. They were based on Shein and O'Grady, the two cops who arrested him at the 115th Street apartment in 1946. The book was on the stands one month after Beiles came to tell Burroughs that Girodias wanted it – something of a record.

The Naked Lunch opens with a flight from narcotics agents and ends with the shooting of officers Hauser and O'Brien. The Hauser and O'Brien routine is a miniature masterpiece of pulp detective fiction. Another routine featuring them, 'The Conspiracy', originally left out but later published in *Interzone*, provides an alternative ending, but Bill's protagonist, Lee, was never in any great danger, as Bill told Allen back in 1955:

> The meaning of Interzone, its space time location is at a point where three-dimensional fact merges into dream, and dreams erupt into the real world. In Interzone dreams can kill – Like Bangutot – and solid objects and persons can be as unreal as dreams. For example Lee could be in Interzone, after killing the two detectives, and for various dream reasons, neither the law nor The Others could touch him directly.

Dream-time reality is not the only weapon in Burroughs' arsenal. In *Junky*, Lee the junkie wises up and finds he has been conned. In *The Naked Lunch*, Lee the junkie becomes Inspector Lee of the Nova Police – a character that is further developed in later books, particularly *Nova Express*. The observer sees many of the situations in *The Naked Lunch* from different viewpoints (youth and age, junkie and cop), but these are liable to subdivide into multiple characters, each with a different view: 'As I was saying before I was interrupted by one of my multiple personalities . . . troublesome little beasts.'

It is not only Lee who has wised up. *The Naked Lunch*, like *Junky*, is intended to educate the reader, and Bill says so directly towards the end of the book: '*The Naked Lunch* is a blueprint, a How-To Book ... How-to extend levels of experience by opening the door at the end of a long hall ... Doors that only open in Silence ... *Naked Lunch* demands Silence from The Reader. Otherwise he is taking his own pulse.'

Bill makes no attempt to create artificial situations or to construct an elaborate plot. The text is simply a record of the writer's consciousness at the precise point of writing, with breaks, mood changes, unpleasant fantasies, mad humour, all described as they flash into consciousness. This is explained in the book itself:

> There is only one thing a writer can write about: what is in front of his senses at the moment of writing ... I am a recording instrument ... I do not pretend to impose 'story' 'plot' 'continuity' ... Insofaras I succeed in Direct recording of certain areas of psychic process I may have a limited function ... I am not an entertainer.

In this, Burroughs joins the ranks of 'garrulous' American authors such as Ezra Pound and William Carlos Williams, whose literary output adds up to a map of the authors' consciousness, recorded over a period of years or even decades. It is confessional literature at its absolute, since it can only work if it is completely honest. Ginsberg has pointed out how Ezra Pound's lifetime work, *The Cantos*, gives a journal-like record of the development of his various interests and concerns, including his economic ideas, his support for fascism and his anti-semitism, all as part of an integrated whole, a 'quantitive map of consciousness'. One doesn't have to agree with Pound to respect his honest revelation of his thoughts.

The links between *The Naked Lunch* as published and the previous manuscripts which bore that name ('Junk', 'Queer' and 'Yage Quest') are extensive. (When *The Naked Lunch* was published in the United States, Grove Press dropped the article and it became simply *Naked Lunch*.) Material frequently intrudes, or flops over, from the already published *Junkie*; for example, the details on how to fix on an airplane are repeated; there is more information about Lupita, Bill's Mexico City pusher (who has to wait until the 1987 *Western Lands* before becoming a major character); Lee awakes, his wife shaking him and holding hot coffee under his nose, as he did in *Junkie*.

In some cases, ideas first aired in *Junkie* are further developed in *The Naked Lunch*: 'Followers of obsolete unthinkable trades, doodling in Etruscan, addicts of drugs not yet synthesised . . .' is a follow-on from a routine in *Junkie*. Another instance – 'My dear, I'm working on the most marvellous invention . . . a boy who disappears as soon as you come, leaving a smell of burning leaves and a sound effect of distant train whistles' – is a development of a nostalgic image first given a straight narrative treatment in *Junkie*.

Many of the images in *The Naked Lunch* are taken from Burroughs' notes on the hallucinations caused by yage, originally written for 'Yage Quest': 'He was in a great cone, spinning down to a black point . . .' (an image, incidentally, virtually identical to the sensation of yage intoxication as described by Allen Ginsberg in *The Yage Letters*). The section describing the City (originally 'Yage City') and The Meet Cafe were both written in a state of yage intoxication and are followed by one of Burroughs' scholarly asides: 'Notes From Yage State'.

A large number of the images in *The Naked Lunch* are the result of drug experimentation: 'Many of the more unpleasant ones [images] I got with N-dimethyltryptamine dim-N. Minraud I got with mescaline. But all of these places also have real origins. Interzone is very much modelled on Tangier in the old international days: it was an Inter-zone, it was no country. The jungle scenes come from my South American explorations. Upper Baboonsasshole is Upper Babanasa actually.'

Burroughs has always been prepared to speak quite openly about his use of drugs for literary purposes, and in 1979 said,

I didn't have any experience with opiates until I was 30 years old. . . What interested me was what interests anyone who takes drugs – altered consciousness. Altered consciousness, of course, is a writer's stock in trade. If my consciousness was just completely conventional, no one would be interested enough to read it, right? So there's that aspect. Now you may not be doing that for literary purposes at all. You may just be doing it because you want to. But of course, altering the consciousness need not be drug related either. We alter our consciousness all the time, from minute to minute. Altered consciousness is a basic fact of life.

Observations and details from the previous decade are scattered across the text: the great city, 'at all levels criss-cross of bridges, cat walks, cable-cars . . .', was inspired by the view of fire escapes in Ginsberg's back yard on East 7th Street, which was also, of course, where he first developed the 'schlup, schlup, schlup' routine which occurs early in the book. In *The Naked Lunch* this is also associated with the notion of men changing into centipedes, an idea first outlined in *Queer*:

What happens when there is no limit? What is the fate of The Land Where Anything Goes? Men changing into huge centipedes . . . centipedes besieging the houses . . . a man tied to a couch and a centipede ten feet long rearing up over him. Is this literal? Did some hideous metamorphosis occur? What is the meaning of the centipede symbol?

Burroughs wrote this about Guayaquil, Ecuador, on his trip with Marker, but has its origin in a fragment of a Mayan codex of unknown source and date which shows a man tied to a couch as a huge centipede rears over him. There is also the obvious influence of Franz Kafka, one of Bill's favourite authors. Kafka's *Metamorphosis* opens with the line: 'As Gregor Samsa awoke one morning from uneasy dreams he found himself transformed in his bed into a gigantic insect.'

Some readers, confused by the chance order of the chapters, the lack of obvious narrative and the multiple viewpoints of the characters, wonder what *The Naked Lunch* is ultimately about and why it is so highly regarded. It was written for the most part in the pre-rock'n'roll, straight-laced Doris Day, Debbie Reynolds era, when the USA had the world's highest standard of living but a very low quality of life. President Eisenhower's caddy accompanied him around the golf course carrying the nuclear button to enable Ike to launch World War Three before teeing off. Segregation was still in force in the South, and crew-cut advertising men controlled American consciousness from Madison Avenue. *The Naked Lunch* was a reaction to all this: a full-scale offensive against the deep-seated hypocrisy, arrogance, naivety and mindless futility which characterised so much of 50s American consumer society.

The Naked Lunch confronted the paranoid Red-baiting anti-communism of McCarthy and the cynical detachment of the creators of the atomic bomb. It drew attention to Anslinger and Hoover for their ugly drug laws which treated addicts as criminals, hounding and persecuting them instead of going after organised crime (in his 40 years as head of the FBI, Hoover refused to act against the Mafia, or even to recognise its existence). It was an attack on the snoopy, interfering, puritan ideology which caused Prohibition and persecuted homosexuality. It revealed the anaesthetised language and hypocrisy which permitted segregation in the South, and attacked the bureaucrats who maintained their positions of power with hanging, the electric chair and the cyanide gas chamber of Californian justice. It was an American confessional: exposing everything from the mundane life of the 50s American housewife to the full horror of capital punishment – as Terry Southern described it, 'An absolutely devastating ridicule of all that is false, primitive and vicious in current American life . . .'

The housewife passage is a good example of Burroughs' masterful understanding of American language: 'AMERICAN HOUSEWIFE (opening a box of LUX): "Why don't it have an electric eye the box flip open when it see me and hand itself to the Automat Handy Man he should put it inna water already . . ." '

The two so-called pornographic sections of the book, which had more or less rendered publication in the United States or Britain an impossibility, were retained. Bill wrote Allen: 'Hassan's Rumpus Room and A.J.'s Annual Party are in and very important part of the whole structure.' 'Hassan's Rumpus Room' is an eight-page homosexual orgy beginning with a mugwump fucking a young boy:

A Near East Mugwump sits naked on a bar stool covered in pink silk. He licks warm honey from a crystal goblet with a long black tongue. His genitals are perfectly formed – circumcised cock, black shiny pubic hairs. His lips are thin and purple-blue like the lips of a penis, his eyes blank with insect calm. The Mugwump has no liver, maintaining himself exclusively on sweets. Mugwump push a slender blond youth to a couch and strip him expertly.

'Stand up and turn around,' he orders in telepathic pictographs. He ties the boy's hands behind him with a red silk cord. 'Tonight we make it all the way.'

The Mugwump fucks the boy, then hangs him. The boy ejaculates as his neck snaps. The scene shifts, Arab boys fight and have sex. Javanese dancers, Negroes, Chinese boys, blond German youths and naked lifeguards, page after page of boys fucking in endless permutations and positions.

Burroughs was particularly opposed to capital punishment. He grew up with media stories of hangings in Missouri and in *The Naked Lunch* he was referring back to the sensational newspaper imagery of his youth. The repetition and permutations of the ghastly act which characterised newspaper reports are continued here, using the journalistic fetish of dates and exact times:

The well filled with dried shit and mosaic of a thousand newspapers . . . The trap was sprung at 12:02. At 12:30 the doctor went out to eat oysters, returned at 2:00 to clap the hanged man jovially on the back. 'What! Aren't you dead yet? Guess I'll have to pull your leg. Haw Haw! . . .'

Burroughs repeats the hanging scene a number of times, using different characters and permutations, writing with unprecedented realism. The explicit heterosexual and homosexual sex acts make the whole scenario as shocking as possible, jolting the reader into a realisation of what actually occurs. This is a loaded subject and Burroughs used everything at his disposal to mount a full assault on the power of the state and its officers: 'Sheriff: "I'll lower his pants for a pound, folks. Step right up . . ." '

It was the Johnny, Mark and Mary multiple hanging scenes in the 'A.J.'s Annual Party' chapter which caused the public outrage at the book: in order to deprive the action of any question of legitimacy, the gallows are set up in a seedy nightclub, far away from the trappings of judge, jury and officers of the law. Johnny is hung by Mary, and ejaculates. Mary is also hung, but only after eating half of Johnny's face. It is interesting that this act of bestiality, uncharacteristic in Burroughs but needed to show the full horror of hanging, should occur in the only extended section of heterosexual sex in his fiction. There is nothing erotic about these passages; everyone involved is shown to be exploited and used. The scene is shown to be a sham, acted out for the satisfaction of the paying customers. The routine ends: 'Mary, Johnny and Mark take a bow with the ropes around their necks. They are not as young as they appear in the Blue Movies ... They look tired and petulant.'

To underline the message, and make sure that the connection between power, the state and the church is absolutely clear, the hanging scene is restyled yet again as a religious ceremony, with Johnny's snapping neck and ejaculation co-ordinated with the rising sun. Critic Eric Mottram has noted that capital punishment has always been the central sacrificial act which men have been prepared to use to preserve their power and control: 'The naked boy victim, the executive priests, the vampiric audience.'

In a 1961 interview Burroughs commented, 'I'm against Capital Punishment in all forms, and I have written many pamphlets on this subject in the manner of Swift's *Modest Proposal* pamphlet incorporated into *Naked Lunch*; these pamphlets have marked *Naked Lunch* as an obscene book, most all methods of Capital Punishment are designed to inflict the maximum of humiliation – note attempts to prevent suicide.'

The connection between religion and the state is one of the themes of Burroughs' work, and *The Naked Lunch* contains attacks on Christianity, Buddhism and Islam. It was Christianity that created the illiberal conditions which caused Burroughs to live outside the United States for 25 years, so it is Christianity that usually receives the full force of his criticism. When asked about Christianity he said: 'I'm violently anti-Christian. It was the worst disaster that ever occurred on a disaster-prone planet, the most virulent spiritual poison ... Fundamentalists are dangerous lunatics. There's really no place for them in an over-crowded lifeboat. They're a menace.'

Burroughs' criticism of society was insightful and prophetic: the image of the burning Negro occurs throughout the text, as does the character of the frog-faced fat Southern Sheriff who at that time reigned supreme. Lynching and burnings still occurred in the South in the 50s and early 60s, and horrific photographs of Blacks put to the torch by Southern bigots still appeared from time to time in the press. Burroughs was one of the few American writers to concern himself with this subject, and the only member of the Beat Generation (except LeRoi Jones, some time later) to do so. This may have been because Burroughs was the only one to understand the South – St Louis, being on the Mississippi, had a lot of Southern attitudes – whereas the other Beat writers were all from the North. Ginsberg didn't mention Blacks and Kerouac had a hopelessly sentimental assessment of their situation. In this sense *The Naked Lunch* was a precursor of the mass civil rights movement in its outrage at treatment of Blacks in the South.

In his description of a society gone horribly wrong, Burroughs could be shockingly prophetic. One passage, 'All benches were removed from the city, all fountains turned off, all flowers and trees destroyed', predicted Pol Pot's destruction of Cambodia to the last horrible detail.

These are serious subjects, and Burroughs felt deeply about them. The reason this weighty subject matter worked in the context of his writing was that it was presented throughout in a picaresque manner. The seriousness of his intent was disguised by humour, even when he spelled it out plain and simple:

Gentle Reader, The Word will leap on you with leopard man iron claws, it will cut off fingers and toes like an opportunist land crab, it will coil round your thighs like a bushmaster and inject a shot glass of rancid ectoplasm.

Burroughs, discussing the themes of his novels in a 1963 interview, said, '*Naked Lunch* could be described as science fiction, though it was simply a development of the themes I see running through all my novels. One of these I would describe as the picaresque theme and that you can trace through Thomas Nashe and Céline of course, who was not generally recognised as a writer of picaresque novels. When I read Céline he immediately struck me as being very funny. But the critics talked about his cry of despair. They seemed to have missed the point entirely.'

The book also holds up because of its inspired writing. Some passages work as prose poems:

Motel . . . Motel . . . Motel . . . broken neon arabesque . . . loneliness moans across the continent like fog horns over still oily water of tidal rivers . . .

Others invoke a whole world in just one sentence:

The Rube flips in the end, running through empty automats and subway stations, screaming: 'Come back, kid!! Come back!!' and follows his boy right into the East River, down through condoms and orange peels, mosaic of floating newspapers, down into the silent black ooze with gangsters in concrete and pistols pounded flat to avoid the probing finger of prurient ballistic experts.

It is the tough-talking language of 40s America:

He follows my trail all over the city into rooms I move out already, and the fuzz walks in on some newlyweds from Sioux Falls.

And, of course, it is the compact efficiency of the one-act-play routine. *The Naked Lunch* contains hundreds of routines, sometimes extended, others concise short exercises. The lunch routine is a classic example where a simple idea – lunch is served – is expanded to finish with the creation of a typically Burroughian character – Autopsy Ahmed – all in just a few lines:

They just bring so-called lunch ... A hard-boiled egg with the shell off revealing an object like I never seen it before ... A very small egg of a yellow-brown colour ... Perhaps laid by the duck-billed platypus. The orange contained a huge worm and very little else ... He really got there firstest with the mostest ... In Egypt is a worm gets into your kidneys and grows to an enormous size. Ultimately the kidney is just a thin shell around the worm. Intrepid gourmets esteem the flesh of The Worm above all other delicacies. It is said to be unspeakably toothsome ... An Interzone coroner known as Autopsy Ahmed made a fortune trafficking The Worm.

The Beats have been accused of wholly negative attacks on society without proposing an alternative. This is not the case, particularly with Burroughs, who, even at this early stage of his writing, proposed what Mottram called, 'A non-subservient model of human nature. His writing has explored the nature of obedience from every angle, in particular the manipulation of human sexuality.'

Burroughs proposed freedom from the dogma and conditioned reflexes of the individual living in authoritarian society. He proposed a society of Johnsons but all he saw were shits. Accordingly he looked for the methods of control which perpetuated this unfortunate state of affairs, for without them such a society cannot exist. He saw them in the church and in the state and, as a Reichian, he immediately identified the role of sexual suppression and repression in keeping the population subservient. In a 1965 interview he said:

I feel that sex, like practically every other human manifestation, has been degraded for control purposes, or really for anti-human purposes. This whole puritanism. How are we ever going to find out anything about sex scientifically, when *a priori* the subject cannot even be investigated? It can't even be thought about or written about. That was one of the interesting things about Reich. He was one of the few people who ever tried to investigate sex – sexual phenomena, from a scientific point of view. There's this

prurience and this fear of sex. We know nothing about sex.
What is it? Why is it pleasurable? What is pleasure? Relief
from tension? Well, possibly.

He also identified another element used in control as simple
need. In *The Naked Lunch* he uses the analogy of junkies and
their need for junk, but as he has pointed out, what he calls the
'algebra of need' is not confined to drugs: 'By "the algebra of
need" I simply meant that, given certain known factors in an
equation, and the equation comprising a situation of absolute
need – any form of need – you can predict the results. In other
words, leave a sick junkie in the back room of a drug store and
only one result is possible. The same is true of anyone in a state
of absolute hunger, absolute fear, etcetera. The more absolute
the need, the more predictable the behaviour becomes, until it
is mathematically certain.' This is a human weakness, exploited
to the full by those in control. Burroughs' investigation into
who exactly was in control was to preoccupy him for many
years to come, and over a number of subsequent books.

When *The Naked Lunch* was published by Olympia in Paris
in 1959, it received no reviews. Three years later, when Barney
Rosset published it at Grove Press in New York, it received a
full appraisal. Herbert Gold, with whom Allen Ginsberg had
spent an entire evening in Paris in 1958, reading aloud from the
manuscript of *The Naked Lunch* and attempting to explain it,
wrote in the *New York Times* of 25 November 1962:

It happens that Burroughs possesses a special literary gift.
Naked Lunch is less a novel than a series of essays,
fantasies, prose poems, dramatic fragments, bitter arguments, jokes, puns, epigrams – all hovering about the
explicit subject matter of making out on drugs while not
making out in either work or love. The black humour of
addiction.
    . . . The literary technique will remind readers of Villon
and Corbière, the gasping, torrid Céline and the furious
Swift, Alfred Jarry and Jean Genet. But in a most American
way, Burroughs rejects their yearnings for form in favor of
a definition of the novel (read: Book) as receptacle.

Repetitions of words, phrases, even episodes remain uncut. It is all there because it was all there in his mind. He offers up a series of drug and sex transports, unseparated from the motion sickness of getting to the fantasy.

... At its best, this book, which is not a novel but a booty brought back from a nightmare, takes a coldly implacable look at the dark side of our nature. Civilisation fails many, many fail civilisation. William Burroughs has written the basic work for understanding that desperate symptom which is the best style of life.

Newsweek said, '... The strange genius of *Naked Lunch* lies precisely in the fact that it is wholly, unmercifully destructive, right down to being hooked on an openly destructive saviour. It is indeed a masterpiece, but a totally insane and anarchic one, and it can only be diminished by attempts to give it any social purpose or value whatever.'

Richard Kluger in the *New York Herald Tribune* commented, 'Here is an American novelist writing in an existentialist idiom that proclaims the essential absurdity of life and reduces it to a flash series of cruel and often pointless charades. Time and place and plot and character are all missing; yet none of this matters, by the standards invoked. What matters, as in all abstract art, are the effects created, and Burroughs' effects are stunning. He is a writer of rare power ... his talent is something more than notorious. It may well turn out to be important.'

Of all the critics, the one that Burroughs had the most time for was Mary McCarthy. Interviewed in London in 1963, Burroughs said:

My own work I see as having a strong satirical and picaresque aspect. The only critic – or perhaps the only one I remember – to have got the point is Mary McCarthy. She said mine was a carnival world, a circus world. Mine are carney characters, con-world short-change artists. I have extended that to interplanetary fields with interplanetary con-men and gunmen, shortchange artists who short-change in terms of space instead of time. This has all come from the world I have had contact with, very much a part of the American scene really, though by no means confined to America.

Paul Bowles was delighted when he received his copy: 'Once it was published and I was able to read it cover to cover, I liked it. I read it three times. I think Bill's the greatest American humorist.'

The original Paris edition of *The Naked Lunch* ended with an 'Atrophied Preface'. The book finished with Bill signing off: ' 'C'lom Fliday' Note. Tanger, 1959' (Burroughs always used the French spelling of Tangier). He was unable to resist a final note, so even this required a final footnote:

Note: Old time, veteran Scmeeckers-faces beaten by grey junk weather, will remember. . . In 1920s a lot of Chinese pushers around found The West so unreliable, dishonest and wrong, they all packed in, so when an Occidental junky came to score, they say.
'No glot . . . Clom Fliday . . .'

This final note was not present in the British and American editions because they used an earlier draft of the text; one sent by Allen Ginsberg to his publisher Lawrence Ferlinghetti at City Lights Books in 1958 when the book was still called *Interzone*. When Grove Press came to publish *The Naked Lunch* in the USA (as *Naked Lunch*) they thought that the Olympia version was too short, and asked if they could include some of the material that Burroughs had edited out of it. Burroughs agreed, but instead of inserting this material back into the Olympia text, they used the old manuscript, moving the different sections around to put them into the same order as in the Olympia edition. In this way they missed the numerous small changes of tense and viewpoint which characterised Burroughs' final version of the text. (Some sections, of course, were not present in the *Interzone* manuscript, and these remained the same.)

Thus, strangely, the American edition, published three years after the Olympia edition, constituted an earlier version of the text; one which was to enter the canon for the next forty years until the Burroughs Estate issued a fully revised edition of the text.

The existence of the 'Atrophied preface' and its note marked the beginning of a pattern which characterises Burroughs' work: the desire continually to update his books. This is in keeping with Burroughs' statement that his work constitutes one long book; consequently, with the publication of each new book, all previous books are affected. Bill, however, often re-worked the texts from one edition to the next, bringing the new edition up to date. *The Soft Machine*, for instance, exists in three distinctly different versions; *The Ticket That Exploded* was rewritten once, and other books have received new additions in the form of introductions, notes, appendices and so on.

As time passed, *The Naked Lunch* became one of the most clothed books in history. When it was first published in the USA in 1962, it contained two new sections: a seventeen-page letter written to Dr Dent, 'Letter From A Master Addict To Dangerous Drugs', which first appeared in *The British Journal of Addiction* in 1956 and consists of a scholarly discussion on the effects of a wide variety of drugs that Burroughs had experimented with. Much of this material was used as footnotes in the Olympia edition, but not all of it. In the Grove edition it was restored to its original text as a letter. This was preceded at the front of the book by an entirely new twelve-page introduction – 'Deposition: Testimony Concerning A Sickness' – designed to ward off potential prosecution for obscenity. In it he spells out, 'country simple' for the authorities, 'Certain passages in the book that have been called pornographic were written as a tract against capital punishment in the manner of Jonathan Swift's *Modest Proposal*. These sections are intended to reveal capital punishment as the obscene, barbaric and disgusting anachronism that it is . . .'

The ruse didn't work, and *The Naked Lunch* was prosecuted for obscenity, finally winning at the appeal court in Boston. This was an excuse for the American publisher to load the book down with even more extraneous material and a transcript of the juicier portions of the court proceedings was added as an appendix in the next edition.

In Britain, publisher John Calder was more cautious and asked Burroughs to prepare a sort of 'reader' to introduce his work to the British public. If this evinced enough critical support, then he felt he could go ahead and publish *The Naked Lunch* and get enough assistance from the literary community to defend it in court if necessary. By this time, Burroughs had written two more books, *The Soft Machine* and *The Ticket That Exploded*, which were already published in Paris. He took sections from all three, and added some new unpublished material, to produce a new book, *Dead Fingers Talk*, which Calder published in 1963. The material in it from *The Naked Lunch* appeared in a different sequence than in the original book, further demolishing any claims that some critics have made for a chronological development in *The Naked Lunch*.

Dead Fingers Talk (taken from the line in *The Naked Lunch*, 'Only dead fingers talk in braille') produced a violent reaction from the sedate *Times Literary Supplement* in the form of a review headed 'Ugh'. In those days *TLS* reviews were anonymous (this one was by John Willett) but his negative review of the three Paris volumes, plus *Dead Fingers Talk*, caused a thirteen-week correspondence, which grew so large that it had to be given its own page. Dame Edith Sitwell attacked *The Naked Lunch*, even though she had not read it; so did the publisher Victor Gollancz, who had. 'Bogus high-brow filth . . .' he puffed. Burroughs was defended by critic Eric Mottram, and writers such as Michael Moorcock and Anthony Burgess, but mostly it was John Calder who kept the spirited correspondence going. The overall effect was that *The Naked Lunch* – using the original title but the American version of the text – was published in London the next year, 1964, without prosecution.

In 1982, however, Calder decided to follow the trend, and published a new edition containing the complete *TLS* correspondence, all 56 pages of it, and a new foreword by himself, which meant that almost a third of the British edition was made up of additional material, defending, explaining and analysing the text. As Burroughs said in his own introduction, 'The title means exactly what the words say: NAKED Lunch – a frozen moment when everyone sees what is on the end of every fork.' A reader wishing to experience *The Naked Lunch* as Burroughs originally intended is recommended to read the book first, then the various appendices, including those added by Burroughs himself. Of course, as Burroughs also pointed out, 'You can cut into The Naked Lunch at any intersection point . . . I have written many prefaces. They atrophy and amputate spontaneous like the little toe amputates in a West African disease confined to the Negro race . . .'

7 Cut-Ups

O ne day in late September 1959, Brion Gysin was in his room at the Beat Hotel, mounting some drawings, slicing through the boards with his Stanley knife and simultaneously slicing through the pile of old *New York Herald Tribunes* he was using to protect his table. When he finished, he noticed that where a strip of a page was cut away, the newsprint on the next page lined up and could be read across, combining stories from different pages, often with hilarious results. Some of the combinations amused him so much that his neighbours in the hotel knocked on the door, thinking that his laughter was a hysteria attack.

Burroughs was away in London, but when he returned a week later, Brion excitedly showed him his discovery. Bill immediately saw its importance and portentously announced it 'a project for disastrous success'.

They began experimenting together, first with the magazines in Brion's room: *Saturday Evening Post*, the London *Observer* and *Time*, then by moving the pages against texts by Rimbaud and Shakespeare. 'I began experimenting,' Burroughs remembered.

Of course, when you think of it, 'The Waste Land' was the first great cut-up collage, and Tristan Tzara had done a bit along the same lines. Dos Passos used the same idea in 'The Camera Eye' sequence in *USA*. I felt I had been working toward the same goal; thus it was a major revelation to me when I actually saw it being done ... Any narrative passage or any passage, say, of poetic images is subject to

> any number of variations, all of which may be interesting and valid in their own right. A page of Rimbaud cut up and rearranged will give you quite new images – real Rimbaud images – but new ones ... Cut-ups establish new connections between images, and one's range of vision consequently expands ...

Cut-ups held an obvious attraction for Burroughs, whose work was already naturally fragmented. *The Naked Lunch*, with its abrupt transitions and random order of chapters, has sometimes been mistaken for a cut-up text even though it was written before their discovery.

Within days, Burroughs and Gysin had introduced Gregory Corso and Sinclair Beiles to the new method and soon the four of them had enough cut-ups, as they called them, to make a selection of the best for a slim volume. *Minutes To Go* was given to Jean Fanchette, the Paris publisher of *Two Cities*, a bilingual literary magazine. Fanchette ran out of money and the book was rescued from the printer by Gaït Frogé at the English Bookshop on the rue de Seine.

Both Burroughs and Gysin took the project extremely seriously, and their whole-hearted endorsement of cut-ups caused tremendous arguments between them, Gregory Corso and Sinclair Beiles. Beiles later reported getting so tense that he had to leave the room to throw up, whereas Corso added an appendix to the book, disassociating himself from cut-ups which he now regarded as an attack on the muse he held sacred. Bill and Brion's position was that, using the cut-up technique, poetry could be produced by anyone who owned a pair of scissors.

A second batch of material, called *Exterminator*, this time written only by Burroughs and Gysin, was sent to David Hazelwood at the Auerhahn Press in San Francisco; Hazelwood was a friend of Ginsberg's and published much of the new Beat poetry. Both titles came out in 1960 and were essentially volumes of poetry, the only time Burroughs worked in the genre. Burroughs soon made the cut-up method his own, and began using it to create prose. He explained his methods in a 1964 interview:

'Brion Gysin, an American painter living in Paris, has used what he calls the cut-up method to place at the disposal of writers the collage used in painting for 50 years. Pages of text are cut and rearranged to form new combinations of word and image, that is, the page is actually cut with scissors, usually into four sections, and the order rearranged.'

Sometimes the page was not cut, but folded so it could then be folded again in a different place:

I take a page of text, my own or someone else's and fold it lengthwise down the middle and place it on another page of text, my own or someone else's, lining up the lines. The composite text is then read across, half one text and half the other. Perhaps one of ten works out and I use it. The fold-in method extends to writing the flashback used in movies to enable a writer to move backwards and forwards in time. Characters and themes are carried over from one to the other, moving back and forth in time and space, making repeated trips through the same space but in previous times.

In addition to introducing him to cut-ups Brion Gysin told Bill the story of Hassan i Sabbah, which was to become another important element in the Burroughs' cosmology. Hassan was the founder of the infamous Ismaili sect known as the Assassins, which flourished at the end of the eleventh century in the valley of Alamut, where he had 60 castles. Al-Hassan b. Al-Sabbah, first Grand Master of the Assassins, was born a few kilometres to the south of modern Teheran. By 1090, using various devious political means, he managed to establish himself in the Castle of Alamut where he surrounded himself with a corps of disciples or fida'is, who became so successful at carrying out his orders that the name assassin, which applied to any follower of Hassan, became synonymous with political murder and intrigue. The name came not from Hassan but from Hashishin, eater of hashish, which was used by Hassan's fida'is during their training. Legend has it that Alamut had a secret garden, the Garden of Delights, within its precincts, and that after the fida'is had completed a successful operation, they were drugged with hashish and taken to spend three days in the garden. They never knew how they entered or how they emerged from it; it seemed like a dream and they thought they had actually been in Paradise. According to Marco Polo, the garden is reputed to have contained sweet-smelling plants and rare flowers; nightingales were specially imported for it and many beautiful young women, though Burroughs maintained that this account was inaccurate: 'No women were allowed in Alamut. The garden was not a three-dimensional place but a vision to which Hassan had the key – conforms perhaps to Egyptian paradise The Western Lands.' It is true that excavations at Alamut found no area which could possibly have been a garden.

The assassins, armed with daggers and poisons, were known as the Nizaris and their chief enemies were the Sunni orthodoxy and the Seljuk Turks. No caliph, emir or vizier was safe, and Hassan's power and influence spread rapidly as his men infiltrated castle after castle. In the course of 35 years, until his death in 1124, Hassan only left his apartments twice, and that was for a walk on the roof.

The story had considerable appeal to Bill, combining, as it did, both drugs and a control system that could reach out invisibly and snuff out a life. He particularly liked Hassan's reputed saying: 'Nothing is true, everything is permitted', which he incorporated into his own mythology, quoting it in letters to friends, and in books. It became his maxim, rather like Aleister Crowley's 'Do what thou wilt shall be the whole of the law'. *Soft Machine*, *Ticket That Exploded* and *Nova Express* all feature material based on Hassan and his Garden of Delights. *Minutes To Go* opens with an epigram by him, 'Not knowing what is and is not knowing, I knew not.'

Brion Gysin was also responsible for introducing Burroughs to the cult of Scientology, a subject which continued to interest him until the early 1970s. Though Burroughs could hardly have been called a believer, many of his friends were disturbed by his deep involvement in the cult. He found some of their techniques of use to him in his writing and, as Gysin said, 'He must be one of the few people who has made more money from them than they made from him.' Bill used Scientologists in short stories, and experimented with textual layouts based on their Q & A questionnaires.

The Church of Scientology was a development from the science fiction novels of American writer L Ron Hubbard. Gysin first encountered the Scientologists in Algiers – to his cost, since one of them managed to gain control of his Tangier restaurant – but the ideas appealed to Burroughs. On 7 October 1959, in a letter to Allen Ginsberg, he wrote: 'Remembering has many levels. We remember our operations under anaesthesia according to L Ron Hubbard. Dianetics went on to Scientology which you would do well to look into.' By 27 October he was much more positive about the system, and told Ginsberg: 'The method of directed recall is the method of Scientology. You will recall I wrote urging you to contact local chapter and find an auditor. They do the job without hypnosis or drugs, simply run the tape back and forth until the trauma is wiped off. It works. I have used the method – partially responsible for recent changes in management . . . and policy.'

Scientology was very rapidly assimilated into the Burroughs scheme of things because only two days later he wrote to Allen again: 'I have a new method of writing and do not want to publish anything that has not been inspected and processed. I cannot explain this method to you until you have necessary training. So once again and most urgently (believe me there is not much time) – I tell you: "Find a Scientology Auditor and have yourself run." ' There is some mention of Scientology in *Minutes To Go* (1960), but it was not until the mid-60s that Burroughs began a serious investigation into Scientology techniques and methods of mind-control.

In the summer of 1959, a young Cambridge undergraduate mathematician called Ian Sommerville was spending his vacation in Paris working at George Whitman's Mistral Bookshop, fixing up its antiquated electrical system and tidying the shelves. The poet Harold Norse, who lived at the Beat Hotel, first drew Bill's attention to him, telling him that Ian liked older men. Burroughs met him there, and they soon struck up a friendship. Ian came from Darlington in the north of England; he was thin and jumpy, with long fair hair which he constantly brushed back with a nervous gesture so it was piled high on the top of his head. He was sharp and birdlike, with a bony face, very pale, translucent skin with strong cheekbones and thin lips. He was always neatly dressed and was obsessively tidy, arranging his pencils in a row, labelling files and numbering tape boxes in his meticulous handwriting: a slightly showy copperplate using a wide-nibbed pen and jet-black ink. He had a brilliant mind and did not suffer fools; his conversation was often elliptical and difficult to follow, largely as a result of nervousness, though he could also be patient and spend hours drawing diagrams to try and explain the principle of free-floating equations.

Bill was trying to kick a codeine habit at the time and Ian moved into the Beat Hotel and nursed him through it. The hallucinations and visions, the sweating and convulsions were all a strange and frightening new experience for Ian, but he was a strict nurse and each day he doled out the apomorphine with a diminishing dose of codeine until Bill had recovered. Ian was to become part nurse, part secretary, lover and collaborator in Bill's life. He set up a filing system, labelling each folder: 'When I first met him he had 20 files, 17 of which were labelled miscellaneous,' he sniffed.

He became technical adviser to both Bill and Brion Gysin in all matters to do with tape recorders, electronics and photography, and Bill later put him in *Ticket That Exploded* and *Nova Express* as 'The Subliminal Kid'. He also appears under the guise of 'Technical Tilly' in other texts. Ian was a product of Cambridge tradition and brought a finely-tuned donnish sense of scientific method to Bill's experiments. Ian saw immediately the possibilities of the cut-up method as applied to tape and photographic collage, but was not impressed with Bill's methodology. Bill may have been to Harvard, Ian pointed out with his youthful arrogance, but the founder of Harvard had been to Cambridge. The pedantic scientific side of Ian could be fussy and sometimes infuriating but it was a meeting of equals: Ian believed Bill to be the greatest writer alive and had tremendous respect for him, while Bill was in awe of Ian's scientific abilities.

Bill was more than twice Ian's age, and he introduced the inexperienced young man to a fascinating world of drugs, avant garde literature and the international bohemian crowd. Ian was an eager pupil: he became something of a connoisseur of hashish and grass, and was quickly converted to the writing of Paul Bowles, Allen Ginsberg and Bill's other friends. Ian and Brion Gysin developed a firm friendship and together they developed the dream machine, a device which reproduced alpha-brain waves using a record player and a light bulb. Ian and Brion adored gossiping and bitching about other people. They both loved meeting famous people and were terrible snobs, though Ian had an element of northern working class solidarity which Brion lacked and could be catty even about princesses, which Brion could never do. This same side of Ian could be giggly and camp and fostered a strong strain of misogyny. He was tremendously loyal to his friends, and though he might utter loud sighs of exasperation at Bill's sloppiness, no one else was allowed to make any serious criticism.

This was the first time since his affair with Allen Ginsberg in 1953 that Burroughs allowed himself to become emotionally involved with someone, and this time it worked out. Ian could be moody and difficult, but Bill wasn't all that easy to get on with either. Though Bill's relationship with Ian eventually faltered, they always remained close friends up until Ian's death (in 1976), and it was easily the most important romantic relationship in Bill's life and probably also in Ian's. In a curious way they were an ideal 60s couple, particularly later, in the mid-60s, with Ian working at the Hewlett-Packard computer think tank while Bill cut up texts and tapes back at the St James's apartment and shopped at Fortnum and Mason's.

In April 1960, the American Embassy contacted Burroughs and warned him – falsely, as it turned out – that the French government was making moves to deport him as the result of a small drugs charge the previous autumn for which Bill had been given a fine of £50. Bill used the warning as an excuse to move to London and spend more time with Ian, who had returned to Corpus Christi College, Cambridge, to complete his studies. Bill sometimes stayed in Cambridge but spent most of his time working on *The Soft Machine* in his cheap room in the Empress Hotel at 25 Lillie Road, in Earl's Court. While he was in

London he also took a second apomorphine cure at Dr Dent's clinic to kick the habit he had yet again allowed to develop in Paris. He told the *New York Post* that he preferred London to Paris, loved the fog, and found English food cheaper and more to his taste.

In Paris Bill got up at midday or later, but in London he was up by nine to get his breakfast, the cost of which was included in his rent. He then worked until six and was usually in bed by midnight. In October of 1960, the first of the Burroughs groupies came knocking at his door. Mikey Portman was a wealthy seventeen-year-old English public schoolboy who latched on to Bill and started copying his every move, from his manner of walking to how he took his tea. Bill was irritated by his presence, but a little flattered, and since Portman was virtually impossible to get rid of he stayed, though Bill drew the line at him getting a room in the Empress Hotel. Ian Sommerville was less than pleased at this latest development but naturally deferred to Bill's decision to let Portman stay. There had been people at the Beat Hotel anxious to befriend Bill and hang around him, as if some talent for writing might rub off on them, but Mikey was the first groupie in the rock'n'roll sense who had read *The Naked Lunch* and just wanted to be with his idol. Bill's friends were astonished at Mikey's behavior. Michael Horovitz remembered how Mikey would show up at his flat in Greek Street, Soho, and shoot up heroin, proudly explaining, 'This is just how Bill does it.' Horovitz was fascinated and revolted.

Portman's own father died when he was fifteen, and part of Bill's attraction was obviously that of a father figure. Mikey was homosexual, a heroin addict and drank too much. He was a complete pest to have around because, like many spoiled, rich young men, he never had any money and treated other people's belongings as his own. He had read *The Naked Lunch* and was determined to worship at Burroughs' feet. Wherever Bill went, Mikey would follow, with his mother eventually picking up the bills left in his wake. Burroughs described him in *My Education*: '. . . selfish, self-centered, spoiled, petulant, weak Mikey Portman.'

Bill now travelled with both Ian and Mikey, using the Beat Hotel as a base, taking any room available, relying on the solid presence there of Brion Gysin, who stored Bill's manuscripts and papers for him in an old sea trunk as he bounced in and out of town: a trip to Amsterdam in July 1960, Cambridge with Ian that autumn, a trip to Oxford, Paris for the winter then the Villa Muniria in Tangier in April 1961, with quick visits to Boston and New York – this time without Ian and Mikey – and then back to London.

Bill was still seen by most people who encountered him as a distant, difficult man. Maurice Girodias gave his impression of Burroughs at that time:

> Bill was leading a very secret life in Paris, a grey phantom of a man in his phantom gabardine and ancient discoloured phantom hat, all looking like his mouldy manuscript. Burroughs was very hard to talk to because he didn't say anything. He had these incredibly mask-like, ageless features – completely cold looking. At this time he was living with Brion Gysin [in the hotel] and Gysin would do all the talking. I would go down to Gysin's room and he would talk and show me his paintings and explain things. Then we'd go back to Burroughs' room and all three of us would sit on the bed – because there were no chairs – and try to make conversation. It was really very funny. The man just didn't hardly say anything . . . I never had much editorial conversation with him. Actually none. He'd just bring in the manuscript and I'd knock it out.

This was the beginning of a strange period in Burroughs' life, which resulted in some of his most difficult, yet most intriguing, works: a trilogy of cut-up novels which all overlapped each other and which were re-written each time a new edition came out. He regarded his books as part of one continuously evolving text, and nowhere was this more obvious than in the trilogy, as chunks of text repeated and permutated from one book to the next.

Readers experience difficulty with the trilogy if they come to it looking for something resembling conventional novel form. Burroughs accepted that people found them problematic: 'I applied it [the cut-up technique] with great enthusiasm and I think in some cases carried it too far. Writers get carried away by a technique and what they can do with it and carry it so far that they lose their readers and I think this happened to some extent in these three books.'

The first cut-ups were poems, and if the cut-up novels are approached as long prose poems, then they become perfectly understandable – a development from the same strand of modernism that begins with Baudelaire's *Twenty Prose Poems*, and continues with Djuna Barnes' 1936 poetic novel *Nightwood*. These are texts where meaning is sometimes fugitive, shifting, and where narrative is essentially replaced by a procession of juxtaposed images. Cut-ups are used as a way of bringing collage to literature and the images in the books are composed in a cubist manner. This applies particularly to the later revisions of the texts which resemble palimpsests, with evidence of erasures and additions, superimpositions and commentaries – a model of the writer's consciousness duplicating the form of his yage hallucinations, and everyday consciousness itself, with its flickering of images and jumps from one mood to another. Burroughs has also compared them to what the eye sees during a short walk around the block: a view of a person may be truncated by a passing car, images are reflected in shop windows, and all images are cut up and interlaced according to your moving viewpoint. The central theme of all the books is the fight against control, though it is dealt with in an immensely complicated way.

The books were composed from Bill's 'Word Hoard', the huge pile of manuscripts, notes and routines left over from *The Naked Lunch* which he assiduously cut up. The first book to appear was *The Soft Machine*, published by Olympia Press in Paris in 1961. *The Naked Lunch* had a calligraphic dust wrapper by Burroughs, showing a marked influence of Brion Gysin. *The Soft Machine* had a wrapper by Gysin himself. The first edition of *The Soft Machine* is now very scarce and few readers will have read that version of the text, which unfortunately appears nowhere else. The second edition, published by Grove Press in 1966 in New York, was completely rewritten. Even then, Burroughs was still not satisfied with it, and the English edition, from John Calder in 1968, was rewritten yet again. Like Walt Whitman and WH Auden before him, Burroughs used each new edition as an opportunity to change the text to reflect his current thinking. The problem for anyone trying to trace the development of the text of *The Soft Machine* is that, in between rewrites, Burroughs wrote *The Ticket That Exploded*, which was again first published in Paris and rewritten for the Grove edition. Thus the English edition of *The Soft Machine*, supposedly still the first volume of the trilogy, has been up-dated to include Burroughs' latest ideas, as expressed in the second rewrite of *Ticket*.

The first edition of *The Soft Machine* shows Bill's enthusiasm for the recently discovered cut-up technique, and is a very dense text, with evidence of endless cuts. This gives rise to some oddly beautiful prose poetry: 'City blocks speed up out in photo flash. Hotel lobbies 1920 Time fill with slow grey film fallout and funeral urns of Hollywood', and 'Wind hand caught in the door' (which occurs twice on the last page), but the book requires the utmost dedication from the reader. Narrative passages in the first edition are mostly retained or are expanded in the later American and British editions.

In the third rewrite – the UK edition – Burroughs explained the book in an 'Appendix To The Soft Machine'.

The soft machine is the human body under constant siege from a vast hungry host of parasites with many names but one nature being hungry and one intention to eat.

If I may borrow the lingo of Herr Doctor Freud while continuing to deplore the spread of his couch no one does more harm than folks feel bad about doing it 'Sad Poison Nice Guy' more poison than nice – what Freud calls the 'id' is a parasitic invasion of the hypothalamus and since the function of the hypothalamus is to regulate metabolism . . .

'Only work here me.'

'Under new management.'

What Freud calls the 'super ego' is probably a parasitic occupation of the mid brain where the 'rightness' centers may be located and by 'rightness' I mean where 'you' and 'I' used to live before this 'super ego' moved in room on the top floor if my memory serves. Since the parasites occupy brain areas they are in a position to deflect research from 'dangerous channels'. Apomorphine acts on the hypothalamus to regulate metabolism and its dangers to the parasitic inhabitants of these brain areas can be readily appreciated. You see junk *is* death, the oldest 'visitor' in the Industry.

Three years before the American edition was published, Burroughs told an English interviewer, 'With *The Soft Machine* I had many complaints it was difficult to read, and going through it again, I felt this was true so I rewrote it completely.' Most people found the new version just as difficult.

Two years later Burroughs described the book as 'an expansion of my South American experiences, with surreal extensions. When I rewrote it recently, I included about 65 pages of straight narrative concerning Dr Benway, and the Sailor, and various characters from *Naked Lunch*. These people pop up everywhere.'

Joan Didion, writing in *Book Week*, said: 'Burroughs is uninfected by any trace of humanistic sentimentality, and his imagery is that of the most corrosive nightmare ... this voice is hard, derisive, inventive, free, funny, serious, poetic, indelibly American ... It is the voice of a natural.'

Burroughs himself explained the book tersely: 'In this work I am attempting to create a new mythology for the space age.' In *The Naked Lunch*, Burroughs first proposed the virus metaphor to represent control, or agents of control (church, state, police). In *The Soft Machine*, there are many examples of virus invasion: the Nova Mob, The Public Agent, Mayan Priests, Johnny Yen, The Board Bastards, The Other Half, Mr Martin – a whole gamut of Burroughs characters, all waiting to permutate. The only way to thwart the intentions of the controllers is to destroy their means of control: their language. The cut-up is a means of escape. 'Rub out the word' becomes a revolutionary slogan in the battles against the controllers which extend across space and time throughout the trilogy. The names are given of the central control agents: The Short Time Hyp, The Mayan Caper and, in *Ticket That Exploded*, The Board Books.

Trak Enterprises, first mentioned in *The Naked Lunch*, are developed in *The Soft Machine*. (Trak is a classic Burroughs word, suggesting both the tracks on the arms of a junkie, and the tract homes, the enormous suburban housing estates built in the USA during the 50s.) The motto of Trak Enterprises is 'Invade, Damage, Occupy'. Written in the days before arbitraged buy-outs, asset stripping and junk bonds, Trak was a prophetic invention. The Trak Home office occupies a black obsidian pyramid in Cut City where they market total addiction:

> The perfect product, gentlemen, has precise molecular affinity for its client of predilection . . . Our product never leaves the customer . . . This is not just another habit-forming drug this is the habit-forming drug takes over all functions from the addict including his completely unnecessary under the uh circumstances and cumbersome skeleton . . .

The protagonist Lee now becomes The Technical Sergeant. This is the beginning of Burroughs' space mythology, and the Novia Kid (sic) in *The Soft Machine*, prefigures the Nova Mob of *Nova Express*. *The Ticket That Exploded* develops these themes which reach their conclusion in *Nova Express*. Burroughs saw mankind as a slave to the linear verbal experience at the expense of non-verbal experience.

In the trilogy cut-ups are seen as the principal weapon against control, and Burroughs makes many claims for them: they are used as a means of bringing the visual art technique of collage to literature (they are not like the automatic writing of Tristan Tzara since they are completely controlled and there is no unconscious element in the method). There is an element of chance but, as Burroughs explained, it is a small one:

> The cut-ups are simply random at one point. That is, you take scissors and cut the page, and how random is that? What appears to be random may not, in fact, be random at all. You have selected what you want to cut up. After that, you select what you want to use . . .
>
> You can't always get the best results. Some cut-ups are interesting and some of them aren't. There is the important

matter of selection to consider. If I were to compose a poem out of cut-ups, I would just choose certain segments and parts that do work, and the rest I'd throw away. Sometimes I have cut-up an entire page and only got one sentence from it.

Bill would move the two cut pages against each other and type out lines or word combinations which looked interesting. This new page of manuscript would then sometimes be cut up itself, or he would maybe read through and underline a few words or groups of words, which would then be typed out. This meant that every word in the finished manuscript would have gone through a lengthy process of selection. This is why Burroughs' cut-ups are so unlike anyone else's.

In his book, *Here To Go*, Brion Gysin said:

William followed by running the cut-ups into the ground, literally. He has a gimlet-type mind and enormous powers of concentration. When he concentrates on something, he burns a hole in it, like someone concentrating the beam of light through a magnifying glass. He is corrosive. He pushed cut-ups so far with variations of his own that he produced texts which were sickeningly painful to read, even to him, mind you. These were texts which had to be wrapped in sheets of lead and sunk in the sea, disposed of like atomic waste, in marl holes (one of his favorites). Used by another writer who was attempting cut-ups, one single word of Burroughs' vocabulary would run a stain right through the fabric of their prose, no matter how they cut it. One single high-powered Burroughs word could ruin a whole barrel of good everyday words, run the literary rot right through them. One sniff of that prose and you'd say, 'Why, that's a Burroughs.'

Cut-ups are seen as a way of duplicating drug states: non-linear, producing irrational or illogical material, they are a way of 'deranging the senses' in the Rimbaud sense, a concept that interested Burroughs from the early 40s on. They free the writer from the tyranny of grammar and syntax. They enable anyone to write poetry, 'Anyone who owns a pair of scissors can be a poet.' They are a way of discovering 'terminal truth', literally 'reading between the lines'. Cut-ups create new juxtapositions, breaking down 'either-or' logic and providing a way of thinking in association blocks. Cut-ups make explicit the actual phenomenon of writing and show it to the reader, revealing the psychological process of what was going on – literally a map of the writer's consciousness, a true confessional.

Here Burroughs can be seen as a post-modernist figure, developing beyond Eliot, Joyce and Pound; revealing the actual structure of writing itself, and, in his opposition to either/or dichotomies and his examination of texts (and not only texts) for hidden and repressed meanings, acting as a precursor of the Deconstructionist philosophers.

In the trilogy, cut-ups serve a number of functions: they defend against attack, and they attack those in control. They provide a convenient way of travelling through time and space without worrying about how your characters got from A to B. Central to *The Soft Machine* is 'The Mayan Caper', a virtually straight narrative which explores the use of cut-ups and fold-ins to travel in time and space. Here cut-ups are used directly as weapons against the Tzolkin ritual control calendar of the Mayan priests. This is reminiscent of the conditions of Interzone where dream time provided the same function by removing the protagonist from the 'either-or' continuum. By removing himself from linear verbal control, the hero can move in time and space:

> . . . next thing we both got busted and sentenced to 'Death in Centipede' – So they strapped us to couches in a room under the temple and there was a terrible smell in the place full of old bones and a centipede about ten feet long comes nuzzling out of one corner – So I turn on something I inherit from Uranus where my grandfather invented the adding machine – I just lay there without any thought intense focus of heavy blue silence and a slow wave went through me and spread out of me and the couch began shaking and the tremors spread into the ground and the roof fell in and crushed the centipede and smashed the couch so the straps were loose and I slipped out and untied Technical Tilly – So we got out of there.

The book is set largely in South America, in that it draws on images going back to Burroughs' explorations in search of yage, and consequently there is an overlap of material from *Queer*. A reference in *Queer* to the lack of calcium salts in the jungle is developed into a proper routine in *The Soft Machine*:

> No calcium in the area you understand. One blighter lost his entire skeleton and we had to carry him about in a canvas bathtub. A jaguar lapped him up in the end, largely for the salt I think.

Another image with an obvious South American genesis is the line 'You win something like jelly fish, Meester', which Bill clearly found very amusing, since the line repeats more than half a dozen times throughout the text. In the latter half of the book the phrase 'Johnny, pants down' also reoccurs time and again, with the repetition providing an intentional rhythm to the text.

The familiar cat-walks from *The Naked Lunch* (Ginsberg's 1953 New York back-yard) get yet another airing:

> . . . a spiral iron stairwell into a labyrinth of lockers, tier on tier of wire mesh and steel cubicles joined by catwalks and ladders and moving cable cars as far as he could see, tiers shifting interpenetrating swinging beams of construction, blue flare of torches on intent young faces . . .

The images of the burning Negro and Southern sheriff from *The Naked Lunch* are replaced by much more overt attacks on Southern racism:

> . . . a Southern Senator sticks his fat frog face out of the outhouse and brays with inflexible authority . . . 'I wanna say further that ahm a true friend of the Nigra and understand all his simple wants. Why I got a good Darkie in here now wiping my ass.'

This prophetic routine was of course written before President Johnson entered the White House and actually invited reporters in to interview him while he sat on the can. Burroughs did not find it particularly significant that some of his imagined scenarios came true. To him, a writer's job was 'to make things happen'. When the things he wrote about did happen, it meant that he was doing his job well – just as F Scott Fitzgerald wrote the Jazz Age into existence, so Burroughs created the Space Age. He constructed a mental landscape that was receptive to what lay ahead in the next century. This is why he sometimes addressed the reader directly. Burroughs' great skill was his ability to deal with serious, controversial ideas, and present them in an amusing yet forceful way:

So the District Supervisor calls me in and puts the old white smaltz on me:
'Now kid what are you doing over there with the niggers and the apes? Why don't you straighten out and act like a white man? – After all they're only human cattle – You know that yourself – hate to see a bright young man fuck up and get off on the wrong track.'

It was shocking material considering it was written when segregation was still in force in the Southern states and the civil rights movement had not yet made significant gains.

The British edition of *The Soft Machine* was completely rewritten and was more accessible than the previous two. The chapter breaks were more logical and included the restoration of a sentence broken in half by the arbitrary opening of chapter two, a break which presumably occurred because Burroughs inserted his chapter breaks at the beginning of a new page of manuscript, without regard for the fact that the break might come halfway through a sentence. (This was the kind of sloppiness Ian Sommerville abhorred.)

Many chapters had new endings, often with much more material. One chapter, '1920 Movies', was renamed 'The Streets of Chance'. A complicated system, by which the original Olympia text of *The Soft Machine* was divided into four units, designated by colour, had already been much reduced for the American edition. In the British edition only vestigial traces remained. This meant that anyone reading a critical review of the book needs to know which edition the critic read. For instance, Alan Ansen's comments on the four coloured units make no sense when applied to the British edition where the text is no longer organised in the same way. The coloured units idea came to Burroughs during a visit to Cambridge to see Ian Sommerville. He stayed for a week in the first days of October 1960 and rented a large room in St Mary's Street, overlooking the market. He recalled it in *My Education*:

> It contained a sofa and one narrow bed, and the landlady was always snuffling around when we made it, so one could never relax.
> Looking out over this market, I got the idea of color separation. Look out there and pick out all the reds; now all the blues; now the green shutters on the stalls, and trees, and a sign; the yellows, a truck, a licence plate, a fire hydrant; the reds, a stop sign, a sweater, some flowers; the blues the sky, a coat, a sign on the side of a truck . . . later elaborated into the 'color walk'. I recall the feeling of strain, of not quite being able to do it.

The longest new addition occurred in 'Where The Awning Flaps' which was given six additional pages of straight narrative. Three pages of narrative were added to the 'Gongs of Violence' chapter and the more obscure cut-up passages were for the most part removed, rewritten in a shorter form, or moved to a more suitable position. Material was sometimes moved from one chapter to the next, for example in 'Dead Fingers Talk'. The book also had a new final line; the previous evocative ending ('The shallow water came in with the tide and the Swedish River of Gothenburg') was now followed by 'He waves his hand sadly from the soft machine, dead fingers in smoke pointing to Gibraltar.'

Burroughs also added an 'Appendix To The Soft Machine', and a thirteen-page document entitled 'A Treatment That Cancels Addiction', concerning the apomorphine treatment which he received from Dr Dent in London in 1955. Burroughs maintained that this system of detoxification, which was based on returning the addict's metabolism to its normal balance, was the only system that actually worked. His interest in apomorphine as a 'metabolic regulator' led him to include it, along with Scientology and cut-ups, in the pantheon as a weapon against control.

The only chapter to sustain a complete reworking of the same material was in the final section, 'Across the Wounded Galaxies', a retelling of the creation myth itself as a powerful prose poem about the pain of creation and birth, in which humanity evolves from the apes. Lines which Burroughs regrettably cut from the British edition include:

> Limestone slopes cover our bodies melting in savanna and grass mud. shit and sperm fed hot till the sun went. The mountain touched human bubbling throats. Torn we crawled out of the mud. faces and bodies covered the purple sex-flesh. and the sickness leaped into our body under-water music bubble in the silver morning frost. faces tentative flicker in ape forms. into the warm mud and water slopes. cold screaming sickness from white time.

The Soft Machine was a book which had to be taken seriously. Burroughs made efforts to make the text more accessible, but ultimately he did not compromise:

> Glad to have you aboard reader, but remember there is only one captain of this subway . . .

8 The Doctor Does a Good Job

With the completion of *The Soft Machine*, Burroughs reached a very strange phase in his investigation of control systems. He was more and more convinced that some outside agency was manipulating events, and that their agents had infiltrated all levels of society. 'I think very definitely that all events are produced because someone or something wants them. That is to say, you're made of about the same material as this table and this table doesn't walk by itself and neither do you.' But who was in control, and precisely how was control exercised?

In part, Bill was investigating his own addiction. As he saw it, the dynamics of interpersonal and institutional control are that need is essential to the imposition of authority: the pusher cannot exist without the junkie's participation; the junkie needs to feel controlled by something more powerful than his own will. This same collusion of need can exist between lovers, between workers and their bosses, between citizens and the government. All systems need acquiescence; a person must cooperate to be controlled. For Bill the mediating factor was language: 'Words are the principal agents of control. Suggestions are words. Persuasions are words. Order are words. No control machine can operate without words.'

Orders come to us down the word lines. Bill began to trace the word lines back to source: immediately identifying the huge clippings dossiers and photographic files of the *Time/Life/Fortune* group, the CIA and other large document deposits as prime suspects. In 1963, Bill told the *Guardian*: 'The Luce magazines are nothing but control mechanisms. They're about as human as a computer. Henry Luce, himself, has no control over the thing now, it's grown so large. Yet all it would take to bring it down is one technical sergeant. That's why the "Word falling, photo falling" image. We've got to break down the police organisation of words and images.'

In a 1965 interview, he compared the Luce system to that of the Mayan priests:

> [Luce] has set up one of the greatest word and image banks in the world. I mean, there are thousands of photos, thousands of words about anything and everything, all in his files. All the best pictures go in the files. Of course, they're reduced to micro-photos now. I've been interested in the Mayan system, which was a control calendar. You see, their calendar postulated really how anyone should feel at a given time, with lucky days, unlucky days, et cetera. And I feel that Luce's system is comparable to that. It's a control system. It has nothing to do with reporting. *Time/Life/Fortune* is some sort of police organisation.

Since words were the vehicle of control, an obvious way of combating control was silence. In the interview with Burroughs done by Allen Ginsberg and Gregory Corso for the *Journal for the Protection of All Beings* in 1961, Burroughs said,

> I feel that the change, the mutation in consciousness, will occur spontaneously once certain pressures now in operation are removed. I feel that the principal instrument of monopoly and control that prevents expansion of consciousness is the word lines controlling thought, feeling and apparent sensory impressions of the human host.
>
> Allen Ginsberg: And if they are removed, what step?
>
> WSB: The forward step must be made in silence. We detach ourselves from word forms – this can be accomplished by substituting for words, letters, concepts, verbal concepts, other modes of expression; for example colour. We can translate word and letter into colour (Rimbaud stated that in his colour vowels, words quote 'words' can be read in silent colour). In other words, man must get

away from verbal forms to attain the consciousness, that which is there to be perceived, at hand.

Gregory Corso: How does one take that 'forward step', can you say?

WSB: Well, this is my subject, and is what I am concerned with. Forward steps are made by giving up old armour because words are built into you – in the soft typewriter of the womb you do not realise the word-armour you carry . . .

The interview was conducted in Tangier, where Bill and his entourage had retreated upon hearing that Allen Ginsberg and Peter Orlovsky were stopping off in Paris on their way to live in India. When Allen arrived at the Beat Hotel in Paris at the beginning of April 1961, looking forward to a grand reunion with Bill, whom he had not seen since 1958, he was shocked and hurt to find that Bill had checked out, leaving no forwarding address. He was soon set straight by Brion Gysin, who told him conspiratorially that Bill had left precisely because he knew Allen was coming. Allen should beware, Brion said, Bill was an assassin, responsible for many deaths. Though this was a reference to Hassan i Sabbah, not to be taken literally, at the time Allen was not to know and worried that something was seriously wrong.

Bill had left without completing work on *The Soft Machine*, so Ginsberg, ever the loyal friend, finished editing it for him, going over the manuscript with Brion Gysin. Brion then designed a calligraphic dust wrapper and Allen wrote a cover blurb. Gysin eventually told Allen where Bill had gone and Allen wrote to him. After a while Bill replied, inviting them to Tangier.

They met up with Gregory Corso and the three of them travelled to the south of France where they attended the Cannes Film Festival at Jacques Stern's expense. They arrived in Tangier expecting to find Bill waiting on the harbour but there was no sign of him. They found him working in his room, indifferent to their arrival. Allen and Peter were saving their money for India and the Villa Muniria was too expensive for their budget. Along with Gregory, they took two rooms around

Heir's Pistol Kills His Wife; He Denies Playing Wm. Tell

Mexico City, Sept. 7 (AP).—William Seward Burroughs, 37, first admitted, then denied today that he was playing William Tell when his gun killed his pretty, young wife during a drinking party last night.

Police said that Burroughs, grandson of the adding machine inventor, first told them that, wanting to show off his marksmanship, he placed a glass of gin on her head and fired, but was too drunk that he missed and shot her in the forehead.

After talking with a lawyer, police said, Burroughs, who is a wealthy cotton planter from Pharr, Tex., changed his story and insisted that his wife was shot accidentally when he dropped his newly-purchased .38 caliber pistol.

Husband in Jail.

Mrs. Burroughs, 27, the former Joan Vollmer, died in the Red Cross Hospital.

The shooting occurred during a party in the apartment of John Healy of Minneapolis. Burroughs said two other American tourists whom he knew only slightly were present.

Burroughs, hair disheveled and clothes wrinkled, was in jail today. A hearing on a charge of homicide is scheduled for tomorrow morning.

No Arguments, He Says.

"It was purely accidental," he said. "I did not put any glass on her head. If she did, it was a joke. I certainly did not intend to shoot at it."

He said there had been no arguments or discussion before the "accident."

"The party was quiet," he said. "We had a few drinks. Everything is very hazy."

Burroughs and his wife had been here about two years. He said he was studying native dialects at the University of Mexico. He explained his long absence from his ranch by saying that he was unsuited for business.

Wife From Albany.

He said he was born in St. Louis and that his wife was from Albany, N. Y. They have two children, William Burroughs Jr., 3, and

William Seward Burroughs in Mexico City prison.

(Associated Press Wirefotos)
The late Mrs. Joan Burroughs— killed at party.

Julie Adams, 7, who he said was his wife's daughter by a previous marriage. The couple had been married five years.

She had attended journalism school at Columbia University before her marriage to Burroughs.

Burroughs, who also had been married before, formerly lived in

Loudonville, a swank suburb of Albany. He is a graduate of Harvard University and worked for two weeks in 1942 as a reporter for the St. Louis Post-Dispatch.

His paternal grandfather laid the foundation of a fortune when he built his first adding machine in St. Louis in 1885.

News report on the accidental shooting of Joan Vollmer, *New York Daily News*, 8 September 1951

Above: Allen Ginsberg, Lucien Carr, William S. Burroughs, at Lucien's apartment, New York 1953 (*Francesca Carr, Allen Ginsberg Archives*)

Below: The beach, Tangier, 1957 – left to right, Peter Orlovsky, Jack Kerouac and Burroughs, reclining (*Allen Ginsberg*)

Above: Burroughs and Brion Gysin outside the Beat Hotel, rue Git le Coeur, Paris, 1959

Below: Maurice Girodias and Burroughs on the rue Git le Coeur in 1959, shortly after Girodias published *Naked Lunch* (*Brion Gysin*)

Burroughs in Paris, 1960

Above: The garden of the Villa Muniria,Tangier, 1961. From left to right: Peter Orlovsky, Burroughs, Allen Ginsberg, Alan Ansen, Paul Bowles (seated), Gregory Corso, Ian Sommerville (*Michael Portman, Ginsberg Archives*)

Below: Burroughs at the rue Delacroix, Tangier, 1964, during his photo-collage collaborations with Ian Sommerville (*Ian Sommerville*)

Burroughs on the fire escape of his loft at 210 Center Street, New York, 1965 (*John Hopkins*)

Alan Ansen and Burroughs, Athens, 1972. Ansen helped Allen Ginsberg type *Naked Lunch* in Tangier, 1957 (*Johnny Brady*)

Above: Burroughs at Duke Street, St James's, London, 1972, working on
Exterminator! (*author*)

Below: Carl Solomon, Patti Smith, Allen Ginsberg and Burroughs at the launch
party for the uncensored Penguin edition of *Junky*, New York, 1977 (*Kate Simon*)

Bill Burroughs, Kansas, 1983 (*Kate Simon*)

the corner at the Hotel Armor, where Allen and Peter had a tiled room on the roof.

'Bill was in a very suspicious mood,' Ginsberg said, 'distant to me, distant to everybody. He was with Ian Sommerville but I think their sexual relationship had stopped, I'm not sure. He was with Michael Portman who I don't think he made out with but was very fond of. Portman was very fond of Bill and my feeling was that they had replaced us in Bill's affections and intimacy. It was they who dictated socially who should come to supper and when.'

Allen wrote to Lucien Carr:

Bill's all hung up with 18-yr-old spoiled brat English Lord who looks like a palefaced Rimbaud but is a smart creep – Apparently Lady Portman his mother gave him into Bill's hands to look after here – platonic anyhoo – But Bill got some kinda awful relation with him and the kid bugs everyone so intimacy with Bill is limited and Bill absent-minded all the time – however very busy with his cut-up experiments and applying it to pictorial collages and taking brownie photographs and very busy and creative – also did new book in cut-up method, very pure experiments and strangely good reading tho oft toneless, 'The Soft Machine'.

Ginsberg remembered that the first thing Burroughs did was interrogate him: ' "Who are you an agent for?" That's literally what he said to me. Bill was thinking very much in terms of agents and smoking a lot of grass.' Bill detected in Allen traces of his father, traces of Lionel Trilling, who was his professor at Columbia, and various Jewish traits. 'It was a little difficult to see old friend Bill looking at me as if I was a robot sent to check him out. And also to be suggested by him that I examine him to see who he was representing, because he assumed that everybody was an agent at that point. Not necessarily for the government at all; an agent for a giant trust of insects from another galaxy actually. Women were suspect as being agents and Burroughs thought that maybe you had to exterminate all the women, or get rid of them one way or another. Evolve some sort of male that could give birth by parthenogenesis.'

Peter Orlovsky, who expressed a preference for women, was found to be a Venusian and subjected to constant ridicule and humiliation by Bill and his boys, whom Ginsberg described to Kerouac as 'scampering and skipping behind his elbows like demons, simpering at us all'. Sommerville and Portman encouraged the anti-women side of Bill's homosexuality. In a drunken WC Fields-style conversation Bill told Peter 'Take a tip from me, kid, and steer clear of 'em. They got poison juices dripping all over 'em. Fishy smell too. Down right pornographic.'

Bill had taken cut-ups far beyond their original role as a literary technique. Bill and his boys had created a hermetic cut-up universe, in which everything was processed. Bill was out on a limb, far removed from his old friends. He was now cutting up people, his anthropological training enabling him to distance himself from his friends and acquaintances. The reality of the situation was that he had developed a cosy little world with his two acolytes, which was not able to admit any outsiders, not even Bill's old friends. The little group particularly objected to Peter Orlovsky's vociferous defence of both women and the idea of love. The arguments were acrimonious and bitchy, with Burroughs scoffing at the very idea of friendship. Ginsberg vaccilated between the two positions, not knowing who to support, with the result that Orlovsky, his lover of six years, decided to leave. It was many months before Ginsberg was able to locate him again in order to continue their journey to India.

Allen Ginsberg saw this development of cut-ups as a continuation of Burroughs' self-analysis, begun in Tangier in 1958 and continued in Paris that year: the constant working through of fantasies and unpleasant obsessions until their power was exhausted and they no longer had any control over Bill's life. Ginsberg said,

In fact, the cut-ups were originally designed to rehearse and repeat his obsession with sexual images over and over again, like a movie repeating over and over and over again, and then recombined and cut up and mixed in; so that finally the obsessive attachment, compulsion, and preoccupation empty out and drain from the image . . . Finally, the hypnotic attachment, the image, becomes demystified . . .

He can finally look at it at the end of the pool; he can look at his most tender, personal, romantic images objectively, and no longer be attached to them.

This was very similar to the elements of Scientology techniques which Bill found useful.

What Allen had not expected was how far Burroughs had extended the idea. Like a routine taken to its ultimate end, Burroughs now suspected that the entire fabric of reality was artificially conditioned and that whoever was doing the conditioning was running the universe, like an engineer running a cinema soundstage with tape machines and films. He assumed that all reality, sight, taste, smell, sound and touch was some form of hallucination and that these apparent sensory impressions were programmed into our bodies. It was another variant on the search for the controllers, the search for the Ugly Spirit that had made him kill Joan.

It is hard to know how real the trust of giant insects on another galaxy was to Burroughs. He always believed in magic, in UFOs and contact with aliens, but the whole construct had more to do with routines than a belief system. It did give rise to some wonderful prose and was even used as the name for a literary magazine – *The Insect Trust Gazette* – and the rock band, Insect Trust. Ginsberg attributed much of it to the same Burroughs inventiveness which enabled his grandfather to invent the adding machine.

These themes – Hassan i Sabbah, Scientology, substituting silence for sub-vocal language, the replacement of words by colours or hieroglyphs and ideographs, investigations of the word-image track, identification of the unconscious agents of control – all made up the subject of the next book, *The Ticket That Exploded*, which was published by Olympia Press in December 1962.

Burroughs has described *The Ticket That Exploded* as being in a 'fictional context extending beyond the planet as we know it. *The Ticket That Exploded* involves the Nova conspiracy to blow up the Earth and then leave it through reincarnation by projected image onto another planet. The plot failed, so the title has both meanings.'

The book opens with a Hassan i Sabbah sequence. The reader is presented with a choice: either stay in the Garden of Delights, drugged, hallucinating, in a phoney, unreal world created by your controllers, or come out of the garden and see grim reality. Burroughs was in no doubt about which course is preferable, and since this is an action book, one of the many narrators takes it upon himself to blow up the Garden, and, since it is also a cut-up book, he does it several times, in different ways:

> The Demolition Squad has arrived. The G.O.D. is being pulled down and stacked in piles for burning. A lean leather-faced man looks sourly at a broken gallows covered with pink tinsel. A tape recorder gasps, shits, pisses, strangles and ejaculates at his feet. He listens his face impassive. He swings his heavy metal tipped boot. The noise stops ... in a darkening valley the Garden of Delights is scattered piles of smouldering rubbish.

It is a dense, difficult book, described by Mottram as 'Burroughs' most complex allegory of his major theme' (the fight against control). The hallucinatory reportage of his experiences with yage, which characterised *The Soft Machine*, continues here – 'The whole trip gave me an awful lot of copy' – but it is presented in a much more controlled manner, particularly the sections 'Black Fruit' and 'In A Strange Bed'. The latter is a complete science fiction story in itself, written in the classic sf straight narrative tradition but of course using Burroughs' unique imagery.

Early in the book, the green fish boys make their first appearance:

> The other green boy dropped his pants and moved in swirls of poisonous colour vapour, breathing the alien medium through sensitive purple gills lined with erectile hairs pulsing telepathic communications.

In the 'In A Strange Room' chapter they are developed in a major sequence:

Beside him sat an amphibious green fish boy shimmering with water from the pool – The creature pulsed with translucent green light that flooded through the flesh in eddies – The head was a pointed dome that sprang from a slender neck on either side of which protruded gills like sensitive spongy wings . . .

Burroughs returned to this theme again years later in *The Western Lands*. *The Ticket That Exploded* has its full complement of Burroughs characters: the Old Doc and Inspector Lee, who becomes the Technical Sergeant in the revised edition of the text. Lee, now cured of his drug addiction, describes the connection between the Nova Mob and addiction.

The Nova Mobster operates through addicts because he himself is an addict – a heavy metal addict from Uranus – what we call opium or junk is a very much diluted form of heavy metal addiction – Venusians usually operate through sexual practices – In short controllers brought their vices and diseases from planet of origin and infected the human hosts very much in the same way as early colonisers infected the so-called primitive peoples.

Two of the mobsters are favourite Burroughs characters: Mr Martin, the Uranian heavy metal addict, and Johnny Yen, the Venusian sex addict who first introduced himself in *The Soft Machine*:

'Hello, I'm Johnny Yen, a friend of – well, just about everybody. I was more physical before my accident you can see from this interesting picture . . .'

Inspector Lee outlines the techniques of Nova in great detail, and this must be regarded as the definitive description, since all five pages of Lee's speech are repeated later, word for word, in *The Wild Boys*, a transitional volume completed in August 1969, long after the cut-up period.

Much of the science-fiction drama of *The Ticket That Exploded* is a record of combat against the Other Halfs, who are represented by orgasm. Sex partners are Other Halfs, an illusion of another body created by the Word. The Other Half exists to create conflicts through 'either-or' polarisations through dualistic thinking. It is all seen as a plot to create conditions of Nova. The specific definition of 'the Other Halfs' as women had not yet been made.

In the section 'Operation Rewrite' Bill explained the concept of the Other Half in some detail. It is an important idea used throughout the Burroughs early canon:

> The 'Other Half' is the word. The 'Other Half' is an organism. Word is an organism. The presence of the 'Other Half' a separate organism attached to your nervous system on an air line of words can now be demonstrated experimentally . . . The word is now a virus. The flu virus may once have been a healthy lung cell. It is now a parasitic organism that invades and damages the lungs. The word may once have been a healthy neural cell. It is now a parasitic organism that invades and damages the central nervous system. Modern man has lost the option of silence. Try halting your sub-vocal speech. Try to achieve even ten seconds of inner silence. You will encounter a resisting organism that forces you to talk. That organism is the word.

Fortunately the Nova Police arrive in the next chapter to combat this invasion. The next routine is called 'The Nova Police' and Inspector J Lee of the Nova Police is introduced.

The question of why man is being held back by this parasite is considered. Who would profit from retarding human development, and keeping humans from exploring space? The answer, Bill discovers, is a parasitic entity that lives in the human body but which could not survive space. In other words, the Word.

In *The Soft Machine*, Burroughs proposed that the sexes be separated and that all male children be raised by men and all female children raised by women. In Bill's view, the less the two sexes had to do with each other the better, as he explained in a later book, *The Job*: 'I think love is a virus. I think love is a con put down by the female sex. I don't think it's a solution to anything . . . I think they [women] were a basic mistake, and the whole dualistic universe evolved from this error.' Burroughs later modified his feelings regarding women, but while he was working on the cut-up trilogy, they were seen very much as the enemy, possibly even as agents from another galaxy. Burroughs' views on women were notorious and dated back to pre-war St Louis society. Burroughs was often very influenced by his immediate associates and the periods of his most extreme misogyny correspond to the times when he lived in close proximity to other extreme misogynists: Brion Gysin, Michael Portman and Ian Sommerville. The kind of woman that Burroughs disliked was the woman still playing the traditional role: demanding security and protection, looking to her man for money, flattery and love, restricting his freedom, tying him down to house and family. It is a form of women-hatred common in America and explains the popularity of writers, such as Charles Bukowski, in whose work women keep their place and men keep their freedom. However, as feminist ideas spread through American society in the 70s, Burroughs recognised that liberated women were no threat to him. In an interview in 1977 he said: 'They [the women's movement] are opposed to the matriarchal society. They don't want to be treated as women. I certainly have no objection to any of their objectives. They say they want job equality and to be treated the same way as men. The difference between the sexes is certainly more sociological than biological. Like the Southern Belle who was put on a pedestal.'

Bill now saw that not all women wanted to be taken care of and began to befriend some of the more independent women who entered his circle. In the 70s he was happy to spend time with Patti Smith, Laurie Anderson, Kathy Acker, Debbie Harry and others.

Friendship itself, male or female, appeared to be suspect at one point – the reason for Bill's coldness to Allen Ginsberg when he arrived in Tangier in 1961. 'There are no friends. I found that out after the crash. I found out before the others. That's why I'm still here. There are allies. There are accomplices.' After being rejected by Allen, and perhaps disturbed by

Ian's promiscuity, Bill clearly no longer believed in love, between men or with women, as he explained in an interview with Daniel Odier: 'I think that what we call love is a fraud perpetrated by the female sex and that the point of sexual relations between men is nothing that we could call love, but rather what we might call recognition.'

Love gets its final comeuppance from Burroughs in a routine included in *The Ticket That Exploded* called 'Do You Love Me?' which is made up of pages of titles and lines from popular love songs of the day, intercut with banalities and clichés:

All the tunes and sound effects of '*Love*' spit from the recorder permutating sex whine of a sick picture planet: Do you love me? – But i exploded in cosmic laughter – Old acquaintance be forgot? – Oh Darling, just a photograph? – Mary i love you i do do you know i love you through? – On my knees i hoped you'd love me too – I would run till i feel the thrill of long ago – Now my inspiration but it won't last and we'll be just a photograph – I've forgotten you then? I can't sleep, Blue Eyes, if i don't have you – Do i love her? I love you i love you many splendored thing – . . .

They gradually get cut up and become progressively more caustic in the process, ending with a predictable conclusion:

Sheets of pain hung oh baby oh i love her sucked through pearly jelly – I've got you under big fat scratching clouds of me – Always be true to your diamond rings – Tell Laura black slow movement but it won't last – I've forgotten you then? Decay breathing? Black lust tearing his insides apart for ants? Love Mary? – The rose of memory shifting colour orgasms back home – Good-bye – It's a long way to go – Someone walking – Won't be two –

Burroughs never lies in his work; there are no opinions expressed other than his own but the complex mixture of fact and fiction sometimes makes it hard to distinguish which is which: a genuinely held opinion or a fictional routine which is just that. In *The Ticket That Expoded*, the connection between what Burroughs says in the book and what he sees going on around him is clearly spelled out in the opening pages, when Old Sarge says:

> I am reading a science fiction book called *The Ticket That Exploded*. The story is close enough to what is going on here so now and again I make myself believe this ward room is just a scene in an old book far away and long ago might as well be that for all the support I'm getting from Base Headquarters.

Once the enemy has been identified, it is a question of warfare. Bill brings out all his weapons: cut-ups, Scientology, apomorphine, tape-recorders and film collage. A curious arsenal, but one which proved effective over the years. (Burroughs used these weapons in real life, including a sabotage run against Scientology's London HQ using tape-recorders and film as weapons. Bill was usually armed to the teeth in a more conventional manner as well. He believed in effective weaponry.)

The section called 'Writing Machine' takes the idea of cut-ups to their ultimate end, a machine which writes without human input.

> A writing machine that shifts one half one text and half the other through a page frame on conveyor belts – (The proportion of half one text half the other is important corresponding as it does to the two halfs of the human organism) Shakespeare, Rimbaud, etc. permutating through page frames in constantly changing juxtaposition the machine spits out books and plays and poems.

Scientology makes an appearance early on in the book in a long straight narrative crime story concerning a mysterious death involving tape-recorders. The Scientologists are transparently disguised as the 'Logos' group:

> They have a system of therapy they call 'clearing'. You 'run' traumatic material which they call 'engrams' until it

loses emotional connotation through repetition and is then refiled as neutral memory. When all the 'engrams' have been run and deactivated the subject becomes a 'clear' . . .

Apomorphine, the metabolic regulator with which Dr Dent cured Burroughs' drug addiction on several occasions, makes its appearance in a discussion of military tactics:

Remember you do not have to organise similar installations but merely to put enemy installations out of action or take them over – A camera and two tape recorders can cut the lines laid down by a fully equipped film studio – The ovens and the orgasm death tune in can be blocked by large doses of apomorphine which breaks the circuit of positive feedback – But do not rely too heavily on this protection agent.

The use of cameras and tape-recorders is gone into in exhaustive detail, based on the experiments with tape-recorder cut-ups conducted initially with Brion Gysin but more extensively with Ian Sommerville. Descriptions of the obvious next step, film collage, only appear in the revised edition of *The Ticket That Exploded*, where English film-maker Antony Balch is thanked in the acknowledgements for his collaborations in the section 'Let Them See Us', a section of cut-ups and fold-ins: 'Now some words about the image track – The Human body is an image on screen talking.'

The Ticket That Exploded was published in a considerably revised form in Britain and the United States. As Burroughs told the *Paris Review* in 1965, 'It's not a book I'm satisfied with in its present form. If it's published in the United States I would have to rewrite it.' This he did. By October 1966, Grove Press were clamouring for the manuscript, but Bill still had not finished work on it. 'I am still working on the corrections and additions which will be considerable,' he wrote to Richard Seaver at Grove. 'It really would be extremely disadvantageous to publish that book as is. The changes I am making could well make the difference between a real setback and a book that will make money.' Considering how difficult to understand most readers found either version of the book, it seems more likely that what Bill really wanted was more time to revise the text and incorporate his new ideas about tape and film collage. As he must have known, there was little danger of the book becoming a bestseller. *The Ticket That Exploded* ended with the writing of Brion Gysin, fading into pure calligraphic gestures, the words dissolving off the page. The revised edition spoiled this effect somewhat because Bill added an appendix in the form of 'The Invisible Generation', a technical essay on how to use tape cut-ups for radical political purposes.

The third of the cut-up trilogy, *Nova Express*, opens, like *The Ticket That Exploded*, with the words of Hassan i Sabbah, denouncing the Nova Mob, demanding retribution:

> Listen all you boards syndicates and governments of the earth. And you powers behind what filth deals consummated in what lavatories to take what is not yours. To sell the ground from under unborn feet forever . . . Pay it all back, pay it all back for all to see.

It is another attempt to wise up the marks, the readers, and throughout the book Burroughs does address the reader rather more than usual – appropriately so, since the book concerns the battle between the Nova Mob and the Nova Police. The details of the activities of the Nova Mob are given again by Inspector Lee, his five-page speech repeated verbatim from *The Ticket That Exploded* – since he said it right the first time, why change it?

The book is a warning against either-or conflict, against cold war, against ecological distortion, a prophetic warning sounded early:

> The death dwarfs are weapons of the Nova Mob, which in turn is calling the shots in the Cold War. The Nova Mob is using that conflict in an attempt to blow up the planet, because when you get right down to it, what are America and Russia really arguing about? The Soviet Union and the

United States will eventually consist of interchangeable social parts and neither nation is morally 'right'.

Yet again Burroughs prefigured later social and political developments, as if his uniquely cynical approach and way of always reading between the lines gave him advance warning of things to come. Burroughs had been outraged at the dropping of the atomic bomb, and had always held the power elite and the miltary-industrial complex (the Nova Mob) in contempt. This clear-eyed view enabled him to see that the ecological damage they caused would one day become a major item on the political agenda.

In *Nova Express* the Nova Mob attempt to escape but the Nova Police are brought in, in the shape of Burroughs' alter ego, Inspector Lee, who immediately begins to behave like police everywhere, providing another dimension to what would normally have been a straightforward science-fiction story. In the 1965 *Paris Review* interview, Burroughs explained:

> Implicit in *Nova Express* is a theory that what we call reality is actually a movie. It's a film, what I call a biologic film. What has happened is that the underground and also the nova police have made a breakthrough past the guards and gotten into the darkroom where the films are processed, where they're in a position to expose negatives and prevent events from occurring. They're like police anywhere. All right, you've got a bad situation here in which the nova mob is about to blow up the planet. So the Heavy Metal Kid calls in the nova police. Once you get them in there, by God, they begin acting like any police. They're always an ambivalent agency. I recall once in South America that I complained to the police that a camera had been stolen and they ended up arresting me. I hadn't registered or something. In other words, once you get them on the scene they really start nosing around.

The Nova Police take the Nova Criminals to the Biologic Courts but the book ends in a stalemate. It is, after all, the readers who are on trial. It is up to them to wise up, to reject the present administration, to free themselves from dependency on the false images of advertising and state power, to act against the advertising agencies and political hacks who run their lives. 'Heaven and Hell exist in my mythology,' said Burroughs. 'Hell consists of falling into enemy hands, into the hands of the virus power, and heaven consists of freeing oneself from this power, of achieving inner freedom, freedom from conditioning. I may add that none of the characters in my mythology are free. If they were free they would not still be in the mythological system, that is, in the cycle of conditioned action.'

Burroughs uses the symbolism of the relationship between the confidence man and his clients, the con man and the marks. It is the 'carny' jargon of the circus and state fair. We are not, however, at the mercy of the con man. Burroughs devotes much of the book to explaining the weapons at our disposal, which are the usual ones of cut-ups, silence, apomorphine, Scientology, and the orgone accumulators of Wilhelm Reich which Burroughs had been building and using since the 40s.

Regarding cut-ups, Burroughs said: 'In *Nova Express* I think I get further from the conventional novel form than I did in *Naked Lunch*,' but he added, 'I don't feel that *Nova Express* is in any sense a wholly successful book.' Fortunately, this time he did not attempt to rewrite it.

Nova Express features the activities of the Subliminal Kid, from *The Ticket That Exploded*, who uses cut-ups as a weapon to disrupt the time–space continuum. The Subliminal Kid was based on Ian Sommerville, who is credited in the acknowledgements as collaborating on the section called 'This Horrible Case' (the introduction to the Biologic Courts) and contributing the technical notes to 'Chinese Laundry'.

The Subliminal Kid moved in seas of disembodied sound – He . . . had recorder in tracks and moving film mixing arbitrary intervals and agents moving with the word and image of tape recorders . . . The kid stirred in sex films and the People-City pulsed in a vast orgasm and no one knew what was film and what was not . . . He took film of sunsets and cloud and sky water and tree film and projected colour in vast reflector screens concentrating blue sky red sun green grass and the city dissolved in light and people walked through each other – There was only colour and music and silence where the words of Hassan i Sabbah had passed –

'Boards Syndicates Governments of the earth Pay – Pay back the Colour you stole –

'Pay Red – Pay back the red you stole for your lying flags and your Coca-Cola signs – Pay that red back to penis and blood and sun –

'Pay Blue – . . . Pay back the blue you stole for your police uniforms

'Pay Green – Pay back the green you stole for your money . . . Pay that green back to flowers and jungle river and sky –

'Boards Syndicates Governments of the earth pay back your stolen colours – Pay Colour back to Hassan i Sabbah –'

This long passage clearly shows Burroughs as proto-ecologist, forecasting the ecology and green movement in 1964, even before Gregory Bateson's speech predicting the Greenhouse Effect, delivered in London in 1967. Though couched in poetic terms, which show how closely Burroughs read his Rimbaud, these are in essence the same radical ideas now promoted by the Green Parties. Burroughs uses the colour arc as a metaphor for nature and natural order and demands retribution for the despoliation of the planet caused by the Nova Mob: the politicians and generals who pollute and destroy.

Much avant-garde experiment grows stale over the years, yet the Burroughs cut-up trilogy is as fresh as ever. Possibly this is because conditions on the planet are now much worse than they were when he issued his warnings, and his message is therefore all the more urgent. Although the trilogy was fiction, Burroughs meant every word he said: 'I do definitely mean what I say to be taken literally, yes, to make people aware of the true criminality of our times, to wise up the marks. All of my work is directed against those who are bent, through stupidity or design, on blowing up the planet or rendering it uninhabitable. Like the advertising people, I'm concerned with the precise manipulation of word and image to create an action, not to go out and buy a Coca Cola, but to create an alteration in the reader's consciousness.'

Silence, freedom from the word and image track, is seen as both desirable and a weapon. In *Nova Express* apomorphine, cut-ups and silence contribute directly to the defeat of the Nova Mobsters and set the stage for their trial at the biologic court. Apomorphine is further extolled (Burroughs issued a small press book called *Apo-33*, concerning the use of the drug as a metabolic regulator, in 1965). In *Nova Express* it is used as a weapon:

> You can cut your enemy off your line by the judicious use of apomorphine and silence – Use the sanity drug apomorphine.

Burroughs explained how:

> [Winkhorst speaking] Apomorphine combats parasite invasion by stimulating the regulatory centres to normalise metabolism – A powerful variation of this drug could deactivate all verbal units and blanket the earth in silence, disconnecting the entire heat syndrome.

Scientology is dealt with in *Nova Express* by the rather transparent device of The District Supervisor interrogating an unnamed recruit:

> 'Repeat what you know about Scientology.'
> 'The Scientologists believe sir that words recorded during a period of unconsciousness ... (anaesthesia, drunkenness, sleep, childhood amnesia for trauma) ... store pain and that this pain store can be plugged in with key words represented as alternate mathematical formulae indicating number of exposures to the key words and reaction index ... they call these words recorded during unconsciousness engrams sir ... The child forgets sir but since the controllers have the engram tapes sir any childhood trauma can be plugged in at any time ... The pain

that overwhelms that person is basic basic sir and when basic basic is wiped off the tape ... then that person becomes what they call clear sir.'

Already Burroughs was adapting Scientology for his own use. Scientology and the theories of Reich were used extensively throughout the trilogy as the means of analysing what was corrupt and affected by the Nova Mob and what was not. In *Nova Express* Burroughs used the same footnotes about Reich to explain the line 'Blue light played over their bodies' as he used to explain the line 'The photos vibrated and welded together in orgone accumulators' in *The Ticket That Exploded*. (This is a classic example of Burroughs' multi-use of texts because the footnote was originally written to explain yet another line, used in an early draft from *The Ticket That Exploded* that appeared in a Swedish magazine.)

In *Nova Express* Hassan i Sabbah was given far-reaching powers, to 'rub out the word forever'; however, a grim warning was issued concerning the Garden of Delights, which was, after all, created by Hassan. Burroughs strenuously urged the reader to reject the Garden of Delights in favour of the 'natural state' induced by apomorphine. (Burroughs had two apomorphine cures from heroin addiction while writing the trilogy.) It is a very moral trilogy: Burroughs wanted everyone to clean up their act:

At the immediate risk of finding myself the most unpopular character of all fiction – and history is fiction – I must say this:
'Bring together state of news – Inquire onward from state to door – Who monopolised Immortality? Who monopolised Cosmic Consciousness? Who monopolised Love Sex and Dream? Who monopolised Life Time and Fortune? Who took from you what is yours? Now they will give it all back? Did they ever give anything away for nothing? Did they ever give any more than they had to give? ... Listen: Their Garden Of Delights is a terminal sewer – I have been at some pains to map this area of

terminal sewage in the so called pornographic sections of
Naked Lunch and Soft Machine . . . Stay out of the Garden
Of Delights – It is a man eating trap that ends in green goo
– Throw back their ersatz Immortality – It will fall apart
before you can get out of The Big Store – Flush their drug
kicks down the drain . . .'

The cut-up trilogy and *The Naked Lunch* (since it was the *The
Naked Lunch* manuscript hoard which produced all four
books) was responsible for the creation of a number of
memorable Burroughs characters, and also for the formulating
of a formidably complex mythology, one which was constantly
changing as Burroughs rewrote and cut up his words, his
friends and his ideas. Many of the characters survived the
trilogy and went on to appear in later books. Burroughs
regarded his characters with considerable affection, as he
explained in *The Job*:

> A novelist is essentially engaged in creating character. He
> needs the reader in that he hopes that some of his readers
> will turn into his characters. He needs them as vessels, on
> which he writes. The question frequently asked of a writer
> is: 'Would you write if you were on a desert island and no
> one would ever read it?'
> I would say certainly, yes, I would write, in order to
> create characters. My characters are quite as real to me as
> so-called real people; which is one reason why I'm not
> subject to what is known as loneliness. I have plenty of
> company.

Because they were so real to him, Burroughs did not find it
necessary to give any background to them: 'There's no character development in my novels. The characters are there, fully
developed. You don't know where they came from or how they
got to be where they are.' The reader may not know, but
Burroughs knew, as he revealed in the *Paris Review* interview:
'Something I've been meaning to do with my scrapbooks is to
have files on every character, almost like police files: habits,
idiosyncrasies, where born, pictures. That is, if I ever see

anyone in a magazine or newspaper who looks like Dr Benway (and several people have played Dr Benway, sort of amateur actors), I take their photographs. Many of my characters first come through strongly to me as voices. That's why I use a tape recorder. They also carry over from one book to another.'

About half of his characters, sets and situations came to him in dreams: 'I get a lot of my material from dreams. I've had narrative dreams; I usually continue a dream. I wake up and go back to sleep and get another instalment. I wake up about five times in the average night. I am a very light sleeper. I get up and write them down or make notes, at least. I've written down dreams for many years, and I do find occasionally they will turn up a future event.' In a later interview, Burroughs also said: 'There is no line between the dream world and the actual world – of course if you get to the point where you find it difficult to cross the road then you should see a doctor.'

Other characters were composites, or based on people that Bill knew, such as Ian Sommerville or Alan Ansen, who helped type up the original draft of *The Naked Lunch* in Tangier and claimed to be the model for AJ in the book. Some characters are found in other writers' work: Burroughs, in his later books, was not just influenced by Denton Welch but used some of his characters. Similarly Salt Chunk Mary in *The Soft Machine* was taken directly from Jack Black's *You Can't Win*, whereas Clem Snide was clearly a parody based on Raymond Chandler: 'The name is Clem Snide – I am a Private Ass Hole – I will take on any job any identity any body – I will do anything difficult dangerous or downright dirty for a price –'

Texts by other writers are also appropriated in a manner now defined as post-modernist, including sections from Joseph Conrad's *Lord Jim*, TS Eliot's *Waste Land*, Franz Kafka's *The Trial*, F Scott Fitzgerald's *A Diamond As Big As The Ritz*, Lawrence Durrell's *Clea*, and Henry Kuttner's *Fury*. Burroughs' copy of *Fury* was inscribed on the title page, 'References from this book in *Ticket That Exploded*. This book also covers a general area in *Soft Machine* and the South American sections of *Naked Lunch*. July 4, 1973.'

Just because Burroughs appropriated characters or even lifted chunks of text from someone else's book, this did not mean they were an influence on him though it probably meant that he liked their work. He often told interviewers that he was more influenced by scraps of overheard conversation, by his friends, or by street observation than he was by images in the books he read.

9 Ian and Tony

The first tape-recorder cut-ups were made by Brion Gysin in room 25 at the Beat Hotel in the autumn of 1959. 'It was simply an experiment of taking material from magazines and cutting at random into his Uher he had at the time,' said Burroughs. 'I was surprised the number of intersections that were very meaningful so that the whole thing, instead of being just a jumble, was quite coherent.' Gysin and Burroughs had spent several months cutting up texts on paper and it was only logical to extend the application to the tape-recorder.

Though he collaborated with Gysin on the tape experiments in the Beat Hotel, it was not until he moved to the Empress Hotel in London, early in 1960, that Burroughs began his own investigations. Ian Sommerville bought and set up a cheap tape-recorder for him; nothing as grand as Gysin's semi-professional Uher. 'I did a number of experiments with that,' said Burroughs. 'Lots of them with Ian Sommerville following Brion's experiments, all sorts of cut-ups, musical cut-ups and sleep recordings.'

As usual, Bill experimented exhaustively, making literally hundreds of hours of tapes over the years. 'We weren't thinking about art, we were thinking about alterations and the, shall we say the potentialities of the tape-recorder for altering addictions, and how they were undoubtedly being used for this purpose by official agencies,' Burroughs told his secretary James Grauerholz in 1981.

The work was all strictly experimental and was not regarded as art work: 'They weren't supposed to be works. It was not an art proposition at all. In fact I have used tape-recorders very little in my actual writing.' A number of these early recordings have now been released, including examples of inching: manually pulling the tape past the recording heads while recording or re-recording, backwards tapes, and experiments made with a throat microphone in an attempt to record sub-vocal speech. As the experiments continued, a second tape-recorder was added, opening up the field for a whole variety of new techniques. Recordings were made cutting in tapes of Moroccan trance music with Burroughs reading from texts. Radio broadcasts were another obvious source of material to cut up. When Philips introduced the cassette recorder in 1965 Sommerville was one of the first people to buy one. He made a point of taking a prototype for a walk each day, recording and playing back street sounds. He returned his own recorder about a dozen times on the grounds of incompatibility (the tape-recorder and he did not get along) but Teletape, the supplier, did not mind because Sommerville was sending them so many customers – rock bands were buying a dozen at a time.

Sommerville had a strange affinity with tape-recorders. Once his machine developed a fault and stopped; he opened it up and soon detected what was wrong. Brion Gysin telephoned him about five minutes later and before he could speak Ian informed him that he knew why he was calling: Gysin's tape-recorder had stopped. Gysin was astonished because he was right. Ian told him how to fix it because he knew that Gysin's machine had the same malfunction as his own. He believed that tape-recorders were all in touch on some mysterious level and that something happening to one was felt by them all. Gysin's cassette recorder had stopped in sympathy with Ian's.

Both *The Ticket That Exploded* and *Nova Express* acknowledged Sommerville's collaboration. In the revised edition of *Ticket That Exploded* his credit reads: 'Mr Ian Sommerville of London pointed out the use and significance of spliced tape and all the other tape recorder experiments suggested in this book.' This was for the technical information contained in the appendix Burroughs added to the book for the 1967 version called 'The Invisible Generation' about the use of tape-recorders as political weapons, a development that occurred some time after the cut-up novels.

The same acknowledgements continued, 'The film experiments suggested I owe to Mr Antony Balch of Balch Films London.' Balch was a young English film-maker who had worked with Burroughs since 1961 on a number of cut-up films. Balch made his first amateur films at the age of ten, screening them in his family living room and charging admission; on the living room door was posted a timetable which he hoped was adhered to even when he was away at boarding school. His mother worked in the film industry and he grew up surrounded by movie-business gossip. This wide knowledge of the business gave him the idea of directing, producing, filming and distributing his own movies, something unknown in the industry at that time. Balch was gay, well dressed with dark hair and an eager smile. After a few drinks he could be quite camp: 'The trouble with fish is that they are so *fisheee!*' he once shrieked in a restaurant, embarrassing Bill. He made money by distributing European 'art' films, many of them soft porn, most of which he spent on making three experimental films with Burroughs and Gysin: *Towers Open Fire, The Cut Ups* and *Bill and Tony*.

He met Burroughs at the Beat Hotel in 1960, introduced by Brion Gysin, who knew Balch's friend Claude de Feugas who lived next door. Their first collaboration, *Towers Open Fire*, was based loosely on the Burroughs text of that name which finally appeared in *Nova Express*, in 1964. It was filmed in London, Paris, Tangier and Gibraltar, with Bill in the starring role, and included some memorable scenes; in one he bursts through a window dressed in combat gear and blasts away at family photographs with a ping-pong gun; in another he glares at a vulture in the Paris Zoo. There is no story line that can be summarised and there is no dialogue. There were no professional actors used, but the film features, among others, Ian Sommerville, Michael Portman and the writer Alexander Trocchi. The film used a number of experimental techniques, including one shot where a series of hand-coloured pink and blue dots descend from the sky on to Michael Portman in this otherwise black and white film. Balch hand-coloured them on to clear leader for every print of the film.

Towers Open Fire was shot over a period of about a year, 1962–3, using a fifteen-year-old De Vry camera. 'It wasn't a total success but it does have some good scenes in it,' Balch said. 'One or two scenes do work: The Stock Exchange crash is a gas, the Dream Machine shots are very beautiful, the boardroom is quite beautiful.' The boardroom scene was shot in the British Film Institute boardroom. Behind the board members were pinned board reports, drawn by Balch with a magic marker, hurriedly copied from the *Egyptian Book of the Dead*. Balch regretted that Gysin had been unavailable to do the drawings which were done at the last minute. 'The cut-up sequence on the quayside in Paris I duped to make it look old; in fact, I should have duped it more, again and again.'

The film was made on a shoestring and the soundtrack is a testament to this. Some of it was done by Bill on a Grundig in London at a hotel in Gloucester Road, where he was living in 1963. Some was done in a recording theatre, some of it was Arab music, and some was music from De Wolfe's music company. The Stock Exchange shots came from Pathé News, who provided the negative, and Balch paid a royalty.

Towers Open Fire was completed in 1964 and submitted to the censor. The exception slip said 'Remove words fuck and shit'. So they did for the English version. A scene of Balch masturbating in the film was passed because the censor didn't realise what he was doing. The film premiered at the London Paris Pullman cinema along with Tod Browning's *Freaks*. It was Balch's first attempt as being a film distributor as well as film programmer but it didn't run long. He later showed it at the Times Theatre, Baker Street, and the Piccadilly Jacey which he programmed in the late 60s. It remains an underground classic, available on video though rarely given theatrical exhibition.

The next film was to be *Guerrilla Conditions*, a 23-minute silent documentary on the lives of William Burroughs and Brion Gysin, filmed at the Beat Hotel in Paris, the Hotel Villa Muniria in Tangier, the Hotel Chelsea in New York and the Empress Hotel in London. For various reasons this film was never completed, though all the footage for it appears to have been shot. The earliest sequences were done in Paris in 1961 and the latest in New York in 1964.

The footage from *Guerrilla Conditions* was then modified and used for the film *The Cut Ups*. Lengths of film, usually from the same shot but not the same frames, were superimposed on each other. Sometimes three separate lengths of film would be superimposed, and sometimes negative film would be used. The triple and negative superimpositions were done last and included footage taken from other films, such as *Bill Buys A Parrot*, a 16mm colour short, shot in Tangier, which appears in black and white negative in *The Cut Ups*. *The Cut Ups* was literally that, with four reels of film being cut into 12-inch lengths and assembled in rotation by a lab technician. This was done with a print of the film, from which an interneg was made because of the impossible grading problems presented by the master print. No artistic judgment was made and Balch was not even present.

The soundtrack was made by Ian Sommerville, Brion Gysin and Burroughs. Sommerville produced permutated phrases to last exactly twenty minutes and four seconds, including the final 'Thank You'.

The Cut Ups opened at the Cinephone in Oxford Street, London, in 1966. Members of the audience rushed out saying, 'It's disgusting', to which the staff would reply, 'It's got a U certificate, nothing disgusting about it, nothing the censor objected to.' The manager, Mr Provisor, had never had so many people praise a film, or so many hate it. It ran for two weeks at the Cinephone, during which time Balch shortened it to twelve minutes because the manager and staff were exposed to it five times a day, as well as having to deal with walk-outs, and Antony thought that was too much for them to handle. There were fewer walk-outs in the evenings when a more appreciative audience attended. (During the two-week run there were an unusually large number of articles, bags and coats, left behind in the cinema by the disorientated audience.) Balch always preferred the twelve-minute version. Some of the techniques used in *The Cut Ups* were used in Nicolas Roeg's film *Performance* starring Mick Jagger, after Roeg asked Balch to show him how he made arbitrary cuts.

The third film that Burroughs and Balch made was *Bill and Tony*, which derived from Burroughs' 'John and Joe' text which, in turn, was based on a 1961 idea of Brion Gysin and Ian Sommerville. At a performance at the American Center in

Paris, Gysin appeared on the stage nude, or so everyone thought. He was wearing a black overall; it was a photograph of his naked body projected on himself. For *Bill and Tony*, Burroughs and Balch shot film of each other's faces which were then projected on to the subject, or on to the other person. They simultaneously experimented with soundtracks, swapping each other's voices, superimposing their image and voice tracks to form a composite person.

Burroughs described what they were doing:

Antony Balch and I did an experiment with his face projected on to mine and mine on to his. Now if your face is projected on to someone else's in colour, it looks like the other person. You can't tell the difference; it's a real mask of light. Brion was the first to do this at the rue Dragon in Paris, and no one would believe how it was done. They thought it was all a film.

Another experiment that Antony and I did was to take the two faces and alternate them 24 frames per second, but it's such a hassle to cut those and replace them, even to put one minute of alternations of 24 frames per second on a screen, but it is quite extraordinary. An experiment I always wanted to make was to record and photograph very friendly and very unfriendly faces and words and then alternate them 24 frames per second. That should have quite an upsetting effect I should think; you don't know until you actually do it.

In *Bill and Tony*, Burroughs and Balch, as talking heads, read two texts: one from a Scientology Auditing manual, the other from the script of Tod Browning's film *Freaks* (which Balch distributed in Britain).

As very early examples of Anglo-American experimental film-making, the Balch-Burroughs films are clearly of great significance since all of these films were made before the 1964 explosion of underground film-making in the United States, and were far more avant-garde than most of the productions of the New York underground film-makers. They were also technically better than any of them, because Balch had training shooting cat-food commercials and other mundane work which gave him a thorough grounding in the technical side of shooting, lighting and grading his prints.

Ideally one would read the cut-up trilogy with Burroughs' cut-up tapes playing in the background, taking time off occasionally to examine a photo-collage or view prints of *Towers Open Fire* or *The Cut Ups*. To get in the right mood it would be appropriate to eat some majoun first, preferably made to Paul Bowles' recipe. In 1961, when he was living in Tangier, Burroughs used to have three radios on around the room, each tuned off the station to play static or a jumble of conflicting shortwave signals. Most people cannot listen to this for more than a few minutes, but it provided an aural environment for reading cut-ups.

Burroughs continued to revise the trilogy up until 1967. In a sense he was attempting the impossible: an actual record of consciousness that was immediately identifiable to the reader. He was optimistic about it:

> When people speak of clarity in writing they generally mean plot, continuity, beginning middle and end, adherence to a 'logical' sequence. But things don't happen in logical sequence and people don't think in logical sequences. Any writer who hopes to approximate what actually occurs in the mind and body of his· characters cannot confine himself to such an arbitrary structure as 'logical' sequence. Joyce was accused of being unintelligible and he was presenting only one level of cerebral events: conscious sub-vocal speech. I think it is possible to create multilevel events and characters that a reader could comprehend with his entire organic being.

In 1958 an extraordinary thing happened to Brion Gysin which he recorded in his journal for 21 December of that year: 'Had a transcendental storm of colour visions today in the bus going to Marseilles. We ran through a long avenue of trees and I closed my eyes against the setting sun. An overwhelming flood of intensely bright patterns in supernatural colours exploded behind my eyelids: a multidimensional kaleidoscope whirling out through space. I was swept out of time. I was out in a world of infinite number. The vision stopped abruptly as we left the trees. Was that a vision? What happened to me?'

Several years later, in 1960, his unusual experience was explained when William Burroughs lent him a copy of *The Living Brain* by W Grey Walter (Duckworth, London, 1953). 'I learned that I had been subjected to flicker,' Brion wrote, 'not by a stroboscope, but by the sun whose light had been interrupted at a precise rate per second by the evenly spaced trees as I raced by. A many million-to-one chance. My experience utterly changed the subject and style of my painting.'

Ian Sommerville had also read the Walter book, and being scientifically minded, decided to re-create the experience experimentally. On 15 February 1960 he wrote to Gysin from Cambridge to tell him,

I have made a simple flicker machine; a slotted cardboard cylinder which turns on a gramophone at 78 rpm with a light bulb inside. You look at it with your eyes shut and the flicker plays over your eyelids. Visions start with a kaleidoscope of colours on a plane in front of the eyes and gradually become more complex and beautiful, breaking like surf on a shore until whole patterns of colour are pounding to get in. After awhile the visions were permanently behind my eyes and I was in the middle of the whole scene with limitless patterns being generated around me. There was an almost unbearable feeling of spatial movement for a while but it was well worth getting through for I found that when it stopped I was high above earth in a universal blaze of glory. Afterwards I found that my perception of the world around had increased very notably. All conceptions of being dragged or tired had dropped away . . .

Using Sommerville's instructions, Gysin constructed a flicker machine in his room at the Beat Hotel. He painted the inside of the cylinder with calligraphic symbols to heighten the effect. The flicker machine reproduces the subject's own alpha rhythm. Sommerville wrote in his article 'Flicker':

The Dream Machine began as a simple means to investigate phenomena whose description excited our imaginations – our faculty of image-making which flicker was said to stimulate. Maximum effect is achieved with a light of at least 100 watts when flicker plays over closed lids brought as close as possible to the cylinder revolving at 78 rpm. This may not produce everybody's exact alpha rhythm but the effects can be astonishing. They continue to develop over a long period of time. More elaborate machines can be obtained. Brion Gysin added an interior cylinder covered with the type of painting which he had developed from his first 'natural flicker' experience, and with eyes open the patterns became externalised, seemed to catch on fire, and lick up from inside the whirling cylinder. In the bigger machines of his design whole moving pictures are produced and seem to be in flux in three dimensions on a brilliant screen directly in front of the eyes. Elaborate geometric constructions of incredible intricacy build up from bright mosaic into living fireballs like the mandalas of Eastern mysticism surprised in their act of growth. The intensity of the effect varies with the individual; melancholics tend to be irritated, some see nothing. The use of opiates and barbiturates would seem to seal off the patterns almost completely. Rhythmic sound, particularly Arab music and jazz, modulate the vision in which patterns keep time with the music.

Brion took out a patent on the machine (P.V. 868,281 18 July 1961, entitled 'Procedure and apparatus for the production of artistic visual sensations') and though he worked the princess circuit very hard to promote the machine and get backers, nothing ever came of it. A number of prototypes were built, however, and feature in both *Towers Open Fire* and *The Cut Ups*.

In early 1962, Burroughs sublet a flat from the publisher Marion Boyars at 52 Lancaster Terrace, in Bayswater, an area of damp, crumbling Regency houses, virtually all of which had been crudely divided into flats. Mikey Portman immediately moved in with him. This was a disaster: Mikey was sloppy and never cleaned, he would leave cabs outside with the meter running and not have the money to pay, he would borrow Bill's clothes and not return them, or leave them in a dirty heap on the floor. When he set fire to the mattress, Bill decided enough was enough. He paid Marion Boyars for the damage and gave up the flat after living there for only a few weeks.

In March, Bill moved a few doors down the street to a basement flat at 5 Lancaster Terrace, which he shared with Ian Sommerville who had now completed his studies, and Mikey moved elsewhere. Life with Ian was much more orderly. With Ian's assistance, Bill taped a text for a multi-media show with Brion Gysin for the Institute of Contemporary Arts on Dover Street, the first time the British were exposed to the cut-ups, and they worked together on tape and photo collages.

In June 1963, Bill and Ian went to Marrakesh, where, after some house-hunting, they unwisely took a $15 a month villa at 4 Calle Larache in the Marshan, with a view out over the Mediterranean. There were no other Europeans living on the block, they did not employ any Moslem servants and Ian soon got a reputation among the local young Arab men. He was going through a promiscuous phase and not being very discreet about it. The neighbours hated them and harassed them continuously. Bill tried to ignore them. He was working on *Nova Express* and finishing off a few details of *Dead Fingers Talk*, the composite text from *The Naked Lunch*, *Soft Machine* and *The Ticket That Exploded*.

Bill's son, Billy, was now sixteen, and Bill's parents were putting pressure on him to take some interest in his offspring. It was decided that Billy would join his father in Tangier and attend the American School there which was run by Ezra Pound's son, Omar. The visit was not a success. On his first day there, Bill asked Ian to take Billy to the market and buy him a hash pipe.

Billy lasted three days at the American School before dropping out. He was listless and uninterested in anything. He had no desire to explore the city or do anything except to sit strumming his guitar. He and Bill had nothing in common and there was an awkward silence between them. Ian took pity on the lost boy and gave him some tutoring in maths. In the end it was Ian who brought matters to a head and told Billy, 'You don't want to live in a household of fags', and suggested that he return to his grandparents in Florida and get his high school diploma. Bill put Billy on the plane in January 1964. They had not talked about anything serious. Bill had been unable to bring up the subject of Joan's death.

'Our time together in Tangiers was strained and hollow,' Burroughs later wrote, 'like the time he called me long-distance from a hospital in Florida after a car accident. I could hear him, but he couldn't hear me. I kept saying, "*Where are you, Billy? Where are you?*" – Strained and off-key, the right thing said at the wrong time, the wrong thing said at the right time, and all too often, the wrongest thing said and done at the wrongest possible time. We never really came close in Tangiers. I remember listening to him playing his guitar after I had gone to bed in the next room, and again, a feeling of deep sadness.'

Life got more difficult on the Calle Larache: 'It looked as though the tide turned against us in Tangier after the assassination of Kennedy,' Burroughs wrote.

Dank rooms, the smell of kerosene, dirty dishes stacked in the dark kitchen, trained beggars banging on the door day and night. They worked in shifts. We were getting the full treatment. My companion in this horrible situation was Ian Sommerville and there was no money to move out. Neither of us was standing up under it very well. I worked in a very small room with a round hole in the white wall for a window and sometimes rain blew in onto my typewriter as I wrote. Ian had built shelves along one wall on which the decorated files took their places.

It was during this difficult period that I began experimenting with newspaper formats and got in touch with Jeff Nuttall who was publishing *My Own Mag* in England. This move seemed to inspire my tormentors to redoubled fury. I remember once when a package of *My Own Mag*s arrived at the door a wooden top crashed through the skylight. It got so bad that Ian and I used to draw straws to see who was going out for kerosene! Run the gauntlet of old orange peel and garbage. The Arabs really know how to harass you: they'd get some rotten old beggar to bang on your door at six in the morning. I guess they thought we were just a couple of long-haired fairies.

Bill was still living on his parents' allowance, but very much wanted to move to a better part of town. Maurice Girodias owed him more than $5,000 but Bill knew he was very unlikely ever to see that money. He arranged with Grove Press that they would pay him his share of the American royalties directly, instead of channelling it through Olympia Press, and in May 1964 he finally got his first large cheque from them.

He and Ian immediately moved to a penthouse apartment in the Loteria Building, at 16 rue Delacroix. They had a wide balcony and a luxuriously appointed living room with leather chairs and plenty of shelf space for Bill's manuscripts. On 17 February of that year Bill started keeping a diary and soon after that he started decorating files with photographs. In March he started keeping scrapbooks in which he pasted newspaper and magazine photographs which related to scenes and characters in his books. Some of these are reproduced in facsimile in *The Burroughs File*, which City Lights published in 1984.

For a while, things went well. Antony Balch arrived during the summer to shoot scenes for his film, but life with Ian was difficult. Bill was getting fed up with Tangier and Ian's moodiness and his Arab boys. Ian even began learning some basic Arabic, something Bill never bothered to do despite living on and off in Tangier for many years. When Bill heard that Brion was going to New York, he decided to join him there.

Brion had moved back to the Beat Hotel, where he had been painting and trying, without success, to sell the dream machines. He thought that we would have better luck in marketing them in the USA since Europe was so unresponsive. Burroughs had meanwhile been asked by *Playboy* to return to St Louis and write his impressions of his birthplace for them. This seemed a worthwhile project and he agreed. Antony Balch, who returned to London from Tangier, decided to come along too and finish filming *Guerrilla Conditions* in New York.

The only problem was Ian Sommerville. His application for an entry permit to the USA was rejected. Possibly the authorities assumed that he wanted to work there illegally, or, as Ian thought, the CIA had noticed his association with Burroughs and Gysin and decided to keep him out. Since both Burroughs and Gysin were American citizens they could not be prevented from entering the country. Ian was extremely upset at being left behind on the venture, since there was no guarantee that Bill would return. He had wanted very much to see New York, and to help market the dream machine, which was, after all, basically his invention. The idea of Bill, Brion and Antony all having a wild time without him threw him into a deep depression. He was a naturally moody person, but he went through a particularly bad period after they left and even talked of suicide.

After visiting St Louis, Bill remained in the US for nine months before returning to England, but by that time Ian had another boyfriend and his relationship with Burroughs never recovered from what he regarded as Bill's casual and unfeeling departure. It was in many ways a pointless separation and a way could probably have been found to get Ian in, possibly through Canada, if they had worked on it. Bill sent Ian $450 in traveller's cheques so he could try to get in as a tourist, but for some reason this plan never worked. By that time Ian had turned petulant and difficult. As it was, the longest and most meaningful relationship that Burroughs ever had was virtually thrown away. By the time Bill returned, Ian had become a good deal more cynical, prickly and difficult to deal with.

Playboy rejected the St Louis piece which was published instead by *Paris Review*, accompanied by a superb interview and illustrated by some of Bill's layouts. Bill, Brion and Antony Balch moved to the Hotel Chelsea, on 23rd Street, New York, where Antony finished shooting *Guerrilla Conditions*. Many sequences were shot in New York, including Bill and Brion in a room filled with revolving dream machines; Bill acting out Dr Benway and pulling down a young man's shorts to conduct a medical examination of his stomach; and Brion paying wads of money to Bill, who looks suitably sinister. There are also some amusing shots of Bill leaving the huge office block of the mighty Burroughs Corporation.

Bill was much fêted by the downtown literary scene in New York; he gave readings and parties were given in his honour.

He decided that he wanted to stay in New York for a while and found himself a loft at 210 Center Street near the downtown financial section. Here he devoted his time to making radio cut-ups (American radio offered much greater scope than the BBC). He filled his folders with clippings from the New York newspapers, particularly those with headlines which included the number '23' (23 October was the date on which Dutch Schultz was shot) – '23 Dead in Plane Crash', 'Bus Plunge Kills 23' et cetera – which he read aloud on tape, cutting into radio news reports and easy listening music. The number 23 became a Burroughs number, recurring frequently in cut-ups made from texts from this period such as '23 Skiddoo', reprinted in *The Burroughs File*.

Much of his time was spent working with Brion Gysin on a technical book called *The Third Mind* which was to include more than 100 collages executed by Bill and Brion, using a grid system that Brion had worked out as the visual base. But after the cut-up trilogy, the last thing Grove wanted to see from Burroughs was an oversize illustrated book which would cost tens of thousands of dollars to produce and in all probability sell very few copies. *The Third Mind* was not published until 1978, thirteen years later, and even then it lacked most of its illustrations.

During his period in New York, Bill published a number of cut-up books through small presses: *Apo-33*, on the apomorphine treatment, was published by Ed Sanders' Fuck You Press; *So Who Owns Death TV?*, a cut-up collaboration with German writer Carl Weissner and French poet Claude Pelieu, was published by Beach Books, Texts and Documents, and *Time*, a cut-up booklet in what became known as the three-column newspaper format, was published by the C Press.

The three-column format was based on the idea that when you read a column of text in a newspaper, the eye also reads the columns on either side, providing an automatic cut-up. 'Cut-ups make explicit a psycho-sensory process that is going on all the time anyway,' said Burroughs. 'Somebody is reading a newspaper, and his eye follows the column in the proper Aristotelian manner, one idea and sentence at a time. But subliminally he is reading the columns on either side and is aware of the person sitting next to him. That's a cut-up.'

Burroughs made literally hundreds of experiments in this style, sending them to little magazines around the world, from San Francisco to Calcutta. His main outlet was *My Own Mag*, the mimeographed magazine edited by Jeff Nuttall in London in which Burroughs had his own section, called variously *The Burrough* or *Moving Times*. Since he wanted the columns to look as much like pages from a newspaper as possible, Bill pasted in photographs torn from real newspapers, and added headlines. The book *Time*, designed to look like a facsimile of *Time* itself, is the best example of this. Some little magazines set the material he sent them exactly as newspapers should look, with very satisfactory results.

The experiments with three-column texts, collaged photographs, tape-recording cut-ups and scrapbooks continued for years, to the general dismay of his publishers, who had found the cut-up novels very hard to sell. The new material was virtually impossible to publish: the literary material was very graphic and often used colour. It would have had to be printed as an art book to do it justice. The tape mutations were unmarketable as the tape cassette had only just been invented, and it was not until the late 70s that films could be distributed on video. However, Bill did not seem to worry that nothing he produced had much commercial value. *The Naked Lunch* continued to sell well in the USA and Britain, and was translated into French, German, Italian and, in the autumn of 1965, even Japanese. He earned enough to get by without having to rely on his parents and told them that he no longer needed his allowance.

The heat of the New York summer got him down, and America turned out not to be very exciting after all. Bill wrote to Ian: 'I have missed you a great deal. Life in America is really a bore. Nothing here really, I just stay in my loft and work.' A month later, at the beginning of September 1965, he landed at Gatwick airport, only to find that his entry permit had been reduced from three months to one. Fortunately Mikey Portman's godfather was Lord Goodman, a powerful man in the Labour Party and Prime Minister Harold Wilson's lawyer. Goodman took Bill's passport to the Home Secretary in person and had it changed. From then on Bill could come as go as he pleased. These formalities, however, took time and after one month, Bill left to spend Christmas in Tangier, where he took an apartment on the Calle Goya.

Back in London in January 1966 with a brand-new visa, Bill moved into the Hotel Rushmore at 11 Trebovir Road in Earl's Court, where he busied himself with his scrapbooks – combining news-clippings with newspaper pictures and photographs with typed and handwritten texts. Sometimes he would give a page a coloured wash and the volumes took on the quality of medieval books of hours.

During the nine months Bill was in New York, Ian had found himself a new boyfriend: Alan Watson from Ian's hometown of Darlington. Alan was an artificial blond (or it looked that way), small, skinny and very affectedly gay. The fashion in 1966 was for hipster trousers, but Alan's were little more than a pair of legs with a belt and very, very tight. He worked in the canteen at Scotland Yard, where the police would encourage him to dance on the tables. He had a nasal, campy voice and absolutely adored opera. In Mason's Yard, behind Antony Balch's apartment in St James's, workmen building the new Cavendish Hotel used to play football during their breaks. Alan would sashay past them, hand on hip, blowing kisses and squeaking, 'Score a goal for me, boys!' The workmen would howl with laughter and shout abuse, but Alan loved it. He was a real exhibitionist.

Bill was distraught. He had tried to reclaim Ian when he returned, but it was no use. He had been the one to walk away and Ian was now making him pay for it. Despite his unhappiness over the situation with Ian, he decided to stay in London, and with the aid of Antony Balch, in July 1966, after a brief stay in the Cavendish Hotel, he was able to take a flat in Balch's building at Dalmeney Court, 8 Duke Street St James's, just up the road from St James's Palace, in the heart of Burlington Bertie country.

It was essentially a *pied-à-terre*; the building was discreet, plain, and not expensive considering its location. It was surrounded by the famous gentlemen's clubs of St James's, and was probably built for gentlemen who for various reasons chose not to stay at their club. There was an art bookshop, the St George's Gallery, on the ground floor and a pub called the

Checkers next door. A very slow, shaky elevator took you to the flats which looked out on to the back of the London Library. There was a kitchenette off the living room, hidden behind a folding fabric screen which pulled out of the wall like a concertina, but as usual Bill ate all of his meals in restaurants and used his kitchen only for making tea and toast. His local shop was Fortnum and Mason's, just up the road.

In 1966, Ian was having a hard time financially. However, one piece of good fortune came his way when Paul McCartney set up a small rehearsal studio to provide facilities for poets and experimental musicians to record their latest work. Paul wanted to release a monthly budget-price record of experimental work in progress: avant-garde music, poetry or whatever. Obviously someone was needed to act as the tape operator and studio engineer, and friends introduced him to Ian.

Ian took great care in buying the equipment: a pair of matched Revox A77s, studio speakers and a selection of microphones with stands. The equipment was set up with the incongruous background of purple watered silk wallpaper in a basement flat in Montagu Square which Ringo Starr was no longer using. Ian and Alan moved into the apartment, using as an excuse the fact that Ian had to be on call at all times. The trouble was that Ian made it very difficult for anyone to use the studio, putting up endless reasons why it was not possible. Even Bill found it hard to record there, though he did manage a series of stereo experiments known as the 'Hello, yes, hello' tapes. The only person whom Ian welcomed was Paul McCartney, who had no real use for the studio, having better equipment at home and access to Abbey Road's multi-track facilities any time he wanted. He did, however, record a few demos there. In the end Paul became discouraged that no experimental material was being produced and closed down the operation, giving Ian all the equipment but inadvertently leaving him with nowhere to live, since Paul was never aware that Ian had actually moved in.

Ian asked Bill if they could live with him, and though he disliked Alan, and knew that the arrangement would make him jealous and miserable, Bill was too infatuated with Ian to resist; in August 1966 they moved in. The one good thing about the arrangement was that Alan did the cooking which, with his Scotland Yard training, he did surprisingly well.

Bill's reaction to the situation was to bury himself even more in the work which already took up most of his waking hours. He told the *Guardian* newspaper in 1965, when he first returned from New York: 'I spend most of my time editing and filing . . . For ten published pages there are 50 pages of notes on file and more on tape. I use a tape-recorder, camera, typewriter, scissors, scrapbooks. From the newspapers and from items people send me, I get intersections between all sorts of things . . . They all tie up, there are connections, intersections.'

10 Language is a Virus

Burroughs lived at 8 Duke Street St James's for seven years, first in flat 22, later moving to flat 18, a smaller, cheaper apartment on the top floor. The living room, in which he also slept, was lit by a west-facing dormer window and he set up his desk to face the room, so that the light poured in behind him. The back room was used as a spare bedroom and for Bill's filing cabinets. Brion Gysin took over flat 22 so that Burroughs, Gysin and Balch were all in the same small building – a sort of St James's version of the Beat Hotel, though with the exception of Eric Burdon, lead singer with the Animals, who lived on the third floor, the other tenants were rather respectable. Bill lived a very quiet life, too quiet in fact, and he was eventually very bored by London.

He had a few favourite restaurants: the Kalamaris in Inverness Terrace, the Capannina on Romilly Street, Lee Ho Fook on Gerrard Street, the Scandia Room in the Piccadilly Hotel, a huge Scandinavian restaurant that was always empty, and the Icelandic Steakhouse on Haymarket, which was also invariably empty – leading Bill to think it must be a front for organised crime. His companion was usually Antony Balch or, later, Brion Gysin. Bill met very few people during his years in London and seemed to like it that way, since he made no effort to make his presence known.

Much of his time was concerned with investigating Scientology and with perfecting his theory of language.

My basic theory is that the written word was actually a virus that made the spoken word possible. The word has not been recognised as a virus because it has achieved a state of stable symbiosis with the host, though this symbiotic relationship is now breaking down ... Is the virus then simply a time bomb left on this planet to be activated by remote control? An extermination program in fact? In its path from full virulence to its ultimate goal of symbiosis, will any human creature survive? Taking the virus-eye view, the ideal situation would appear to be one in which the virus replicates in cells without in any way disturbing their normal metabolism. This has been suggested as the ideal biological situation toward which all viruses are slowly evolving.

In 1974, Burroughs gave a number of interviews to magazines on this subject. In *Kontexts*, he noted that if a virus were to attain a state of wholly benign equilibrium with its host cell it is unlikely that its presence would be readily detected or that it would necessarily be recognised as a virus. He suggested that the word is just such a virus. Burroughs said that apes can not talk because they do not have the vocal cords to produce words. He could, however, imagine an illness that would make these changes, and which would then genetically convey the changes to make it possible. He called this 'a virus of biological mutation', a virus which occasions biological alterations in those who survive, and through whom mutations are then genetically conveyed.

It must be said that no known virus acts in this way at the present time, but Burroughs suggested that there might have been a different factor at some time in the past – a million years ago, or 500,000 years ago – because the process of evolution itself does not seem to be in operation at the present time. 'I mean, you don't know of any species that is in the process of evolving into something else. So there may have been another factor there, possibly another kind of radiation.'

This is yet another part of the Burroughs cosmology: according to ancient legend, Burroughs said, the white race resulted from a nuclear explosion, which occurred some 30,000 years ago in what it now the Gobi desert. The civilisation that produced the explosion was destroyed, along with its technology, and the only survivors were slaves who lived on the margin of that advanced society but had no knowledge of its scientific techniques.

Radiation from the explosion caused them to become albinos. They migrated in a number of different directions, colonising Persia, northern India, Greece and Turkey. Others continued further west into Europe where they settled in caves. The descendants of the cave-dwelling albinos are the present western Europeans and north Americans. The white settlers had contracted a virus in the caves which made them what they are today: 'a hideous threat to life on this planet'. The virus, an ancient parasite, is what Freud called the unconscious, spawned in the caves of Europe on flesh already diseased from radiation. Anyone descended from this line is basically different from those settlers who did not have the cave experience.

Burroughs: 'I think that the cave experience, which was only undergone by certain whites, was a very decisive one. The whites who went to India and Turkey didn't have the cave experience . . . the Arabs are whites and they didn't have it. I talked to a psychoanalyst who is analysing Moroccans and he said that they simply did not have an unconscious. Their whole inner structure is basically different.'

He was asked if he regarded this unconscious feature of the white race as a disease. 'It would seem to me to be so.' Combating the word virus is obviously an extremely difficult task as Burroughs demonstrated: 'We must find out what words are and how they function. They become images when written down, but images of words repeated in the mind and not the image of the thing itself. Try reading something silently without saying the words subvocally. It's hard to do. Gertrude Stein's statement: "A rose is a rose is a rose is a rose", is true only if written down; but Korzybski says, a rose (flower) is, whatever it is, not a rose (word).'

Burroughs points out that there is very little difference between the written word and the spoken word.

We in the west have lost sight of the fact that the written word is a symbol as can be seen very clearly in a pictorial or character language like ancient Egyptian or Chinese.

That the word is, in point of fact, an image. If you know a hieroglyphic language, no matter what your spoken language is, you can immediately communicate with anyone in writing because they may have ten different spoken words for that symbol. But the symbol remains the same. As Chinese or Arabs, with mutually incomprehensible dialects can, if they know the classic Chinese or Arabic, communicate in writing or on a typewriter, by slides or whatever. So a spoken word is something that refers to a written word. Because of this I suggest that writing may have come before talking. That the concept of writing is implicit in talking which is, very simply, representing something by a symbol. And once you do that, you can make information known to anyone over any period of time.

A syllabic language forces you to verbalise in auditory patterns. A hieroglyphic language does not. I think that anyone who is interested to find out the precise relationship between word and image should study a simplified hieroglyphic script. Such a study would tend to break down the automatic verbal reaction to a word. It is precisely these automatic reactions to words themselves that enable those who manipulate words to control thought on a mass scale.

Burroughs was asked if he had been able to think for any length of time in images, with the inner voice silent?

'I'm becoming more proficient at it, partly through my work with scrapbooks and translating the connections between words and images. Try this. Carefully memorise the meaning of a passage, then read it; you'll find you can actually read it without the words making any sound whatever in the mind's ear. Extraordinary experience, and one that will carry over into dreams. When you start thinking in images, without words, you're well on the way.'

Burroughs suggested that a special use of words and pictures could induce silence and that his scrapbooks and time travel were exercises to expand consciousness, to teach him to think in association blocks rather than in words. He began studying

177

hieroglyph systems, both the Egyptian and the Mayan, and experienced a whole block of associations that he had not previously thought of. 'Words, at least the way we use them, can stand in the way of what I call non-body experience. It's time we thought about leaving the body behind.'

Burroughs told *Rolling Stone* in 1972 why it was desirable to not verbalise:

> Verbalisation has got us precisely where we are: war is a word. The whole war universe is a verbal universe, which means they've got us in an impasse. And in order to break out of that impasse it would seem desirable to explore alternative methods of communication ... The more precise your manipulation or use of words is, the more you know what you are actually dealing with, what the word actually is. And by knowing what it is, you can supersede it. Or use it when you want to use it. Most people never stop talking – 'talking to themselves' – as they call it. But who are they actually talking to, and why? Why can't they simply lapse into silence?
>
> Silence is only frightening to people who are compulsively verbalising .... Personally I find nothing upsetting about silence at all. In fact it can't get too quiet for me. I would say that silence is only a device of terror for compulsive verbalisers.

As the 60s got underway, Burroughs' ideas became more radical. His rejection of what the hippies called 'straight' society made him a leading theoretician of the emerging youth culture. His nonmaterialist stance, his rejection of the Nova Mob, meant hippies, political radicals, drug experimenters, ecologists and rock musicians all found that the Burroughs world view held many of the explanations and answers they were looking for. In the mid-60s, it was Burroughs who provided part of the philosophical base for the movement, and it was interviews and articles, such as the following one in the London *Guardian*, in 1965, that attracted the young people to his books and ideas:

They use sex as an addiction for control, just as they use alcohol and drugs – a programme of systematic frustration in order to sell this crock of shit as immortality, a garden of delights and love. In our civilisation alcohol is the other accepted narcotic since it also induces sleep. And as a crime-producing 'drug' it has no rival. This is the world they want to make us live in and like, where they can use the word, the photo, sex, narcotics, and alcohol. And power addiction, many policemen are addicts for power, if it got taken away from them they'd go through agony. Those are their weapons. And the monopoly has records pertaining to anybody that they feel could be of use to them, or who might endanger them.

Burroughs did not, however, agree with all the ideas of the hippies, particularly that of giving flowers to policemen: 'The people in power will not disappear voluntarily, giving flowers to cops just isn't going to work . . . The only way I'd like to see cops given flowers is in a flower pot from a high window.' Though he later modified this view: 'You erase one [policeman], there are others, an inexhaustible supply. But when you erase your involuntary subservience to authority, the extreme manifestations of authority lose their power to affect you.'

When the underground press started up in 1966 and 1967, Burroughs immediately recognised it as a sympathetic and alternative medium for his ideas. He gave interviews and wrote many articles and book reviews for them, particularly the London-based *International Times* and, a little later, the New York *Rat*. He was happy to talk at length to magazines such as *Rolling Stone*, then much more radical than today, in order to reach a wide audience of young people:

The control machine is simply the machinery – police, education, etc. – used by a group in power to keep itself in power and extend its power. For example in a hunting society, which can only number about 30, there's nothing that could be called a control machine in operation. They must function effectively as a hunting party in order to survive, so leadership is casual and you have no control machine. Now as soon as you get an agricultural society, particularly in rich land, you will tend to get inequality. That is, the advantage of slave labour then becomes apparent and you may have, as with the Mayans and Egyptians, workers and priests – in other words, stratification, repression, and you have a control machine. As I said, the ancient Mayan had almost a model control machine through which about one or two percent of the population controlled the others, without police, without heavy weapons. The workers all had such weapons as were available, stone axes, spears, etc. So it was pure psychological control.

Burroughs had tinkered around with Scientology since 1959 but, in 1967, he at last decided to investigate it thoroughly and took a beginners' course at their London headquarters. In mid-January 1967, he took the two month solo audit course at Scientology World Headquarters at Saint Hill Manor, an elegant eighteenth-century country house with mock-Norman additions, in East Grinstead, 50 miles south of London. He stayed at the Brambletie Hotel, where he was convinced that his room was haunted and started a ghost story about it.

Burroughs came to regard the E-meter as a useful device for deconditioning, though he had growing reservations about some of the other Scientology technology, and grave reservations about their policy as an organisation. (He was later expelled from the Church for, among other crimes, running 'squirrel techniques' on himself instead of having an auditor ask the questions.) 'They have a great deal of very precise data on words and the effects produced by words – a real science of communication. But I feel that their presentation has been often deplorable and that as a science, a body of knowledge, it is definitely being vitiated by a dogmatic policy . . .'

The E-meter was a type of polygraph machine, a lie-detector, though the Scientologists refused to acknowledge the fact. It was used to audit lists of questions and to identify unconscious blocks, or engrams, that the subject might have in certain areas. Engrams are words stored in the unconscious during periods of pain and anxiety that can still cause trouble. They can be detected using the E-meter and dealt with. Only when all the engrams had been erased was the subject pronounced 'clear', and able to go on to higher levels. 'Scientology was useful to me until it became a religion,' Burroughs said, 'and I have no use for religion. It's just another one of those control-addict trips and we can all do without those.'

His negative attitude to L Ron Hubbard was sometimes detected by the auditors, who got a reading on the E-meter at the mention of his name. 'Well, I just can't help being jealous of someone who is so perfect,' ad-libbed Bill, and the auditor was satisfied. 'All that time I don't know how I managed to avoid getting a with-hold [adverse reading on the E-meter] on hating Hubbard's big fat face,' said Burroughs. 'I would be sitting in a reception room and some shiny-faced new pre-clear would say, "What do you think of Ron's new directives?" and I'd say, "Oh, I'm sure Ron knows what he's doing, heh, heh!"'

Bill passed the course and became a 'clear'. The Scientologists were initially pleased to welcome such a distinguished name to their ranks, and publicised the fact that Burroughs had become a clear. Later, when he began to write a series of critical articles about them in *Mayfair*, a mass circulation men's magazine, they wished they had been more prudent.

After witnessing the police riot at the Democratic Convention in Chicago, in 1968, which he covered for *Esquire* magazine, Bill became more interested in the practical applications of his cut-up weapons:

Deconditioning means the removal of all automatic reactions deriving from past conditioning ... all automatic reactions to Queen, Country, Pope, President, Generalissimo, Allah, Christ, Fidel Castro, the Communist Party, the CIA ... When automatic reactions are no longer operative you are in a condition to make up your mind. Only the deconditioned would be allowed to vote in any thinking society and no hostess can be asked to put up with the man who has not been deconditioned there he is on about student anarchy and permissiveness such a bore. Very promising techniques now exist suitable for mass deconditioning and we'll all be less of a bore.

The actual methods used to achieve this deconditioning were of course the subject of many of Burroughs' articles. He spoke at length about the use of tape-recorders as a revolutionary tool: 'It's more of a cultural takeover, a way of altering the consciousness of people rather than a way of directly obtaining political control ... Simply by the use of tape-recorders. As soon as you start recording situations and playing them back on the street you are creating a new reality. When you play back a street recording, people think they're hearing real street sounds and they're not. You're tampering with their actual reality.' He found that by making recordings in or near someone's premises, then playing them back and taking pictures, various sorts of trouble occurred. He immediately set out to exploit his discovery.

'I have frequently observed that this simple operation – making recordings and taking pictures of some location you wish to discommode or destroy, then playing recordings back and taking more pictures – will result in accidents, fires, removals, especially the last. The target moves.' By 1972 Bill decided that his dissatisfaction with the Scientologists merited an attack on their headquarters. Bill carried out a tape and photo operation against the Scientology Centre at 37 Fitzroy Street in London, and sure enough, in a couple of months they moved to 68 Tottenham Court Road. However, a follow-up operation he carried out there did not work and they still occupy the building.

The most successful operation was carried out against the Moka Bar at 29 Frith Street, London W1, beginning on 3 August 1972. The reason for the operation was 'outrageous and unprovoked discourtesy and poisonous cheesecake'. Bill closed in on the Moka Bar, his tape-recorder running, his camera snapping away. He stood around outside so the proprietor could see him. 'They are seething in there. The horrible old proprietor, his frizzy-haired wife and slack-jawed son, the snarling counterman. I have them and they know it.'

Bill played the tapes back a number of times outside the Moka Bar and took even more photographs. Their business fell off and they kept shorter and shorter hours. On 30 October 1972, the Moka Bar closed and the premises were taken over, appropriately, by the Queen's Snack Bar.

Buoyant from the effectiveness of his attack, Bill went on to hypothesise what could be done in a location such as a rock festival: 'You could cause a riot easily. All you have to do is take the tape-recorders with riot material already recorded and then record any sort of scuffle that goes on. When you start playing it back, you're going to have more scuffles ... a recorded whistle will bring cops, a recorded gunshot when they have their guns out – well – it's as simple as that.'

For one year Burroughs even exempted himself from the western calendar, in the manner of the French Revolution, and lived by his own, known as the Dream Calendar. The Dream Calendar was started on 23 December 1969, and each month consisted of 23 days, based on the Mayan calendar system. There were supposed to be ten months but the system began with only eight separate months, and they came around in a little different order the second time, with a new month, Wiener Wald, added. Burroughs used the system for a year, dating all MSS and letters that way. Unfortunately, the days somehow got miscounted in several of the months, making dating of letters from that period a little difficult; sometimes the Dream Calendar date would be up to five days off.

The months were: Terre Haute, Marie Celeste, Bellevue, Seal Point, Harbor Beach, Niño Perdido, Sweet Meadows and Land's End. Wiener Wald was added after Seal Point on the second pass. Knowing the starting date enables one to calculate any Burroughs date against the regular calendar, for instance Bellevue 3 would be 19 January 1970.

'The starting date used is 23 December 1969 which is Terre Haute 23 in this calendar. Calculations from this date can be made into the past or the future. We could for example calculate on what date Terre Haute 23 fell on 77,000,000,000 years ago ... nodding listlessly in doorways on a mild gray day they died of an overdose of time.' Books from the period such as *Port of Saints* sometimes refer to the calendar but without an explanation to the reader. Fortunately, when writing to friends, Bill usually gave the conventional date as well.

11 The Return to Narrative

*T*he *Naked Lunch*, *The Soft Machine*, to some extent *The Ticket That Exploded* and even *Nova Express* were all part of more than a thousand pages of Ur manuscript. Burroughs had now exhausted the mother lode and the familiar characters did not carry over into the next novel – *The Wild Boys*, which was published in 1971 by Grove Press in New York. It was unusual for Burroughs to run out of material, as he told Gerard Malanga: 'In a sense, all my books are one book. It's just a continuous book ... whenever I publish a book – the book is 200 pages – I'll usually have 600 which will overflow into the next book. Often I find that what I've decided to put in is not as good as what has been left out ... I use them in a subsequent book.'

In the creation of a new set of characters, Burroughs made a major change in his own role in the books. He was no longer Inspector Lee of the Nova Police, but now took on the position of the author, appearing in a variety of alter-egos and sometimes addressing the reader directly. In the Burroughsian universe this is a position of tremendous responsibility, because writers make things happen, after all: 'In the beginning was the word'; the universe itself was written into existence. Even allowing for what the various alter-egos get up to in his texts, Burroughs' work can now be seen as a continuous autobiography of his ideas: the shifting planes of areas of interest interconnected in a complex web, like a three-dimensional grid that his mind moves around in. There are various centres, or intersection points, consisting of Scientology, Wilhelm Reich, flying saucers, virus theory, cut-ups, shamans, the Mayan codices, Egyptian hieroglyphs, the *Time/Life* image bank, et cetera, all connected in a vast cosmology. Since this is a map of his own thought process, the very act of describing it is confessional. It means that he can jump from a fictional character to a piece of scientific theory without disturbing the structure of his work. He can move from the written word, to painting, tape-recordings, even acting in films, and it is all part of the great work.

In *The Wild Boys*, Burroughs' autobiographical image of himself as a child is a character called Audrey Carsons, though the sources of the imagery are, as usual, varied. Burroughs said 'Audrey Carsons is very much patterned on Denton Welch,' and also described Welch as his greatest stylistic influence. So it is an idealised childhood, based on another of those characters that Burroughs discovered waiting for him in someone else's books.

Welch, who died in 1948 at the age of 33, was the author of *Maiden Voyage*, *In Youth Is Pleasure*, *A Voice Through a Cloud*, as well as several volumes of journals, all written during the 40s. He was a homosexual, and his books are permeated with a wistful nostalgia for youth which was obviously very appealing to Burroughs. It is now fairly common in literature to have real people turning up as characters, but Burroughs went one further and even dedicated *The Place of Dead Roads* to Welch as an acknowledgement of his debt to him.

'I read Denton Welch in 1948, about the time of his death,' Burroughs said in an interview in *Washington Review*. 'I didn't realise the extent to which I'd been influenced by Denton Welch stylistically until I reread him in 1974 or '75, just about when I was starting *Dead Roads*. He is certainly the writer who most directly influenced my work.' Welch's influence on Burroughs is seen in two ways: first, in Welch's 'No Art for Art's sake, but Art for my sake'; second, in his manner of construction. Welch eliminated scenic description in favour of presenting the narrative as a series of vivid anecdotes and experiences.

As a character, Audrey first makes an appearance in *The Wild Boys*, and continues through *Exterminator!* and *Port of Saints* to the first volume of the trilogy, *Cities of the Red Night*. In the second volume, *The Place of Dead Roads*, he ages to become Kim Carsons, the pseudonym of a New York writer called William Seward Hall. Burroughs could not have made it much clearer. The final volume, *The Western Lands,* uses the same characters and is essentially a second volume of *The Place of Dead Roads.*

Burroughs began writing *The Wild Boys* in the middle of March 1967, at Duke Street St James's, but the flat was so crowded, and he found Alan to be such a nuisance, that in May he took off for Tangier, where he checked into the Atlas Hotel with his typewriter, his clippings folders and a plentiful supply of majoun. The 'Gran Luxe' section was begun there and amplified in Marrakesh in June and July of that year. It was there that the book first took shape. The published version of *The Wild Boys* was completed in London on 17 August 1969. In these two years, the plan of the book underwent many changes and only a fraction of the material was used.

Burroughs had originally planned a book called *Academy 23* which would have combined 'wild boy' material with the technical material he had been publishing in his regular monthly column in *Mayfair.* His column 'The Burroughs Academy' ran for 21 issues and dealt with Scientology, low frequency killer whistles, immortality and all the usual Burroughsian concerns – the sort of fringe science of popular magazines, given a special twist. The book would also have contained his voluminous writing on cut-ups, and other literary techniques.

The material was too disparate to put into one book. Burroughs considered linking it by using some of the interviews conducted by French literary journalist Daniel Odier, who was preparing a book of interviews with Burroughs for Editions Pierre Belfond in Paris. Burroughs discussed the idea with Odier in the spring of 1968, but abandoned this plan and decided to assemble the technical material as a separate book, called *The Job,* which would still include much of Odier's interview material.

There was a huge amount of 'wild boy' material. In edition to *The Wild Boys* itself, it overflowed into the *Revised Boy Scout Manual* (unpublished); an illustrated book with Malcolm McNeill called *Ah Puch Is Here* (published as *Ah Pook Is Here* without its illustrations); and *Port of Saints* which is really *Wild Boys II* (published in original and revised editions).

During the two-year period he worked on *Wild Boys*, Burroughs made a number of layouts relative to the book, selecting pictures of boys from magazines and newspapers who could play wild boy roles, and also including photographs of boys he actually knew who appeared as characters in the book. 'Your own photos or photos in newspapers and magazines may suggest a narrative. I got the "Frisco Kid" section in *The Wild Boys* from an 1882 photo which has been lost of Front Street, Nome, Alaska. And of course various models can represent the same character. Audrey, Kiki, Ali, Jerry, Pinkie, Ginger, Old Sarge are composites of dreams, photos, films . . . pieces of an old movie.'

The first draft of 'The Dead Child' section of *The Wild Boys* was produced in East Grinstead, where Bill took the so-called 'Power Processing' course at Scientology headquarters: 'A writer always gets his pound of flesh even out of old Mother Hubbard with her bare cupboard,' he wrote. Hubbard, alas, was not in residence, though Bill did snoop around his quarters in the hope of an encounter.

There were two important sources for the material appropriated for the cut-ups that went into *The Wild Boys*. The first was *Twilight World*, by Poul Anderson:

A world that may be literally just around the corner from us . . . World War III newsflash . . . There are reports of strange mutations of the human species . . . A physical and mental examination of these freaks is being undertaken at the present time . . .

The other was the story 'The House By The Water' in *The Fourth Ghost Book* edited by James R Turner, which was a source for Audrey and the Dead Child. 'In both cases I experienced a cold tingle of recognition,' wrote Burroughs. '*I was waiting there in someone else's writing.*' (Burroughs' own emphasis.)

Another source for Audrey, John Hamlin, the Frisco Kid and the Dead Child was the writings and legend of Peter Webber.

Burroughs heard stories of this young man in Tangier and Paris but never met him. Peter Webber died at the age of 21 and somehow his papers fell into Bill's hands. He made a number of cut-ups from them.

Several young men acted as models for characters in the book, literally acting out scenes and posing for photographs, as in Bill's 1938 collaboration with Kells Elvins. One was John de Chadenedes, who acted as a model for Audrey Carsons in a scene for 'Ah Puch Is Here' which was set in Palm Beach. 'John De Chadenedes, Angelo and Fred MacDermott visited me over Christmas [London, 1971] and New Year. John posed for some scenes in Ah Puch Is Here and soon became one of my fictional characters identified with Peter Webber, Audrey, John Hamlin, the third mate of the Mary Celeste, the POLISH rider.' (Burroughs met John de Chadenedes at the University of the New World at Haute Nendaz, in Switzerland, on 15 October 1971. This was an ill-fated venture where Burroughs and other celebrities were hired as teaching staff. After giving two lectures, Bill bailed out fast when it became obvious that no one was going to get paid, but he did get to know some of the would-be students.)

The Wild Boys consists of eighteen separate stories, episodes or routines which together make up the book. It is again a prophetic book. Colonel Bradley uses a photograph of a gang dousing a middle-class family with gasoline and burning them as an advertisement for the cigarette used to light the gasoline. The wild boy in the photograph becomes the focus for a cult of BOY posters, shirts, knives, et cetera. In real life, Malcolm McLaren's BOY shop on Kings Road, Chelsea, spawned the Sex Pistols and the wild boys of the 1976 British punk movement.

The book is treated as if it were a movie script, showing its construction with jumps in time and space-like jump-cuts, fades and flashbacks in the cinema. Most of the early routines have little to do with the Wild Boys theme: 'Tio Mate Smiles' is a complete short story that could just as easily have appeared in *Exterminator!* or another collection of short stories. It is set in the ruined future Mexico City of 1988 and 1989, the distant future in 1969, the time of the book's writing.

'The Chief Smiles' is a 'Mayan Caper' routine which may be the original, or based on the original, of many of the Mayan cut-ups in *Nova Express*. The chief is some sort of CIA agent, who transports himself back to Mayan times and brings back the secret of their control system, presenting the five-star generals with a Mayan Death God. There is a lot of unpleasantness involving centipedes and priests.

'And Bury the Bread Deep in a Sty' is the kind of sf story that Michael Moorcock has made his own, with time and space shifts which enable the protagonist to rewrite history. It is a complete narrative, again owing little to the rest of the book; it does however introduce the book's hero, Audrey Carsons, in a story based on Burroughs' own St Louis childhood which reoccurs again in both *Port of Saints* and *Exterminator!*

A feature of *Wild Boys* is a recurring section called 'The Penny Arcade Peep Show', in which the previous chapter or chapters are folded in and cut up, reduced to a filmic flashback or summation. There are five of them in the book. The first one also includes an extraordinary SF sequence in the flesh garden, where erotic plants are milked of their semen.

'Le Gran Luxe' is Burroughs in top form, taking the division between rich and poor in some undefined future to enormously exaggerated lengths, a perfect vehicle for Burroughs' humour. Set in Morocco, it was enacted for real 20 years later by an all-star cast of celebrities and jet-setters, when Malcolm Forbes held a party in Tangier costing an estimated two million pounds. Once again Burroughs was writing the future into existence:

The chic thing is to dress in expensive tailor-made rags and all the queens are camping about in wild-boy drag. There are Bowery suits that appear to be stained with urine and vomit which on closer inspection turn out to be intricate embroideries of fine gold thread. There are *clochard* suits of the finest linen, shabby-gentility suits, Graham Greene outfits for seedy agents who are bad Catholics on a mission they don't really believe in, felt hats seasoned by old junkies, dungarees faded on farm boys . . .

This routine develops into gimmicked suits, suits booby-trapped with a nest of scorpions, cobras and so on. The whims of the idle rich are taken to wonderful extremes: 'I maintain my railroads for the train whistles at lonely sidings, the smell of worn leather, steam, soot . . .' It is in some ways a re-working of the charcter AJ from *The Naked Lunch*, who was also used by Terry Southern in *The Magic Christian* in a parallel act of Burroughsian appropriation.

Though they are not yet named, the Wild Boys themselves finally make an appearance a third of the way through the book. They wear a recognisable costume of Mercury sandals and helmets, and from then on the book is scattered with dozens of homosexual acts, described in greater or lesser detail and performed by astronauts, golf caddies, settlers in Alaska in 1898 and the participants in blue movies. The characters Mark and Johnny are central to the action. In *The Wild Boys*, sexuality finally becomes the central metaphor in Burroughs' work, replacing drug addiction, though both have always been important and there are still plenty of drugs yet to come.

Halfway through the book, the Wild Boys are finally named, and the book begins to hold together more as a narrative. Bill's sympathies are clearly with the Wild Boys. The battle between the American army and the Wild Boys is described in breathless *Boys Own Paper* detail, prefiguring the *Cities of the Red Night* trilogy. The Wild Boys are smart, quick, filled with boyish grace. The American army represents Mom and Apple-pie, everything that Burroughs hates. In the next volume, *Port of Saints*, there is a passage which spells it out. The troops are talking:

'We like apple pie and we like each other, it's just as simple as that.' Jolting along in the truck . . . 'Oh God, isn't mother a grand person? She's got all the good qualities . . .' Muttering squirming bursting into maudlin song.

In 1972 Burroughs was asked if he considered the *The Wild Boys* to be a prediction. 'I hope so. Would I consider events similar to the Wild Boys a scenario desirable? Yes, desirable to me.'

In *The Wild Boys* the population of the world has been reduced by about three-quarters by some disaster or plague. The streets are all empty, communications have broken down, there's very little gasoline, people are going back to signal drums and other primitive communication systems. It is a fictional guide to future catastrophe and its aftermath, a monolithic society in the hands of an all-male youth cult (with obvious origins in the militant youths Burroughs saw while reporting on the Chicago police riots of 1968), an amoral Dionysian army free from any of the normal constraints of family, society, church or government. Everything is permitted (as Hassan i Sabbah may have said). It is an alternative world where there are no women to fight for or over, no families to protect. 'I was merely proposing this as one experimental line that I would be most interested to follow, in the direction of mutations from the present humanoid form,' Burroughs said. 'That is, boys who had never had contact with women would be quite a different animal. We can't imagine what they would be like. I certainly have no objections if lesbians would like to do the same.'

With *The Wild Boys*, Burroughs' writing style underwent a subtle change: 'In The Wild Boys I was really quite deliberately returning to older styles of writing,' he said. 'Quite a bit of it is really nineteenth century. It's a different style of writing.' Some of the descriptions have a faintly Victorian adventure book quality:

> The pack stood around the dying boy in a circle and a technician deftly removed the helmet, I saw then that the helmet was an intricate piece of electronic equipment . . . [It turns out to be an electronic Reichian orgone accumulator.]

The book still made use of cut-ups, but sparingly and with much more care taken in selecting the phrases: 'There are literary situations in which they are useful, and others in which they are not. Now in recreating a delirium, they're very good, because that is what is happening. In high fever the images cut in, quite arbitrarily. So I used that in the dream section where the boy is dying in the jungle.'

Burroughs was also becoming more casual about introducing intimate autobiographical material. This is in keeping with the idea that his books are one long autobiography, written in a cubist, cut-up form to model human perception. *The Wild Boys* contains many such passages, including one which is written from the point of view of his son, describing life in Mexico City before Joan's death:

> I don't like to go home. My father is taking morphine and always tying up his arm and talking to this old junkie who has a government script and mother drinks tequila all day and there are kerosene heaters that smoke and the smell of kerosene in the cold blue morning.

Port of Saints, first published in 1973 in a limited edition and later revised for regular publication, is a direct continuation of *The Wild Boys*, using the considerable left-over material – in fact, *Port of Saints* has more material about the Wild Boys than *The Wild Boys* itself; about two-thirds of the book is devoted to their exploits. The two books could be easily joined, like a Victorian double decker.

Port of Saints revives the cut-up method used in *Nova Express* by having narrative passages followed by a cut-up of the same text. This book paves the way for the great un-named trilogy: *Cities of the Red Night*, *The Place of Dead Roads* and *The Western Lands*, with many of the themes which make up the trilogy getting an early airing. We get old favourites from previous books, such as the walking corpse routine which is brought out for another turn, and much new material: Ka appears for the first time, developed later in *Ali's Smile* and the trilogy:

> Audrey knew that this boy was his adolescent Ka who had come from a great distance through terrible pain and sadness.

There is much shifting of the narrators' viewpoint and travelling in time and space, and there is a delicate story which owes much to Denton Welch, which is repeated later on in an abbreviated form and with a totally different ending:

It was a morning in late May, the 26, I think – a cold clear day, wind from the lake. I had walked down to the railroad bridge to fish in the deep pool underneath it. Too cold to sit still, I gave up the idea of fishing and wound my line back onto a spool which I wrapped in oil cloth and shoved into my hip pocket. I could feel someone behind me and I turned around. It was a boy of about my own age. I recognised him as one of the summer people . . .

This was written while Burroughs was living according to his own Dream Calendar system and was dated in the book 'Wednesday, Harbor Beach 2, March 4, 1970'. A number of other passages still retained their date tags: Mary Celeste 9, Bellevue 8, Sweet Meadows 1, Harbor Beach 17, though Bill made no attempt to explain them to the reader. They are part of the mechanical apparatus of the book which he deliberately allowed to show through. Only in the subsequent collection of short stories, *Exterminator!*, was there an explanation of the system, and that was quite perfunctory.

Tio Mate makes a few brief appearances in a three-page section obviously taken from the same source material that made up the original 'Tio Mate Smiles' chapter in the early part of *The Wild Boys*.

In a reworking of the routine which first appeared in *The Wild Boys*, Audrey Carsons goes off with John Hamlin, who leads him to the Wild Boys, and the main theme of the books begins to be developed. The position and identity of Audrey change from time to time, though he is obviously Burroughs' alter-ego, but, as Burroughs reveals early on,

And here's your script Audrey . . . You're the writer. Well write a wild boy takeover. You can start in a modest way with the state of New Mexico, using your old radioactive Alma Mater Los Alamos as your headquarters. . .

Audrey travels to Mexico using a typical Burroughs method – the walls of Burroughs' London apartment dissolve to reveal the new location:

April 3, 1973. Room 18, 8 Duke St., St. James extends and opens at the sides. Outside trees and a river bed with a thin trickle of water – pools here and there – a highway in the distance.

When he gets there, however, Audrey writes in the third person.
Several narratives run simultaneously throughout the book, with little apparent connection. There is again much use of autobiographical material but it is disguised and taken out of context; for example:

Bernabé throws money on the bar and orders Old Pharr Scotch for the house. He turns to the American tourists.
  'Practically everybody in Mexico drinks Scotch.' . . .
  Now they go into a Mexican cop shakedown act. Bernabé pops a huge embossed golden badge into his mouth and snarls his lips back from it . . .

Bernabé Jurado was the lawyer in Mexico City who defended Burroughs and got him out of jail after Joan's death. Jurado had to leave the country after a boy died following a traffic accident involving Jurado and his Cadillac. Even Old Pharr Scotch has an autobiographical element: Pharr was the small town in the Texas Rio Grande where Burroughs and Kells Elvins had their citrus plantation. The real brand is called Old Parr, and Burroughs probably originally intended to call it that when a mnemic slip brought up the Texas ranch.
  There is another, more powerful, and sadder, autobiographical reference towards the end of the book in the section called 'I Had A Dog His Name Was Bill':

The apartment on Calle Cook where the boy died . . . There is a wounded animal in the courtyard. At first it looks like a dog then turns into a boy. Very slowly the boy stands up and walks toward the door that opens onto the courtyard. I can see now that . . . the rooms around it are in ruins. I am standing in the doorway as he walks toward me, a strange sad fixed smile on his face . . . Now I can see his face clearly. He has come a long way . . . he has come a long way to die here . . . When I open the shirt I see that there is a knife wound in the chest and the shirt is caked with blood . . . Sad shrinking face. He died during the night. He died very unhappy.

This appears to be about Bill's Tangier boyfriend, Kiki, whom Bill was obviously very fond of since he appears in dreams and texts over a 30-year period. Had Bill not gone to London in 1955 to take the apomorphine cure, then Kiki would not have taken up with the Cuban bandleader who murdered him. Even though Burroughs was in no way responsible for Kiki's death, this does not stop his feelings of remorse. The address given is that of the Villa Muniria at the corner of Calle Cook and Magellanes.

The most obvious fragment of autobiography is a very minor occurrence which reads almost as if it were taken straight from Burroughs' journal, or strayed into the book accidentally:

October 15, 1972. On the way to the Angus Steak House, as we were passing through St James's Square, John B. found the cap of a gasoline tank still smelling of gasoline, reminding me of an unwritten section I had planned for *The Wild Boys* in which the Dead Child kills a CIA man by loosening the cap on his gas tank – brush fires by a bumpy road.

This undoubtedly happened – Johnny Brady, Bill's boyfriend at the time, and Burroughs had to pass through St James's Square to reach the Angus Steak House on Haymarket. The story of the CIA man occurs about 25 pages later. The mechanics of writing are exposed, the book is turned inside out like the Pompidou Centre; a form now labelled as post-structuralist.

As with Burroughs' other books, the method of composition deliberately allows passages to repeat: a story concerning the English consul (*sic*) and a seaman called Mr Kelly which appeared at the opening of the book, intercut with various other narratives, is suddenly repeated intact, word for word. No words are changed in the three-page reiteration but the paragraph spacing is different. However, this time the story is allowed to continue a little further. The reader senses that if the book continued indefinitely, the story would continue to repeat at greater and greater length and would eventually be concluded. As it stands, it continues outside the frame of the book. This is a new form for Burroughs and very effective.

Port of Saints, like all Burroughs' work, is a profoundly moral book, and one of its major themes concerns an attempt, using cut-ups and other methods, to rid the world of atomic weapons. Audrey (Burroughs) goes back in time to try and alter the time lines sufficiently so that the atom bomb does not get invented. He is ultimately unsuccessful:

> 'Now look, you are in past time. You see this air line leading to present time?'
> 'But Sarge we're changing the whole course of history. It won't happen like that now.'
> 'They still have enough atom bombs in present time to blow us out of past time. They got a hundred years saved up even if we murder Einstein in his cradle before he can pull a Moses-in-the-bullrushes . . .'

The book does, however, end with a utopian scene:

> All around the square are open-air restaurants, vine trellises, baths and sex-cubicles. The boys walk around the square propositioning each other and comparing genitals. The Academy boys compare theories of war and population control. How to implant concepts and direct hatred. How to produce epidemics, hurricanes, earthquakes. How to collapse currencies. The final strategy is stopping the world, to ignore and forget the enemy out of existence . . . No troops can get through the Deserts of Silence and beyond that is the Blue Light Blockade. We don't need the enemy any more . . . The last carnival is being pulled down . . .

The Wild Boys theme reoccurs throughout Burroughs' work from now on. One very successful example was his 1979 book *Blade Runner: A Movie*, which was written as a screenplay treatment and was inspired by Alan Nourse's novel *The Bladerunner.* (The film *Blade Runner*, by Ridley Scott, was made from the Philip K Dick book *Do Androids Dream of Electric Sheep?* and has nothing to do with Burroughs or Nourse – except that it uses Nourse's title.) It is the perfect theme for Bill's imagination to take off: a right-wing world where medicine has gone underground in a half-destroyed 21st-century Manhattan where both Harlem and downtown are divided off from midtown by walls.

Bill worked simultaneously on the Wild Boys material and the book of technical essays called *The Job*, many of which he had originally intended to include in *The Wild Boys* before the sheer quantity of material swamped him. *The Job* began as a series of interviews with French journalist Daniel Odier, and was first published in French as *Entretiens Avec William Burroughs* by Editions Pierre Belfond in their Collection 'Entretiens' in 1969. Parts were published in *Evergreen Review* and it became obvious that the book should be issued in English. Burroughs revised the text of the interviews, adding some new material and sometimes illustrating his answers with quotes from his texts. Sometimes he had already answered the questions in his books and so he inserted the published material in place of his original reply. 'The result is interview form presented as a film with fade-outs and flash-back illustrating the answers.'

Naturally, as expected, Bill revised the book itself after publication to bring it up to date, so the 1973 paperback edition included several new texts, including 'Playback From Eden To Watergate'. Virtually all of Burroughs' theoretical texts were included, and it is the best guide possible to Burroughs' books and ideas. 'I've written an actual treatise on revolutionary tactics and weapons,' Burroughs told *Global Tapestry* magazine in 1970.

That is, a treatise on the actual methods and various revolutionary techniques. A great deal of revolutionary tactics I see now are really nineteenth-century tactics. People think in terms of small-arms and barricades, in terms of bombing police stations and post offices like the

IRA of 1916. What I'm talking about in *The Job* is bringing the revolution into the twentieth century which includes, above all, the use of mass media. That's where the real battle will be fought.

The last frontier is being closed to youth. However there are many roads to space. To achieve complete freedom from past conditioning is to be in space. Techniques exist for achieving such freedom. These techniques are being concealed and withheld. In *The Job* I consider techniques of discovery.

Subjects discussed included the work and persecution of Wilhelm Reich, a very laudatory survey of Scientology, a description of the Mayan Control Calendar, the seven-hertz killer whistle, capital punishment, censorship and the vested interests of power and money:

The medical profession has a vested interest in illness. They suppress any discovery that strikes at the roots of illness. The real-estate lobby has a vested interest in the housing shortage. They sabotage any attempt to provide good cheap housing. An example of this suppression is the Lustron house. A man named Lustron devised a prefabricated house of porcelain steel, with a layer of insulation in the middle. This house was termite-proof, rust-proof, age-proof. It would still be there a thousand years from now. Lustron planned to put this house out for five thousand dollars. He only manufactured a few hundred Lustron houses before he was forced out of business by the real-estate lobby. They blocked him from obtaining the necessary materials ... The Tucker car never hit the open market. Other examples are the blocking of the ramie industry by the Duponts and other manufacturers of synthetic fabrics. Where are the bicycle helicopters we were supposed to have by now? Where are the aluminium houses? The police have a vested interest in criminality. The Narcotics Department has a vested interest in addiction. Politicians have a vested interest in nations. Army officers have a vested interest in war ...

By the summer of 1968, Bill had his Duke Street, St James's flat all to himself. To Bill's obvious relief, Alan Watson had flown off to the south of France with a rich boyfriend, and Ian had found a rather dingy, very overpriced flat at 55 Red Lion Street, just around the corner from Rossetti's house on Red Lion Square. Ian was doing research with computers which placed him in a happier frame of mind. He had finally found Bill impossible to live with because of Bill's obsessive interest in Scientology. 'When he fixes me with that Operating Thetan stare I just can't stand it,' Ian said. 'I can't get out of the room fast enough.' As far as Ian was concerned, Bill was wasting his intelligence and his time on an utterly spurious movement. Bill claimed that he was only investigating it, but as far as Ian could see, Bill was well and truly hooked. If there was a time when he and Ian could have been reunited, this was it, but Bill was too interested in clearing his engrams.

Ian moved to a rather opulent flat, filled with chintz and overstuffed furniture on Kensington Square, just off Kensington High Street. His huge metal Revox speakers stood balanced on gold footstools with red velvet tops. There was a nearby Moroccan restaurant which had belly dancing where Ian liked to eat. He was doing very well as a computer operator. He still saw Bill, but refused to discuss Scientology.

Bill, meanwhile, had met John McMasters, the first ever 'clear' and the man who set up the Church of Scientology with Hubbard. McMasters was a quiet-spoken, white-haired Englishman who presented himself as the victim of a power struggle, and claimed the Sea Org (Hubbard's actual command post, based on a yacht off Casablanca) were out to get him. As proof he showed Bill the bruises where he had been thrown out of bed by massive psychic forces entering his bedroom. The only time Bill showed real scepticism was over dinner one day at the Cucaracha Mexican restaurant on Greek Street in Soho. Bill gave the guitarist a pound to sing the usually banned verse of 'La Cucaracha' which is about marijuana smoking and sang along, wildly out of tune. McMasters, who like Bill had had rather a lot to drink, leaned over and told Bill conspiratorially, 'Bill, did I ever tell you that in a past incarnation I was Rudolph Valentino?'

Bill pursed his lips and murmured, 'Really, John? Most interesting.' None the less, with McMasters he had the inventor of many of the Scientology techniques as a teacher and spent hours self-auditing with his E-meter. By the time Bill was thrown out of Scientology he was in what they called 'a condition of treason'.

Burroughs' next book, *Exterminator!*, published in 1973, was a collection of short pieces, most already published, concentrating on more recent material, mostly from *The Wild Boys* period. The book was described by Burroughs as 'very much a continuation of the Wild Boys . . . a sort of homosexual Peter Pan'. Although it is subtitled 'a novel' there is little or no connection between the chapters, which range from straightforward reportage to routines which could have appeared in any number of books. The book was assembled quickly from tear-sheets and photocopies of articles. All Bill had to do was decide on the order they would appear.

The section 'The Teacher' used material from *The Last Words of Dutch Schultz*, a screenplay first published in 1970 by Cape-Goliard in London. A much-enlarged edition was published by Viking in New York later, using screenplay layout of two columns of text, one for action and one for sound. The material in 'The Teacher' was taken from the original working of this material.

The chapter 'Ali's Smile' was published as a separate, bilingual book in Germany, and in Brighton, England, in a limited-edition volume with a recording of Burroughs reading it. It is a very funny routine based on Burroughs' experience at the Saint Hill Scientology centre in East Grinstead, but stands on its own and is really better as a separate short story.

It is unusual for a piece of straight reportage to appear in the middle of a novel, yet Burroughs included his coverage of the 1968 Chicago convention, 'The Coming Of The Purple Better One' (originally published in *Esquire*), as a chapter. It develops from factual reportage of the police riot into an amusing fictional routine. It is this freedom to include whatever material he feels like in his books that characterises Burroughs' later work. With *Junkie* he was concerned about moving from first person to third person speech; by the early 70s he was breaking every rule in the book and getting away with it. All of this characterises Burroughs as a true post-modernist. He had no respect whatever for the normal restraints and limits of a particular genre, and was always happy to develop ideas in whichever direction they took him – into film, photography, audio-tapes, collage or painting.

As usual, there is autobiographical material in the book: 'End Of The Line' recalls the time when Burroughs and Ian Sommerville were living at 4 calle Larachi in Tangier and the locals were throwing garbage at them. The completely unjustified suspicion that Paul Bowles had encouraged the attack gave rise to a funny routine written in the Bowles manner, and ending like one of his stories:

> When Agent W.E.9 returned from London he found his quarters bugged, his assistant and technician I.S. on the verge of collapse, owing to continual insults and harassment in the street ... The Arabs called I.S. the 'Mad Woman'. He was jeered at in the streets and very near such a complete breakdown as *westerners in contact with Arabs habitually undergo in the novels of Mr. P.* [Burroughs' own emphasis]

In *Exterminator!* the dream calendar system was explained by having it invented by one of Burroughs' many multiple personalities:

> The Colonel decides to make his own time. He opens a school notebook and constructs a simple calendar consisting of ten months with 26 days in each month to begin on this day February 21, 1970, Raton Pass 14 in the new calendar. The months have names like old Pullman cars in America where the Colonel had lived until his 18th year ...

Needless to say, Raton Pass is not one of the months used in Burroughs' own dream calendars, which in any case had 23-day months.

One of the most interesting pieces in the book is the story 'Astronaut's Return' in which Burroughs outlines his cosmology in some detail, including the story of the white virus and the beginning of the word which he had discussed in a number of interviews since 1966. These are a set of interlinked ideas which form a subtext to all of his books from the cut-up trilogy onwards.

Exterminator! was Burroughs' final book before leaving England to live in the United States, and Bill's feelings for Britain were well expressed in the chapter 'What Washington? What Orders?' in which Bill fulminates against the royal family:

> Never go too far in any direction is the basic rule on which Limey Land is built. The Queen stabilises the whole stinking shithouse . . .

This was but one of his routines against the Queen, some of which were much more amusing – 'Bugger the Queen', for instance, which appeared in one of the later incarnations of the London underground newspaper *International Times* with which Bill had a long association. This piece was supposed to appear in the collection of short pieces *The Adding Machine* but publisher John Calder, who in the 60s campaigned against censorship, insisted that it be taken out. When Bill heard the Sex Pistols' number-one hit record 'God Save The Queen' in 1977, he sent them a congratulatory telegram. It seemed to him the first positive sign to come out of England for years.

By the early 70s Bill really hated London: he hated the fact that he could not get a meal late at night, he hated the absurd licensing hours which deprived him of an afternoon drink, he hated the miserably small measures of spirits and their exorbitant prices and the fed-up licensee bellowing 'Time, gentlemen, please!' He hated the surly shop assistants who referred to each other as 'my colleague' and the public transport system which ground to a halt at midnight as if London was some provincial town. He hated the rotten weather and the fact that Britain still didn't have central heating; his St James's apartment used night storage heaters which gathered heat at night and gave it out in the morning and afternoon, leaving the flat cold in the evenings. These eventually broke completely and he told the janitor to tear them out and get him a regular electric heater. He hated the titillating yet prudish attitude of the press and lack of any real pornography. He hated the high cost of everything and the terrible service in shops and restaurants. 'The only service in England is Senior Service,' he would snarl, referring to his favourite brand of cigarettes. But he was stuck, trapped in static time, needing a new collaborator or something to jolt him out of his stasis.

12 The Return of the Prodigal Son

L ife in London became more and more intolerable for
Burroughs. Brion Gysin and Antony Balch were good
friends, but they had their own lives and Bill often found
himself eating dinner alone in an empty restaurant with only the
waiters to talk to. There were a few compensations; a friendly
doctor prescribed bottles of tincture of cannabis: the drug came
suspended in alcohol. A few drops on a cigarette made it into
a potent joint, though it also dyed the cigarette green. Legal
cannabis was prescribed for paranoia: cannabis is illegal,
therefore users suffer from the paranoia that they will get
busted. The paranoia is cured by prescribing it legally.

Bill had a live-in boyfriend, Johnny Brady, but Johnny was a
Dilly boy – a Piccadilly Circus hustler – who was known for his
violent side. Bill gave him five pounds a day and tried to turn a
blind eye to the girls who sometimes pushed past him to the
bathroom in the mornings. Johnny was a strong, sturdy young
man, with a thick Irish country accent and black hair brushed
forward low over his eyebrows in a Beatles cut. He was not
much of an intellectual companion. He had not read Bill's
books, or any books, but entertained Bill with stories about his
sightings of 'the little people' back home in the south of Ireland,
which he took very seriously. They liked to sit on the broad
leaves of a hedgerow and sun themselves, he said. They made
an odd couple, though Johnny usually went out if Bill had
guests.

Ian had left London to work as a computer programmer
at a pork pie factory in the West Country. This was a surprise
move, particularly coming from someone who complained

vociferously when the first astronauts to walk on the Moon ate bacon sandwiches and took their first step with their left foot – their unclean side. Ian moved to Bath, in Avon, where he shared rooms with John Michell, an expert in ley lines and geomancy, and author of *The Flying Saucer Vision* and *City of Revelation*. Bill visited for the 1972 summer solstice at nearby Glastonbury, but never felt any great interest in the mystical numerology as described by Michell. Bill preferred more practical magic.

Allen Ginsberg visited London in 1973 and was horrified to see what a low ebb Bill had reached. On his return to the States, Ginsberg approached CCNY (City College of New York), which was offering three-month courses by distinguished writers, and suggested that they get Bill to teach there, thinking that it might galvanise him into moving back to the city. They offered Bill the February–May 1974 course, at a fee of $7,000, and he accepted at once.

Bill flew into New York in January and sublet a loft at 452 Broadway, north of Canal Street. He worked hard preparing his courses but the students were a dull group, and not worth the effort. Bill swore that he would never teach again, but the money was good and the job had taken him out of London. In New York he had friends and admirers and there was no shortage of dining companions. Allen Ginsberg even provided him with a secretary, a young man called James Grauerholz, who had arrived in New York from Kansas only two days before.

James was 21 years old, a tall, well-built Midwesterner with clear blue eyes who, despite a period at college as a pot-smoking hippie and as a guitarist in a rock group, the Almighty Buck Band, still believed in the Midwestern values of hard work and efficiency. There was no question of Bill staying in London when New York offered so much. When his teaching stint ended in May, all that remained was for him to make a quick trip back to Britain to close down the flat.

In London there was a problem of what to do about Johnny Brady. Over the years they had visited Greece and Tangier together and, difficult as he often was, Bill had become used to having him around. Johnny was not all that pleased to have his home sold out from under him and had been pestering Antony Balch for money while Bill was away. For a while there was talk of him accompanying Bill to New York, where he thought he could get a job as a policeman. He and Bill spent long hours discussing this possibility, with Bill assuring him that the Irish ran the police in New York and it was a sure thing. Both of them knew that it would not happen. It was an example of the Midwestern nature described by Peter Ackroyd in his biography of Eliot as 'Yanquee toughness and shuddering sensitivity'.

Bill put his archives in store at Harrods, sold most of his books and disposed of the lease. Johnny disappeared back into Piccadilly. Bill arrived in New York, ready to make a fresh start. He was 60.

He quickly found that he was in great demand for readings. Unlike Britain, where he was lucky to get £25 and a glass of sherry, on the American college reading circuit he was offered as much as a thousand dollars a time, and never less than $500. James's experience as a rock guitarist meant that he knew how to organise a reading tour efficiently and professionally. He insisted that Bill be treated with respect, and demanded proper posters, transport, accommodation, sound and lighting equipment. James was also good at getting the money. Burroughs estimated that over the years he did more than 150 readings in all parts of the country and at various European arts festivals.

It was fortuitous chance that brought James Grauerholz and Burroughs together. Though Grauerholz made several attempts to stake out a separate life for himself in the music business, he eventually decided that working for Burroughs could also be creative and devoted himself to the task with characteristic thoroughness, painstakingly guiding a career that never had commercial success as its main objective. Sometimes Grauerholz acted more as a rock'n'roll manager than a secretary, and over the years he built a solid business to take care of Bill's needs.

James came from Coffeyville, Kansas, down by the Oklahoma border. He attended the University of Kansas at Lawrence where he studied oriental philosophy and poetry, though, as he says in *Cows Are Freaky When They Look At You: An Oral History of the Kaw Valley Hemp Pickers*, edited by David Ohle, Roger Martin and Susan Brosseau (Wichita, 1991), 'Despite my great academic potential, the university expelled me. Didn't go to any classes except a Zen class.' While he was there he wrote to both Allen Ginsberg and Burroughs: 'There was never a more ardent follower of the Beats.' Ginsberg replied, asking for a photograph which James sent; Allen wrote back enclosing his phone number. Obviously Allen liked James's looks.

They met when James visited New York in May 1973. Allen tried to get him into bed but James resisted. James returned to the Midwest and got a factory job in Kansas City, but by February 1974 he could stand it no longer. He loaded his Volkswagen van with his books and stereo and set off on the long drive to New York. He arrived in Brooklyn and called Allen, who remembered him.

Ginsberg thought he was just the sort of person that Bill needed to help him with his teaching job and gave him Bill's number, explaining that Bill had just arrived in town and needed an assistant. It was an amazing piece of luck, though James, at the time, had no idea that this was going to become his life's work.

Within days James and Bill had become lovers, though this only lasted a few weeks. James preferred men near his own age and after a problematic period during which he resented James's young lovers, Bill realised that James was of more use to him as a secretary and friend. In James he had another Brion Gysin, another Ian Sommerville: a collaborator to encourage and stimulate him.

When he returned to New York after closing down his St James's flat, Burroughs rented a loft at 77 Franklin Street, near Church. It was here that he began work on *Cities of the Red Night*, the first part of his acclaimed trilogy. Whereas London had been too dull, New York was possibly too exciting. There were dinner parties with Charles Henri Ford, Janet Flanner, Christopher Isherwood and other literary celebrities. He saw a lot of Allen and was in constant demand for out-of-town readings. He was a natural performer and went over very well with audiences. In *The Naked Lunch* he wrote, 'I am not an entertainer', but now he said, 'I did become an entertainer and a performer when I started doing readings'. He usually picked humorous passages such as 'Dr Benway' which he could act out and give the audience a good time.

Life in New York was quite expensive, however, and the readings were not bringing in enough to live on comfortably. Bill began writing a regular column for *Crawdaddy* magazine to supplement his income, just as he had written for *Mayfair* in London. Unfortunately, the teaching and all the other side activities had the disastrous result of producing an intractable writer's block, which in turn threw Bill into a deep depression. *Cites of the Red Night* ground to a halt. For a whole year he couldn't remember his dreams. He tried going without pot to no avail. James complained that he sat for hours in his chair at the end of the loft doing absolutely nothing. He described his writer's block in *My Education*: 'The pages and pages with nothing in them: the writer has been nowhere and brought nothing back. The false starts, the brief enthusiasms. Books that died for the lack of any reason to stay alive after ten pages.'

In 1975 he was awarded a CAPS (Creative Artist Public Service) grant of $4,000 by New York State, which was useful because his return to the States had produced an unexpected drain on his funds in the shape of his son, Billy Jr. Billy was now in his thirties, but after a failed marriage he had become little more than a Bowery bum. He had grown up to be a deeply disturbed young man with a very self-destructive attitude. He regarded his father with deep suspicion, though one part of him wanted Bill to admire and approve of him. Mostly Billy spent his time drinking, taking whatever drugs he could lay his hands on, bad-mouthing his father and causing difficulties for himself and those around him.

His life was not entirely fruitless, however. In the late 60s he wrote an autobiographical novel, *Speed*, about hippie life, which was published in 1970 by Olympia Press which had now moved to New York. The parallel between this and his father's own autobiographical first book, *Junkie*, was obvious, right down to being named after the drug they were addicted to. The choice of publisher, however, was probably more to do with Ginsberg, who wrote an introduction to the book. Billy followed *Speed* with *Kentucky Ham*, published in 1973, but a third autobiographical volume, the final part of the trilogy, *Prakriti Junction*, was not published in his lifetime.

Allen Ginsberg had become involved with the Naropa Institute in Boulder, Colorado, set up by the Tibetan Buddhist teacher Chögyam Trungpa. Ginsberg and the poet Anne Waldman founded a poetry department, named the Jack Kerouac School of Disembodied Poetics, and invited Burroughs to lecture there during the 1975 summer term. Bill, James and their friend, Steven Lowe, arrived in May, with Bill hoping that a change of scene might help him in his writing. Steven Lowe had already helped him to break his writer's block. Lowe was interested in pirates, one of the main subjects of *Cities*, and had been engaged to help research the subject. He uncovered a lot of material that Bill did not know about, and which Bill gradually absorbed into the book.

Though Burroughs was not a Buddhist, he was sufficiently interested in the subject to undertake a two-week solitary retreat, held that August at one of Trungpa's other centres: the Tail of the Tiger in Barnet, Vermont. Trungpa would not permit him to take a typewriter into the retreat cabin, but Bill insisted on a notebook and writing materials to record his dreams. Each day he took long walks through the wooded grounds, enjoying the solitude. He later used his dream notes as the basis for *The Retreat Diaries*, first published by James Grauerholz through his City Moon press and later included in *The Burroughs File*. He dreamed frequently of Ian Sommerville and Kiki.

Back in New York that November, Burroughs moved to 'The Bunker' – originally the locker room of a YMCA at 222 Bowery, later converted into lofts and artists' studios, where his friend, the poet John Giorno, lived. It was a large concrete space, lacking windows but with a fridge and air-conditioning which buzzed and hummed, amplified by the bare walls and floor, giving the room peculiar acoustics. The bathroom still had its row of urinals and lavatory stalls, with Bill's single toothbrush in a glass on one of the sinks. You could almost hear the echoes of long-ago basketball games, the slam of the ball on the concrete walls.

The room was always artificially lit and in order to reach it the visitor had to step over the Bowery bums and wait for

Burroughs to open the metal gates which guarded the front door. Three more locked doors had to be negotiated in order to reach his rooms. 'We must defend the bunker at all costs!' Bill proclaimed.

Cities of the Red Night, subtitled 'a boy's book', divides into three plots, each from a popular genre: a boy's adventure story, a science-fiction tale and a detective mystery. The boy's adventure is a pirate story, a utopian pirate community dedicated to the invention of new weapons. For this Burroughs used a flat, pedestrian style, all action, fighting, guns and endless descriptions of weapons. There is a section set in a prehistoric city which is written in an SF mode, whereas the contemporary mystery is written like the thrillers of Frederick Forsyth and represents a return to the hard-bitten formula of *Junky*. All three stories utilise popular occult and New Age images from Castaneda, *The Egyptian Book of the Dead*, and the writing style of marginal science books. *Cities* is essentially a thriller with three main story lines; however, the stories are never completed. The characters and images begin to overlap and appear in each other's narrative. The three narrators merge into one: Audrey Carsons, Bill's image of himself as a child.

The action takes place largely in South and Central America, source of some of Burroughs' favourite imagery. Just as consciousness changes from moment to moment as moods change, the writing presents these changes, a precise map of consciousness as it really is, always shifting, never staying on one subject for long, returning to major themes, often distracted, dwelling on sex or fantasies or retreating to memories. All Burroughs' major themes make an appearance, often overlapping to create an even more complex cosmology: Dr Benway, Wilhelm Reich's 'Death Orgone Radiation' theories, and Bill's lawyer from Mexico in 1951 are all there. There are many descriptions of cities and towns but they are populated entirely by youths and boys, fishing, strolling, drinking. Women are absent except for the occasional mention of a whorehouse and the evil lesbian city of Yass-Waddah, which naturally gets destroyed.

Several familiar themes are woven together to provide another attack on the concept of Love, identified this time as a viral enemy:

'Ladies and Gentlemen of the Board, I am here to give a report on preliminary experiments with Virus B-23 ... Consider the origins of this virus in the Cities of the Red Night. The red glow that covered the northern sky at night was a form of radiation that gave rise to a plague known as the Red Fever, of which Virus B-23 was found to be the etiological agent ...

'Now let us consider the symptoms of Virus B-23: fever, rash, a characteristic odour, sexual frenzies, obsession with sex and death ... Is this so totally strange and alien?'

'I don't follow you.'

'... Are not the symptoms of Virus B-23 simply the symptoms of what we are pleased to call "love"?

' ... I suggest that this virus, known as "the other half," turned malignant as a result of the radiation to which the Cities of the Red Night were exposed ... After many thousands of years of more or less benign co-existence, it is now once again on the verge of malignant mutation.'

Bill's Raymond Chandler private detective, Clem Snide ('I am a private asshole'), makes a welcome reappearance and commands most of the action in the battle against the Other Half. In the course of the book, he runs into many characters from Bill's past, such as Lupita (Lola La Chata), Bill's old drug connection from Mexico City, who first appeared way back in *Junky*, but is now developed more fully as a character:

Lola La Chata sits in a massive oak chair facing the door, three hundred pounds cut from the mountain rock of Mexico, her graciousness underlining her power. She extends a massive arm, 'Ah, Meester Snide ...'

Memories of Mexico City bring back yet another character, this time Bernabé Jurado, Bill's old lawyer:

I start towards the table and recognise Bernabé Abogado.
'Clem!'
'Bernabé!'

'We go into an embrace and I can feel the pearl-handled 45 under his glen plaid jacket. He is drinking Old Parr scotch and there are four bottles on the table. He pours scotch into glasses as I introduce Jim and Kiki . . .'

Bernabé beckons to a young Indian policeman who has just received a thin envelope. The policeman approaches shyly. Bernabé pounds him on the back. 'This cabrón get cockeyed borracho and kill two people . . . I get him out of jail.'

This is a discreet reference to Bernabé getting Burroughs out of jail after Joan's death. Burroughs no longer has any qualms about the direct use of autobiography in his texts: Kiki was of course the name of his Spanish boyfriend in Tangier. As Bill once told Tennessee Williams, 'When someone asks me to what extent my work is autobiographical, I say "Every word is autobiographical and every word is fiction." ' The work is now filled with overlapping levels of personal and fictional material and they inform each other.

The move to New York brought about a sea change in Burroughs' writing. The London period was still European: experimental, related to the avant-garde tradition, to do with cut-ups, tape-recorder experiments, photomontage, and inextricably mixed in with his friendships with Brion Gysin and Antony Balch, whom he saw virtually every day, and Ian Sommerville, who remained an invisible presence.

In New York all this was stripped away. It was a fresh start which, after a difficult beginning, enabled a great fund of images to surface, as if waves of memories were coming to the surface of his consciousness in overlapping, superimposed layers. Everything was in flux. As happened previously in *The Ticket That Exploded*, the book itself even makes an appearance in the text:

She went to the filing cabinet and handed me a short pamphlet bound in heavy parchment. On the cover in red letters: Cities of the Red Night.

Clem Snide is offered a million dollars to find the original manuscript of the book:

'Why do you want the originals? Collector's vanity?'

'Changes, Mr Snide, can only be effected by alterations in the original. The only thing not prerecorded in a prerecorded universe are the prerecordings themselves. The copies can only repeat themselves word for word. A virus is a copy.'

Burroughs had a lot of trouble in editing *Cities of the Red Night* down to a final draft, and it was returned to him for further work by his publisher Richard Seaver at Holt Rinehart & Winston, after his first submission. The narratives set in the present and the pirate narrative were originally presented in 48 intercut sections, switching every few pages, and one of the things that Seaver was not satisfied with was the editing of these cuts, which he thought occurred too frequently and without particular narrative reason.

James Grauerholz undertook the task of creating a new draft on William's behalf:

In William's original manuscript the cross cutting was two and three pages at a time, maybe two to four pages of the pirate story, two to four pages of Clem Snide, very cutty. He just took a folder on one story, a folder of the other, and just took a few of this and a few of that back and forth. And I said, 'Woah, Nelly. Let's just undo this,' and I uncut – as I so often have done – 'the man who uncut the cut-ups'. I reassembled the original folders and I said, 'Suppose we break the stories into the scenes and movements of the story and let's suppose we give the reader at least 15–20 pages of each story so that he or she can get into that venue and into that setting so that something happens there and it comes to a nice little ending vignette, then you go to the other one and I slowed the cutting pace and I made it much much more readable.

The choice of cuts in the final book bears no resemblance to the original manuscript version and the order of material has also been changed around. All of the rewriting within the sections was done by Burroughs, but the final edit can be credited to

Grauerholz. Burroughs said, 'I told James to take out every-thing he considered not essential, and he removed 100 pages from the manuscript. Twenty pages went back but most of his editing was final.'

Approximately 1,000 lines of text were substantially revised between this version and the final book, and around 2,500 lines were cut from the original MS and do not appear in the final version of the book at all. About a third of the material cut consisted of sex scenes, including several hangings, which are one of the themes of the book. If we regard all of Burroughs' books as one long book, in theory one would have to regard all of his manuscripts as part of that text as well. Burroughs was always casual to the point of sloppiness in the final assembly of his books and about proofreading them, as if he was still keeping open the possibility of revision. His mind was already on the next book.

The published draft, which finally appeared in 1981, is still not as developed as the two subsequent volumes of the trilogy, but it shows Burroughs' mastery of the language and his ability to draw a scene in just a few succinct lines:

A purple twilight lay over the sad languorous city. We were driven to a villa on the outskirts of Lima. The house was surrounded by the usual high wall, topped with broken glass like sugar crystals on a cake. Two floors, balcony on the second floor, bougainvillea climbing over the front of the house.

There are loving descriptions of an idealised life, in which men work efficiently at fixing up a house: 'No wasted movements, no getting in each other's way, no talking . . .'

Work was followed by shooting practice in the back yard. It is a fantasy male world taken from a boy's adventure book, a life that a part of Bill aspired to, and which, it must be said, he did to some extent achieve.

Cities of the Red Night took almost seven years to write, the work being interrupted by several unforeseen developments: the protracted illness of his son, writer's block and Bill himself once more becoming a heroin addict. The period 1975–81 was a difficult one for Burroughs. Though he had shaken off the torpor of London, he now faced a series of incidents which depressed and worried him, making it difficult to concentrate on his work and encouraging him to drink and take drugs.

The first serious blow was the news of Ian Sommerville's death. On 5 February 1976, Bill's 62nd birthday, Ian drove to the post office in Bath and sent Bill a greetings telegram: HAPPY BIRTHDAY. LOTS OF LOVE. LOTS OF PROMISE. NO REALISATION. As he drove home, he was hit by a car going the other way which had signalled a left turn but had made a right turn across his path. Later that day, Bill received a second telegram, this one from Antony Balch, which read: IAN SOMMERVILLE KILLED IN CAR ACCIDENT FEBRUARY 5. FUNERAL 12, BATH. Bill did not attend the funeral. Ian had been the greatest love of his life, a constant presence, an invisible support; now he was gone. Shortly after Ian's death Bill began drinking heavily.

That July, Bill and James went again to Naropa for the summer session with Allen Ginsberg, Gregory Corso and various other old friends. Billy Jr was living there. He was in poor health and was always drunk and difficult to be around. In the spring of 1976 he had left a detox clinic in California and moved to Boulder at the invitation of Allen Ginsberg, who created a job as teaching assistant for him at Naropa. Not long after he arrived, his excessive drinking landed him in the emergency ward, throwing up blood. He was diagnosed as having cirrhosis of the liver. In August at a party at Allen's apartment, he again vomited blood and was rushed to the hospital. This time his condition was diagnosed as critical and he was referred to the Colorado General Hospital in Denver, 30 miles away, which happened to have the only surgical team in the world who were able to perform a liver transplant. He was in a coma for eight days before being given the liver of a young woman in a complicated fourteen-hour operation.

The years that followed were difficult for everyone. Bill flew back and forth between New York and Boulder as Billy lurched from one crisis to another. He had to undergo many backup operations to deal with infection and was constantly depressed and in pain. He resumed his heavy drinking and became a morphine addict. He lived the life of a derelict hippie with matted hair and beard, dressed in filthy clothes he found in garbage cans. He was on welfare, and Bill sent him an allowance, but he was determined to self-destruct. On 3 March 1981 he was found dead in a ditch. He had finally drunk himself to death. His new liver added four more years of suffering to his life.

Though Billy had been separated from his wife for many years, she took charge of his remains. She blamed Bill for his son's self-destructiveness and did not want him to have Billy's ashes. Instead she sent them to Allen Ginsberg for disposal. Ginsberg organised a Tibetan Buddhist ceremony at the Rocky Mountain Dharma Center. He took the ashes to the Karma Dzong shrine room at Naropa and placed them on the altar, where they remained for the traditional 49-day purification period. On 3 May, Billy's ashes were scattered at Marpa Point, on the mountain high above the Dharma Center. It was raining heavily. Billy's father did not attend the ceremony.

The years spent travelling between New York and Naropa during Billy's illness were very stressful for Bill, and were marred by constant worry and guilt that he not been a good father. He and Billy had never been able to have an honest, face-to-face conversation, even in the face of death.

Bill was also concerned about Brion Gysin, who was in poor health after a protracted fight against cancer. In 1974, Brion was operated on at the Royal Free Hospital in Hampstead, London, where they removed his colon and anus. He had a private room where they looked the other way when he smoked pot. He did his best to be charming and witty to visitors, but even as he spoke, tears would pour down his cheeks from the pain. His conversation was sometimes interrupted by deathly groans from a neighbouring ward. When he was told that he would have to undergo at least three more operations he broke down and attempted to kill himself but was restrained. In April 1975, suffering from deep depression, Brion returned to Paris and concentrated on putting his affairs in order.

Ever since Jack Kerouac died a drunkard's death in October 1969, Bill's old crowd had been slowly fading away. Jane Bowles had died in Malaga in 1973, Ian's death in 1976 was followed by that of Antony Balch, who died of cancer in 1980.

By February 1979 James was feeling restless. He had been with Bill for six difficult years and was still not sure that he really wanted to devote his entire life to being Bill's secretary. He took a sabbatical back in Lawrence, Kansas, where he had attended college and had many friends. James continued to handle the business side of things while he was away but Bill's day-to-day needs were taken care of by friends. John Giorno, who lived in Bill's building, was prepared to make sure Bill was eating, and during the six years he had been in New York, Bill had developed a group of friends who would take care of his social life. These included Stewart Meyer, a young writer who first attended Bill's writing class back in 1974, and British journalist Victor Bockris, who was making a book of transcriptions of conversations with Burroughs.

No sooner had James left than Burroughs began chipping with heroin. It was the punk period and Bill lived right in the centre of the downtown punk neighbourhood, only two blocks south of CBGBs on the Bowery where they all hung out. The New York punks thought that heroin was very glamorous, and many of the bands, and even more of their followers, used it. Ever since Lou Reed pretended to shoot up on stage while singing 'Heroin', and members of the New York Dolls appeared on stage barely able to stand up, it was regarded as very cool to be strung out – 'elegantly wasted' as Keith Richards put it.

Whether he liked it or not, Burroughs was regarded as the father of this scene and there were many young kids who idolised him in this role. Pretty soon the Bunker was filled with junkies. Bill grew thin and wasted, and work on the manuscript of *Cities of the Red Night* slowed to a snail's pace. When James returned for a visit in June he was horrified to find the place filled with strangers and Bill staring at the end of his shoe. Unfortunately James had family problems that he had to deal with and he was not able to return to New York immediately, so the madness was allowed to continue.

Bill's 'punk phase' lasted for almost two years. It adversely affected his health, it drained his bank account, and very little writing got done. In September 1980, Bill finally decided to go on a maintenance programme. The clinic was way uptown on 92nd Street, and it gave him a certain satisfaction to ride the express subway up from the Bowery early in the morning to get his little plastic cup of methadone. It was almost like the old days, going to score. Bill knew that he was tempting fate to continue seeing his junkie friends. A couple of weeks after getting onto the methadone programme he visited Lawrence, Kansas, with James to do a reading, and realised that a small university town like Lawrence might be the ideal place to live: away from the distractions of the city, where land was cheap and he could once more get his own house.

Off junk, Bill set to and finished *Cities*. It took seven years, far longer than any previous book, and had become something of a burden which is probably why there were problems with it at editing stage. *Cities* was published by Holt Rinehart & Winston in the spring of 1981, and it was just as Bill was about to leave on a three-week promotion tour when the news came in that Billy Jr was dead. It came as no surprise and may have even been a relief to know that Billy was no longer suffering.

That summer Bill and James spent six weeks in Lawrence, and Bill found he liked it even more than on his first visit. He entertained the idea of settling down there. After a summer teaching session at Naropa he returned to New York in September to find that his rent had doubled from $355 to $710. This was the event needed to precipitate Bill into moving. He and James had a long discussion and it was decided that Bill would accompany James back to Kansas. Bill was 68 and needed a proper home. Living on the Bowery could not continue indefinitely. In fact the court declared the rent increase illegal, but the decision had been taken and at the end of 1981 they moved to Lawrence. There is no doubt that the fast-paced New York life, with the cocaine and junk and the pressures of celebrity, would have seriously affected Bill's health had he lived there for very much longer. Bill's New York friends tended to blame James for taking their idol away, knowing that James preferred living back in his home state where he was well known in the local community, but it was ultimately Bill's decision, and he knew it was time to go.

13 Return to the Midwest

The small university town of Lawrence, Kansas, is only 270 miles west of Burroughs' birthplace in St Louis. People expect Kansas to be flat but East Kansas defies the Midwest stereotype. When the first pioneers came down the Oregon Trail, this area was treeless and grass grew six to nine feet high; now dusty country roads cross low rolling hills dotted with small woods and lakes. The landscape is big and sparsely populated, and the buildings look flimsy in comparison. This is the population watershed of America, its geographical centre, and from here on west, there are very few people until you reach the Pacific ocean.

The Kansas–Nebraska Act, passed by Congress in 1854, organised the territories of the two states, giving them the right to self-determination on the vexed question of slavery. The New England Emigrant Aid Company was started in Worcester, Massachusetts, to lead northern resistance against the pro-slavery south, and the first Company pioneers arrived on the Oregon Trail in August 1854. They called their settlement after Amos Lawrence, a Massachusetts financier of the Emigrant Aid Company. A large rock in the college campus marks the site of the early wagon-train camp fires.

Lawrence is a typical small American college town. Three blocks of Massachusetts Street, the main street, are defined as 'Downtown', and filled with shops, offices, and one old-fashioned grand hotel, the Eldridge; but the streets either side quickly give way to old wooden houses, some of them dating back to the first years of the settlement. The university has 28,000 students and naturally dominates the social and cultural life of the town. There are dozens of pizza and hamburger joints, New-Age hippie eateries and gift shops filled with Ansel Adams posters and scented candles you can smell half a block away.

Half the vehicles on the wide streets are pickups and everyone drives real slow. Across the river from City Hall, a huge multitower grain silo is a reminder that Kansas is a corn-belt state. All through the night the town echoes to distant train whistles as the long freight trains pull slowly past the bridge over the Kansas River. Bill had returned to the Midwest.

He rented the Stone House, a nineteenth-century cottage set on a ridge in the countryside near Lawrence. As it was outside the city limits he was able to set up a shooting range and fire his guns. He had no car so James, or one of his friends, shopped for him and chauffeured him around. There were a lot of centipedes in the house and Bill set out to kill them all. 'I'd wake in the middle of the night and I'd know there's a centipede in this room. And I couldn't go to sleep until I killed it.'

William Burroughs Communications had offices downtown, above a 1910 opera house, now a rock venue, on Massachusetts Avenue which previously housed the offices of a law firm. This allowed Bill to get on with his work at home without being bothered by the day-to-day management of his affairs. The oak-panelled rooms of the office were stacked with piles of archives and folders, some to be sold to institutions, some texts to be anthologised, others for use by Bill. James installed an Apple Macintosh on which he typed the final drafts of Bill's various articles and texts and kept track of business. When Allen Ginsberg visited for a week in June 1983 he was deeply impressed. It was the kind of set-up he had always dreamed of.

It was Bill's intention to settle, and in 1982, after a year in the Stone House, he was able to purchase a two bedroom single-storey wooden frame house on Leonard Avenue. Like many of the other houses in the neighbourhood, the house was originally bought from the Sears–Roebuck company back in the 20s and assembled on site. There was a small front yard where four squirrels lived in the tree next to the driveway. A covered porch faced the street and the screened front door led straight into the living room. Bill used the front bedroom, looking out onto the porch, as his painting studio and writing room, and the back one to sleep in. He hung his Brion Gysin paintings, arranged his collection of walking canes near the door, set up his typewriter and continued working on *The Place of Dead Roads*.

The house soon had a comfortable, lived-in feeling. He furnished it from thrift stores and garage sales. The furniture was well-worn but comfortable: an old television on top of a file cabinet next to the settee, a comfortable green imitation-leather armchair, purchased for five dollars in a yard sale, a side table on which a lamp was always burning, a drum container for Bill's collection of canes and walking sticks. Until 1992 a human skull sat on a shelf, but Bill was told by a Navajo Indian shaman that he should bury it in the garden because it was a gateway into the house for bad spirits.

Piles of magazines were stacked on every available surface: *Gun Test, Gun World, American Survival Guide, UFO Universe, Soldier of Fortune, National Geographic*, and subscription copies of the *International Herald Tribune* which Bill always read in London and Paris. There were several glass-fronted bookcases where books and magazines overflowed from the double-stacked shelves: *Basic Stick Fighting for Combat, Deadly Substances, Firearms of the American West, How To Kill, vol. Five, Life History and Magic of the Cat, The Complete Book of Cats* . . . a large grey cat slept on top of the fridge; a long-haired cat claimed the battered sofa. It felt like home, the first real home Bill had had in many decades.

A small creek ran down the side of his property, and there was a fish pond in the garden which he stocked with goldfish. Raccoons and skunk frequently made forays on to his land and he installed a cage to trap them in case they attacked his cats. If any were caught, the Animal Protection League would come and collect them within two hours. They took them to a halfway house where they were weaned off garbage and trained to fend for themselves, before being released into the wild.

There was a busted-down old settee in the backyard across from the garage where he could sit and enjoy the clean air and sunshine. The garage was used as an art studio for making his spray paintings, which were too messy to do indoors.

Bill took to dressing in a blue work shirt, baggy blue jeans, peak cap and an oversize Gap denim jacket – in which he habitually carried a knife and a tear gas canister – rather than in the neat anonymous business-suit of earlier days. The purpose of the suit always *was* anonymity and of course in Kansas there was no better way to pass unnoticed than to dress from the LL Bean catalogue.

Burroughs had joined the methadone programme in New York and had to make a weekly trip to Kansas City to get his supplies. Every Thursday James, or one of the volunteers, would drive him to the clinic where he would take 60 mg orally, and carefully put away his allocation for the following week. He always saved a little from the bottle in order to build up an emergency supply should they be snowed-in or for some reason be unable to get to the clinic. He did not want to let his habit get too high, and at the time of his death he was still only taking 70 mg a day, though he permitted the hospital to give him a booster dose from time to time. After his medications they would head over to Nichols' Diner on Southwest Trafficway where, for fifteen years, Burroughs always ate the same breakfast – two fried eggs straight up, medium, three slices of bacon, hash browns, white toast and three cups of coffee.

His other medications included 200 mg of vitamin B a day, because that is the vitamin knocked out by alcohol and Dr Murphy in Miami had told him it would go a long way towards warding off liver trouble. Similarly he took 1000 mg of vitamin C each day, which is needed to counter perspiration, and drank a pint of milk at lunchtime.

One of the attractions of moving to Kansas was that Bill could indulge in his passion for guns and over the years he accumulated quite a collection, including eight hand guns, two shotguns and three rifles. He had a 'Peacemaker' Colt .45 replica, a Police Special with a two-inch barrel instead of the standard issue four-inch and a vest pocket revolver with a two-inch barrel which fired five rounds. 'I'm not really a collector,' he said, 'I like guns that shoot and knives that cut. I have a couple of flintlock pistols that work, they work very well. It's a lot of trouble getting them all ready, but it's fun to shoot them.

They are plenty accurate.' He used his guns only for target practice, though he always had one handy in case of intruders. His friend Fred Aldrich had a shooting range at his place in the country and Bill went out there most weeks to practise. Weapons became one of the principal themes of *The Place of Dead Roads*.

Bill had already begun work on the second volume of the trilogy in New York, but now that he was free of all interruptions the pages began to pile up. He explained the book in an interview:

> *Place of Dead Roads* is a sequel to *Cities of the Red Night*. What happened was commandos were parachuted behind enemy lines in time and they sort of cleaned up and drastically altered South and Central America. *Dead Roads* is the same sort of thing applied to North America. They did South and Central America and the Catholic Church, now they're doing North America and the protestant ethic and the Bible Belt ... There's drastically fewer sexual scenes in *Dead Roads* than *Cities of the Red Night*. There's really not that many at all. It's really concerned with weaponry more than anything else. Weaponry on all levels. The whole theory of weaponry and war. The history of this planet is the history of war. The only thing that gets a *homo sapien* up off his dead ass is a foot up it! And that foot is war! Now there are more advances in medical sciences, say, in one year of war than there are in 20 or 30 years of stagnant peace. That's where all the big advances come from. People need pressure to get anything done.

The material that provided the starting point for *The Place of Dead Roads* was contained in the hundreds of pages of manuscript left over from *Cities of the Red Night*. 'So that overflowed into the next one.' The beginning and the end sections of *The Place of Dead Roads* were written in the fall of 1980 in New York. The book begins and ends with a shoot-out on the mesa between Mike Chase and 65-year-old William Seward Hall, a New Yorker who writes westerns under the name of Kim Carsons. The book ends with both men being shot down by an invisible unnamed gunman.

Burroughs then began to write the middle of the book, in order to find out why Hall was there in the first place. As things worked out, Hall played a very small role in events, since the book returns to its original setting and characters only in its last five pages. Kim Carsons, however, is the hero of the book and, like Audrey in the previous volume, he has a strangely androgynous name. Carsons is in part Burroughs in his idealised youth: well endowed, always ready for sex and possessed of a fast shooting arm:

> Kim decides to go west and become a shootist. If anyone doesn't like the way Kim looks and acts and smells, he can fill his grubby peasant paw.

But Carsons has another, unusual, origin, as Burroughs explained in his introduction to *Queer*: 'When I was writing *The Place of Dead Roads*, I felt in spiritual contact with the late English writer Denton Welch (1915–48) and modelled the novel's hero, Kim Carson, directly on him. Whole sections came to me as if dictated, like table tapping.'

The book is about time travel, which turns out to be quite a complicated procedure. Kim does it by travelling on 'associational networks'. Burroughs explained, 'Actually time travel is something all of us do. You just have to think about what you were doing an hour ago and you're there.' Having gone forward in time, Kim now starts backwards and in doing so he upsets the whole order of the universe. He leaves a series of disasters behind him: the vacuum left in his place when he transports himself to a different time and space causes earthquakes, riots, stock market crashes.

> We are squandering time and time is running out [Burroughs said]. We must conceive of time as a resource. That is one of the concepts central to this book. Another is that people are living organisms as artifacts made for a purpose, not cosmic accidents, but artifacts created for a purpose . . . Leaving the planet. We are here to go. This first chapter shows you the concept of living beings as artifacts which is developed much more in the rest of the book . . . *The Place*

of Dead Roads. The planet Earth, place of dead roads, dead purposes . . .

Unusually, Bill gave a definition, albeit at the very end of the book:

> And what is a dead road? Well senor, somebody you used to meet, *un amigo, tal vez* . . .
>
> Remember a red brick house on Jane Street? Your breath quickens as you mount the worn red-carpeted stairs . . . The road to 4 Calle Larachi, Tangier, or 24 Arundle Terrace in London? So many dead roads you will never use again . . .

A Place of Dead Roads is somewhere which has served its function:

> Puyo can serve as a model for the Place of Dead Roads: a dead, meaningless conglomerate of tin-roofed houses under a continual downpour of rain. Shell had pulled out, leaving prefabricated bungalows and rusting machinery behind.

It is clear that Burroughs felt that the planet itself can be defined the same way as this dead town, first described in the *Yage Letters*. The actual mechanics of fulfilling our destiny and leaving the planet do not come as much of a surprise to the readers of Bill's previous books:

> As a prisoner serving a life sentence can think only of escape, so Kim takes for granted that the only purpose of his life is space travel. He knows that this will involve not just a change of locale, but basic biologic alterations, like the switch from water to land. There has to be the air-breathing potential first. And what is the medium corresponding to air we must learn to breathe in? The answer came to Kim in a silver flash . . . *Silence*.

It is as if Burroughs' return to his Midwestern origin completed a circle of exploration. Now, at almost 70 years old, he had a full cast of characters, provided by a lifetime of travel. One aspect of the final trilogy which is a little unsettling is how many of Bill's characters make walk-on appearances as if they were taking a curtain call and this was to be his last work: in *The Place of Dead Roads* Pantapon Rose now runs a cathouse and gets a few lines; Tio Mate gets three pages; Hassan i Sabbah gets a name check and Salt Chunk Mary gets a complete re-run of her role in Jack Black's *You Can't Win*. The two sections are unashamedly alike, as Burroughs was the first to point out and acknowledge:

> Salt Chunk Mary ... she keeps a pot of pork and beans and a blue porcelain coffee pot always on the stove. You eat first, then you talk business ... She names a price. She doesn't name another. Mary could say 'no' quicker than any woman Kim ever knew and none of her no's ever meant yes. [*The Place of Dead Roads*]

> 'Did you eat yet?' was the first thing you heard after entering her house. 'I have a pot of beans on the stove and a fine chunk of salt pork in them.' ... She could say 'no' quicker than any woman I ever knew, and none of them ever meant 'yes'. [*You Can't Win* by Jack Black]

In fact, *The Place of Dead Roads* uses the pulp-fiction language of that era of writers: Sax Rohmer, Max Brand, and particularly of Jack Black: 'rod-riding yeggs and cat burglars, bank robbers on holiday ...' The connection with Black's book is not just a stylistic one. The central plot of the book is essentially appropriated from *You Can't Win* and turned upside down. In *The Place of Dead Roads*, Jack Black's Johnson Family stand a good chance of winning, given the Burroughsian weapons at their disposal:

> Kim didn't fit, and a part that doesn't fit can wreck a machine. These old pros could see long before Kim saw that he had the basic secrets of wealth and power and would become a big-time player if he wasn't stopped. That his dream of a takeover by the Johnson Family, by those who actually do the work, the creative thinkers and artists

and technicians, was not just science fiction. It could happen.

This was what Burroughs has always wanted in real life. Here he was doing his best to write it into existence. Kim Carsons, after all, had certain advantages over Jack Black, as Burroughs explained in a 1981 interview: 'The only thing not prerecorded in a prerecorded or prephotographed universe is the prerecordings themselves. So my hero, Kim Carsons, begins tampering with the prerecordings. In other words, he cuts in on God's monopoly. And that's one of the things the book's about, and how he is able to move about backwards and forwards in time under certain very stringent terms.'

The flatness of some of the language and the ultimately simplistic plot are more than compensated for by the abundant imagination and humour in the book:

Kim recruits a band of flamboyant and picturesque out-laws, called the Wild Fruits. There is the Crying Gun, who breaks into tears at the sight of his opponent.

'What's the matter, somebody take your lollipop?'

'Oh senor, I am sorry for you . . .'

And the Priest, who goes into a gunfight giving his adversaries the last rites. And the Blind Gun, who zeroes in with bat squeaks. And the famous Shittin' Sheriff, turned outlaw. At the sight of his opponent he turns green with fear and sometimes loses control of his bowels. Well, there's an old adage in show biz: the worse the stage fright, the better the performance.

It is not just Bill's characters that make walk-on appearances. People from his own life appear with greater frequency here than in previous books. They enter his thoughts therefore they enter his books; maybe it is a function of age. Graham Greene, at the age of 63, felt quite free to include M Felix, the proprietor of the restaurant in Antibes in which he ate luncheon every day, in a story in *May We Borrow Your Husband*. In *The Place of Dead Roads*, Burroughs uses Madame Rachou, the proprietor of the Beat Hotel in Paris, as a character:

Kim heard the blast as he had an afternoon pernod with Madame Rachou, his landlady at the theatrical hotel where he lived in his song-and-dance capacity.

Locations are treated in the same manner. Places from Bill's past are used as settings for his characters. At one point Kim moves to London, and stays in Bill's old digs at the Empress Hotel, 23 Lillie Road, near West Brompton tube station. The London interlude is used as an excuse for one of Bill's attacks on England:

Kim's hatred of England is becoming an obsession ... What hope for a country where the people will camp out for three days to glimpse the Royal Couple? Where one store clerk refers to another as his 'colleague'?
    Licensing laws left over from World War I: 'Sorry sir, the bar is closed.'

Nor does he forget his old school, though in this instance Bill is content to just sing a few lines of the old school song:

Far away and high on the mesa's crest
Here's the life that all of us love the best
Los Alamos
... They have to stay outside until five o'clock.

The theme of the book – the Johnson family versus the shits – is summed up succinctly by Burroughs in one paragraph, addressed as much to the reader as to any of the book's characters:

Now your virus is an obligate cellular parasite, and my contention is that what we call evil is quite literally a virus parasite occupying a certain area which we may term the RIGHT centre. The mark of a basic shit is that he has to be right. And right here we must make a diagnostic distinction between a hard-core virus-occupied shit and a plain ordinary mean no-good son of Bitch.

Towards the end of the book, what was later identifiable as *The Western Lands* material begins to intrude, particularly as Kim Carsons begins to investigate the *Egyptian Book of the Dead*:

> Most immortality blueprints are vampiric, directly or covertly, so Kim surmises that the Egyptian model is no exception, though no Egyptologist has ever suggested such a thing. Dismissing the mummy road and the Western Lands as primitive superstition, they never ask themselves how such a system could work.

The answer to these questions and others were to be found in the final volume of the trilogy. Before Bill could get to this, however, there was the usual problem with editing. Among his other duties, James Grauerholz had an important role as Burroughs' editor:

> On *Place of Dead Roads* I made a reassembly of the whole thing, of his raw stuff. Dick Seaver who was now at Holt Rinehart & Winston was pushing for a draft and we ended up sending them a transcription of the manuscript. We sent Draft Five, meanwhile I continued working on it. Well, I came around with what's called Draft Six. Dick thought that Draft Five was beautiful poetry and so perfect, and there was a lot of arguing about it. I remember Dick Seaver's comment was, Draft Six is more commercial, Draft Five is more poetic – that was his comment.

It was Draft Six that was published. For some time afterwards Bill wondered if Draft Five could be published as a limited edition because it is a substantially different approach to the material.

Bill began writing *The Western Lands* in 1983, beginning with the 800 pages of overflow material from *The Place of Dead Roads*. 'I always had material to draw on for the next one, so in a sense, the next one is well under way by the time I finish the one I'm doing,' Bill told an interviewer.

William Burroughs

The new book, *The Western Lands*, is considered by many to be his finest work after *The Naked Lunch*. It is accessible, and often deeply moving, and deals with grand themes: immortality, time and space. At a time when the trend in American fiction was towards minimal brand-name suburban dramas set among the shopping malls of the sun-belt – Frederick Barthelme and company – Burroughs could not have been further away from the mainstream. A number of science-fiction writers were preoccupied with the same subject matter, but Burroughs was not using these themes just as a good vehicle for fiction, he was stating his own carefully worked-out opinions on these matters:

> I consider that immortality is the only goal worth striving for: immortality in Space. Man is an artifact created for the purpose of Space travel. He is not designed to remain in his present state anymore than a tadpole is designed to remain a tadpole. But man is in a state of arrested evolution.
>
> Time is that which ends, and Man is in Time.
>
> The transition from Time to Space is quite as drastic as the evolutionary transition from water to land . . . Immortality is something you have to work and fight for . . . The Old Man of the Mountain discovered that immortality is possible in Space, and this is the Western Lands of the Egyptian Book of the Dead.
>
> The Western Lands is a real place. It exists, and we built it, with our hands and our brains. We paid for it, with our blood and our lives. It's ours, and we're going to take it. [Boulder, July 1982 – *Statement on the Final Academy*]

Burroughs was unimpressed with the space programme because it was not adapting to space in the sense that certain fish adapted to land: first developing an air-breathing potential, then climbing out on to the shore. The astronauts went into space, but they went there in an aqualung. There was no real transition from land to space. He told the *Sunday Times*, 'I see that dreams are the lifeline to our possible biological and spiritual destiny. Dreams sometimes approximate space conditions. That's what *The Western Lands* is about.'

In order to assist in this exploration, Burroughs creates a secret service without a country, Margaras Unlimited, which has its own agenda: to provide aid and support for anything which favours or enhances space programmes and space exploration, simulation of space conditions, exploration of inner space or expanding awareness. It is also the job of Margaras to extirpate anything going in the other direction: 'The espionage world now has a new frontier.'

At the end of *The Place of Dead Roads*, Burroughs, as William Seward Hall, ended up dead. In *The Western Lands* we find out who killed him:

> Joe the Dead lowered the rifle ... Behind him, Kim Carsons and Mike Chase lay dead in the dust of the Boulder Cemetery. The date was September 17, 1899.

The story of *The Western Lands* concerns his attempt to transcend this unfortunate condition: 'So William Seward Hall sets out to write his way out of death.' Kim is summoned to the office of the District Supervisor and sent to find the Western Lands. His mission was to find out how they were created and what caused the Egyptians to go wrong and get bogged down with mummies and the need to preserve the physical body.

Kim returns with the textbook answer:

> Because they had not solved the equation imposed by a parasitic female Other Half who needs a physical body to exist, being parasitic to other bodies. So to maintain the Other Half in the style to which she has for a million years been accustomed, they turn to the reprehensible and ill-advised expedient of vampirism.
>
> If on the other hand, the Western Lands are reached by the contact of two males, the myth of duality is exploded and the initiates can realize their natural state. The Western Lands is the natural, uncorrupted state of all male humans. We have been seduced from our biologic and spiritual destiny by the Sex Enemy.

Thus Burroughs pulls together a number of his themes and finally allows his misogyny to reach its final conclusion: that women have halted evolution and are preventing the human race from mutating into a form where space conditions would not be inimicable. It is the old dualism of men being of the air, the adventurous spirit, and women being earthly, the homemakers, taken to a typically Burroughsian extreme. He outlined it earlier in the book:

> Joe is tracking down the Venusian agents of a conspiracy with very definite M.O. and objectives. It is antimagical, authoritarian, dogmatic, the deadly enemy of those who are committed to the magical universe, spontaneous, unpredictable, alive. The universe they are imposing is controlled, predictable, dead.

There is, of course, a reverse argument that suggests that it is women who have always been the repository of magical knowledge, of witchcraft, the priestesses in touch with nature and the emotions, while it is men who create rigid authoritarian structures of state and the military. But this is not an argument that Burroughs cared to consider.

As in the earlier volumes of the trilogy, Burroughs includes autobiographical details so that characters as diverse as Brion Gysin's cook, Targuisti, and Allen Ginsberg make an appearance, though they are more integrated into the text than previously. Ian Sommerville makes a walk-on appearance – it is truly a book of the dead. However, the most unexpected autobiographical detail comes early on with a reference to Bill's mother, Laura Lee Burroughs:

> Outside a Palm Beach bungalow waiting for a taxi to the airport. My mother's kind unhappy face, last time I ever saw her. Really a blessing. She had been ill for a long time. My father's dead face in the crematorium. Too late. Over from Cobblestone Gardens.

These lines are culled from a text called *Cobblestone Gardens*, dedicated to his parents, which was first published by a small press in 1976.

Many of the settings in *The Western Lands* are in Central and South America; however, they also seem to have New York street signs: LITTERING IS DIRTY AND SELFISH, DON'T DO IT. The journey begins in Gibraltar, as most of Burroughs' journeys did when he was living in Tangier. Bill clearly hated Gibraltar almost as much as he hated living in England and describes its inconveniences and ugly citizenry with relish:

What am I doing in Gibraltar with my sulky Ba? Waiting, of course. What does anyone do in Gibraltar? Waiting for a boat, a bank draft, a letter, waiting for a suit to be finished, waiting for a car to be fixed, waiting to see an English doctor.

Among the many dangers along the road are book reviewers: Anatole Broyard writing in the *New York Times*, on 15 February 1984, said: '. . . While *Naked Lunch* had flashes of humor, the only joke in *The Place of Dead Roads* is on us. You might say that the comedy lies in people taking Mr Burroughs seriously as a writer . . . For a celebrated author to publish a novel as bad as *The Place of Dead Roads* requires a degree of collusion or encouragement on our part . . . What we ought to ask ourselves is whether we want to go on inspiring books like *The Place of Dead Roads*.'

Anatole Broyard was once classified as a Beat Generation writer, and his 'Sunday Dinner in Brooklyn' appeared in Feldman and Gartenberg's 1958 anthology *The Beat Generation and the Angry Young Men* in the Beat section. His career as a writer apparently failed and he became a professional book reviewer. At the *New York Times*, which claims to have unbiased reviewers, he made a point of always reviewing Burroughs' books, then attacking them so vehemently it was almost as if he were trying to erase his own past.

In *The Western Lands*, Julian Chandler, book reviewer for 'a prestigious New York Daily', has chosen the so-called Beat Movement for his professional rancour and can always be counted on to perform a clever demolition job. Burroughs has him followed by a small black dog which is visible only occasionally, but just often enough to cause Chandler's previously friendly doorman to view him with great suspicion. Chandler can no longer get a good table in his favourite restaurants because head waiters are convinced that he has somehow sneaked in a pet. Chandler's life, after his attacks on the Beat Generation writers, is no longer a happy one.

Not surprisingly, there is also a lot of death in *The Western Lands*. As Burroughs points out:

> The road to the Western Lands is by definition the most dangerous road in the world, for it is a journey beyond Death, beyond the basic God standard of Fear and Danger. It is the most guarded road in the world, for it gives access to the gift that supersedes all other gifts: Immortality.

Dangerous as it may be, the sheer number of deaths begins to assume the farcical excesses of the Marquis de Sade, particularly during the five annual duel days in the border town of Last Chance. Centipedes provide another inconvenience, and in a letter from a learned professor on the subject we are told more than any reader could possibly need to know about them.

Of Burroughs' old characters the only one to make an appearance here is Hassan i Sabbah, who plays an important role:

> 'Ancient Egypt is the only period in history when the gates to immortality were open, the Gates of Anubis. But the gates were occupied and monopolized by unfortunate elements . . . rather low vampires.
>
> 'It is arranged that you will meet the man who will break that monopoly: Hassan i Sabbah . . . HIS.'

His mission was to find out if one could confront death and reach the Western Lands without actually physically dying. Hassan i Sabbah seems to have got there, but did not have a very successful visit, because a dozen pages further on, Burroughs wonders:

> Did HIS have as bad a time in Egypt as I had in the Empress Hotel? Immediately I knew that the answer was Yes!

Hassan seems to have brought out the prophetic element in Burroughs' writing and though he did not write the Salman Rushdie affair into existence, he did take notice of the adverse conditions pertaining in the Islamic world:

> So Allah overwrote a thousand years, and now he can't write anything better than Khomeini. I tell you, those old mullahs got a terrible look in their eyes ... This is nasty writing, Allah, and speaking for the Shakespeare Squadron, we don't like it.

Several old cut-ups from 1960 also appear in the text: 'Professor killed, accident in US.' This is an old cut-up from *Minutes To Go* (1960), waiting all these years for its place in the Big Picture jigsaw puzzle where it would precisely fit. There are also a few conventional cut-ups in the early part of the book, but Burroughs appears to lose interest and they are not repeated. They were possibly only there as a means of travel for his characters.

When the book came out, critics seized upon the ending, in which it appeared that Burroughs was signing off as a writer, perhaps resigning from this mortal coil entirely. At the time it was a very convincing performance, only marred by the appearance of subsequent books. He ended *Western Lands* with his characters, memories and fantasies flickering before his consciousness, and his cats seemingly the only thing keeping him from leaving for outer space:

> He [Kim] is already in space, very far out there in icy blackness and at the same time here in this prop town. The whole town of Lawrence is for sale ... His only link with the living earth is now the cats, as scenes from his past life explode like soap bubbles, little random flashes glimpsed through a Cat Door. It leads out and it leads back in again ... the cat snuggles against me and raises his paw to touch my stomach.

He wrote as if he were already dying, his past flashing before his eyes: 'The Big House at Los Alamos. God it was cold on those sleeping porches.' He signs off resignedly; the book ends on a note of despair, and with a quote from his fellow writer from St Louis, TS Eliot.

I want to reach the Western Lands – right in front of you, across the bubbling brook. It's a frozen sewer. It's known as the Duad, remember? All the filth and horror, fear, hate, disease and death of human history flows between you and the Western Lands. Let it flow! My cat Fletch stretches behind me on the bed . . . How long does it take a man to learn that he does not, cannot want what he 'wants'? . . .

The old writer couldn't write anymore because he had reached the end of words, the end of what can be done with words. And then? . . .

In Tangier the Parade Bar is closed. Shadows are falling on the mountain.

'Hurry up, please. It's time.'

14 Shotgun Art

B ill used the small front bedroom as his painting studio. A life-sized Mugwump from David Cronenberg's movie of *The Naked Lunch* sat in a chair in the corner. Piles of paintings done on thick shiny card were stacked on racks, organised according to size. One of Gysin's Sahara scenes hung on the wall.

The success of Burroughs' new career as an artist produced a phenomenal amount of paperwork: the documenting and photographing of each piece, keeping track of it, and the arranging of literally dozens of exhibitions, meant William Burroughs Communications outgrew their downtown office space and had to get their own building.

Burroughs was not a skilled artist in the sense of knowing how to draw, as his self-portrait in Burt Britton's 1976 *Self-Portrait: Book People Picture Themselves* shows; however, the same criticism could easily be applied to many of the New York 'neo-expressionists'. Burroughs' skill lay in his visual editing, the collaging, the cutting, the investigation and exploration of the visual surface. His paintings did not appear over-night; they had a genesis stretching back to the 50s, and during that time his visual work went through a number of stages and developments, though it was not until the late 80s that it was treated as anything other than secondary to the writing.

The first example of his visual work to be seen publicly was on the dust wrapper of the original Olympia Press edition of *The Naked Lunch* in 1959; thick black calligraphic gestures on a purple and yellow ground very similar to the work of Brion Gysin. Burroughs credited Gysin with teaching him 'how to see pictures'. The advent of cut-ups produced more calligraphic drawings, with texts often dissolving into hieroglyphic-like gestures as the words were replaced or absorbed by signs. Soon Burroughs began to fill whole pages with hieroglyphs, arranged much as words on a page, as if the words had been completely replaced by the glyphs. The glyphs began to run into one another, and he began to draw them with a brush instead of a ball-point pen.

In Tangier, beginning in 1961, he filled sheets of quarto-size typing paper with calligraphic squiggles, often on a background colour wash and usually in blue or brown water colour. Again, the obvious over-riding influence was Brion Gysin's desert work where glyphs vibrate on coloured fields, rather like the early work of Rothko or Tobey. Burroughs' paintings were cruder and more obvious, but had a strangely distinctive Burroughsian flavour to them. He produced a great many works, and was sometimes pleased enough with the results to sign them. The writing had become painting. 'It didn't go very far,' Burroughs said in 1991, 'I never sold any of them, it wasn't really a very serious intent.'

Burroughs made a number of attempts to incorporate these visual experiments with his written work, notably in a series of texts in which words were replaced with coloured dots. But the experiments were not a success, though the pages themselves were visually very beautiful. Burroughs quickly identified the problem: 'As soon as you get an alphabetical language where the word has nothing to do with the object then you get this separation of painting and writing. For one thing, writing must be read sequentially. Doesn't make any difference in Egyptian, you can read it this way and that way but it's got to read in sequence, whereas in painting you can see the whole thing at once.' When he was painting – filling an entire page with calligraphy – different factors came into being.

'I don't know what I'm painting until I see it,' Burroughs said of his work in 1991. 'In fact I've done a lot with my eyes closed. But in writing, you have to know, you can't help but know because there it is in front of you. Unless you're attempting some sort of trance or automatic writing which I've never been able to do at all. There are a number of very definite differences.'

The next development on the visual side was again an extension of the cut-up technique. Burroughs had been experimenting with cut-up tape recordings, and in Tangier in late 1961, with the active assistance of Ian Sommerville, he applied the same ideas to photography. They were not concerned with photographic collage of the sort devised by Heartfield and the Surrealists. Burroughs had been working with fold-in texts, literally folding the paper instead of cutting it, and it was this method they applied to the visual image. They worked together on a series of endlessly folded-in photographic collages, the best known being Sommerville's 'Mr & Mrs D'. Ian Sommerville described the technique in *Gnaoua* (1964):

Imagine a two-dimensional plane covered with a rectangular grid. Further imagine that each pair of rectangles which have a side in common are such that each of the pair is the mirror image of the other, being reflected across their common side. ['Mr & Mrs D'] is a piece of such a grid. A three rectangles by three rectangles slice of an infinite sheet, wherein each rectangle is a collage of photographs which are in turn collages of photographs etc. The recipe is the reverse process. Take your entire photo collection and reduce it to a single picture by a multiple collage process, adding any other images of particular interest until the basic rectangle is obtained. Nine prints are necessary, five printed normally, four printed under exactly the same conditions but with the negative reversed, the prints are then trimmed to form perfect rectangles and then collaged together as described. The process may of course be continued.

It was continued, to the extent that the original elements in the images became so small that the resulting pattern was caused largely by irregularities in the grain of the photographic paper. However, with the aid of some powerful hashish, it was possible to see faces, demons, in fact virtually anything you wanted in the work. Visitors reported Burroughs and Sommerville spending many hours studying the prints, making remarkable discoveries.

As a natural extension of the photographic 'fold-ins' with Sommerville, Burroughs began working on photographic 'layouts' in which he would arrange a series of images – street maps, book covers, photographs and news-cuttings – and photograph them. He would re-arrange them, making small changes, and rephotograph them until he had a whole series. It was the photographic record that counted; the actual arrangement of objects was only temporary and was never preserved. Nor was there any 'final' arrangement; the point was to create a series of images.

Sometimes actual books were used, or objects placed in an open briefcase in different configurations, the briefcase making a natural frame. One entire series of photographs consisted of different views of a saw, hanging from a nail against a bare brick wall. Another 1964 sequence concentrated on the play of light and shadow from a Venetian blind across a newspaper. These had a certain resemblance to the early 1930s photographs of arranged objects by Piet Zwart. As with all of his other experiments, Burroughs worked at it exhaustively, exploring every possibility. He produced hundreds of photographs of collages.

Under the technical guidance of Ian Sommerville, Bill was able to superimpose negative images over positive ones, a strip of negative appearing as an element in the collage, reversed out, or with the contents of each frame showing. Sometimes strips were overlapped. The early series were all photographed, presumably by Sommerville, from directly above, at 90 degrees to the surface to fit the photographic frame as a true rectangle. With Ian there to translate Bill's needs into reality by giving the printers careful instructions on what to do to the negatives, they quickly became very sophisticated, even though they were only being developed and printed by the local Tangier Kodak lab.

Burroughs moved from Tangier to New York and the work from this period, photographed by Burroughs himself, is usually taken at an angle and uses none of the reversals or photographic special effects of the first layouts. Unfortunately, in the mid-60s it was virtually impossible to publish this sort of material except as an art book because the costs of reproduction were too high, so an important development in Burroughs' work went unseen by the public.

It was in March 1964, when Bill and Ian were living at the rue Delacroix in Tangier, that Bill began work on yet another extension of the cut-up technique. This time it involved keeping folders on different subjects: these could be numbers, such as the number 17 or 23; places and associational pictures or news-clippings concerning that place, which could be imaginary or a setting for something in a book – 'sets' he called them. There were folders on Bill's characters containing photographs of friends, sometimes specially posed, or news-clippings which suggested specific characters. Other folders contained notes towards new characters; news-clippings, news photographs, and handwritten notes. They were like police files: dossiers on characters and incidents. Bill began decorating the covers of the folders with collages.

Next he filled entire scrapbooks with collages: combining handwritten diary notes and dream journals with news photographs and real snapshots. Sometimes he would add a coloured wash or calligraphic brushwork to the page. One of these, *Scrapbook 3*, was published in a limited edition of only 30 copies by Claude Givaudan in Geneva in 1979. Another, with particularly luminous colour washes and brushwork, was known as *The Book of Hours*. These constitute some of the most beautiful artworks that Burroughs ever did. Facsimile pages from one of the scrapbooks can be found in *The Burroughs File*, published by City Lights in 1984, and many more are beautifully reproduced in colour in Robert Sobieszek's Los Angeles County Museum of Art catalogue *Ports of Entry, William S. Burroughs and the Arts*, where they are labelled as being by Burroughs and Brion Gysin. In fact Gysin had nothing to do with the scrapbooks, though he and Burroughs did collaborate later on the illustrations for the abandoned large format Grove Press edition of *The Third Mind*. A few fragments of the scrapbook collages also appeared in small magazines or small press publications at the time, notably accompanying the 1965 *Paris Review* interview, but most people remained unaware of them.

At the same time as working on the photographic collages in Tangier, Buroughs began to develop the three-column technique. He noticed that as one reads down one column of text in a newspaper, the eye subliminally reads the columns to the left and to the right of that column, producing an automatic cut-up. He began to produce texts which exploited this fact and, as usual, did a great number of them. He began a diary in February 1964 using the three-column technique. If he were to take a trip to Gibraltar, which he did frequently, he would write an account of the trip in one column, just like a normal diary entry: what was said by the officials, what he overheard on the airplane. The next column would present his memories, 'what I was thinking of at the time, the memories that were activated by my encounters'. The third column would be his reading column, quoting from the books that he had with him. His trips to Gibraltar alone provided him with a book-length manuscript, though it has never been published and the material was probably reused in other ways.

He took to pasting in photographs from newspapers to make the three-column texts look more like newspapers, and gave some of the texts newspaper titles and headlines. Jeff Nuttall's special 'Dead Star' issue of *My Own Mag*, London, 1965, reproduced an entire three-column manuscript, complete with its pasted-in pictures. The C-Press in New York published *Time*, a 1965 three-column text with photographs of collages dropped in, combining the two concurrent experiments. It did not much resemble *Time* magazine, however, because it was reproduced in facsimile of Burroughs' own typing rather than re-set as a newspaper.

Also in 1965, during his nine-month stay in New York, Burroughs gave his three-column book *APO-33* – about Dr Dent's apomorphine treatment – to Ed Sanders for him to publish through his infamous Fuck You Press 'located at a secret location in the Lower East Side'. This was hardly a success, either, because Sanders reproduced it in facsimile using electronic stencils for his mimeo machine. The technology did not exist to reproduce the photographs on the stencils so they were done separately and Peter Orlovsky, Allen Ginsberg's lover, was responsible for cutting each one out and sticking them on the finished pages. Unfortunately Peter was on amphetamine at the time and set about his task with furious energy, scattering pictures and glue everywhere. When Burroughs was given one of the first copies off the press he thought that it was some sort of proof or paste-up. When told that this was the finished book he was horrified and took the project away from them. Mary Beach, publisher of Beach Books, Texts and Documents, quickly did a normal off-set litho facsimile edition of the manuscript. But all these were small press editions, not available to most people, though a number of these texts are now available, collected in 1984, in *The Burroughs File*.

Work on the folders and scrapbooks continued until the mid-70s, and James Grauerholz estimates that Burroughs filled more than twenty scrapbooks, most of which are now in private hands.

In 1981, Burroughs gave a series of texts from *Cities of the Red Night* to Robert Rauschenberg for a set of prints called 'American Pewter with Burroughs'. Though Burroughs had no hand in the visual side, it again raised the possibilities of a visual dimension to his literary images in his mind. The next year he made the breakthrough that enabled him to paint. He had recently moved from New York to Lawrence and was living in the Stone House in the country. Bill was shooting at a plywood target with a double-barrelled ten-gauge shotgun with an eighteen-inch barrel; there was no recoil and it really kicked. When Bill looked at the target afterwards, the plywood had been torn away to reveal different layers of wood. 'I said "That looks like art." I called it "Sore Shoulder."'

This same method had previously been used by Niki de Saint Phalle in her 'Tir' series where she shot at assemblage paintings by Robert Rauschenberg and Jasper Johns with a .22 rifle. 'Gun art', it was called. Bill knew about her work, but did not make the conscious connection when he first began his shotgun paintings.

Burroughs quickly developed the idea, introducing cans of spray paint as a medium, not sprayed directly on to the surface but exploded by a shotgun blast in front of the plywood panel. 'Now that's a real explosion of colour – sometimes it'll throw the can 200 feet: a literal explosion of colour when the blast hits the can.' The random principle at work here is closely allied to the principles of the cut-ups and, just as he did with cut-ups, Burroughs began to explore every possible avenue of experiment:

As soon as you get away from representation in painting, then there's many ways of introducing chance into the equation: there's drip canvas like Pollock. Yves Klein set his paintings on fire sometimes and put the fire out, I did quite a lot of experiments like that, and also tracing outlines with gunpowder, so on and so forth. It's just an extension, shall we say, of any randomising technique. If you think about it, there are lots of different ways in which you can randomise your procedure. Using a shotgun blast to hit the pressurised spray paint is just an extension of the random principle since it's really practically impossible to foresee for yourself what will happen. Particularly when you explode several colours. Sometimes I've seen it throw the can a hundred feet. They blow up. Hit by a shotgun blast or a high velocity rifle or pistol cartridge, Booom! It usually blows out to the sides.

Bill normally used a number six, twelve-gauge shotgun, having found that pistol cartridges did not explode reliably; they just made a hole, and the paint came out of the hole rather than exploding sideways; however, a high velocity cartridge always worked. Burroughs experimented with many ways of shooting at the paint: sometimes he used several cans, or arranged them in different positions and shot across the surface, or exposed a number of surfaces to the blast at the same time. 'That way you get different exposures to different blasts of colour, mixtures and dripping down and so on.'

Very occasionally the result was satisfactory without any further work and was left at that: 'The shotgun blast reaches the little spirits compacted into the layers of wood, releases the colours of the paints to splash out in unforeseeable, unpredictable images and patterns.' In most cases, however, Bill added brushwork, silhouettes or collage material in order to complete the work.

The silhouettes were made by spraying round everyday objects: leaves, his hands, masks, saucers, grilles, whatever came to hand, spraying from different angles to vary the density of colour and sharpness of the outline formed. He also used stencils, usually of recognisable objects: trees, ships, cars, faces, cats, a metal grille. 'Start with your stencils then randomise them. It gives you a number of different possibilities.' He enjoyed using intense fluorescent colours and released two limited-edition serrographs of his spray work through the Canadian gallery Obro. The collage material was similar to the scrapbooks of earlier years and consisted mostly of images torn from newspapers and magazines pasted onto the plywood.

From adding paint work to a wooden panel to painting directly on a sheet of paper was but a small step, and it was not long before the majority of his art work was executed on paper. Burroughs had no preconceived idea when he began a painting: 'There might be something on my mind, I try to just let the hand do it, see with my hand. And then look at it, see what has happened. I may see quite clearly in there something that I've seen recently in a magazine or a newspaper, whatever, emerging ... See, I can't consciously draw anything. I can't draw a recognisable chair – it looks like a four year old's.'

Burroughs often recognised faces or people in the randomly created paint surfaces: 'Some are absolutely recognisable, and end up as portraits of certain people.' Sometimes he had these photographed and used the photograph in other work, harking back to the photographic experiments of the early 60s: 'I use the photographs in the pictures, so I have a picture of a face from a red picture then I can use that in other red pictures or I can make collages of those pictures which I have done ... any number of combos.'

In a classic Burroughsian coincidence, he was to have a show at the Paul Klein Gallery in Chicago and made an association between the gallery owner's name and that of the artist Yves Klein. 'I had an odd thing happen,' he said. 'I'd just written down on the typewriter "Yves Klein set his pictures on fire," and put them out at some point. And James [Grauerholz] came here to tell me that the gallery had burned down in Chicago. The Paul Klein Gallery. Well the whole block burned down as a matter of fact. It was a real disaster. A whole block of galleries and stored pictures, and we collected the insurance but the pictures were completely destroyed. That's an interesting little juxtaposition.'

This connection to Yves Klein is significant because it strengthens the association between Burroughs and the Nouveaux Réalistes which, if one should want to locate

Burroughs in an art movement, is where one would place him. The comparison of his work with that of Yves Klein has been made on a number of occasions and Burroughs agreed that they seemed similar. Though Burroughs had no formal ties with Les Nouveaux Réalistes, and was only vaguely aware of the work of Yves Klein, Arman and Niki de Saint-Phalle, there are many parallels in their work. The School of Nice owed a lot to neo-dada and Duchamp, and paralleled Pop Art in its attention to the 'material surfaces of contemporary life'.

Burroughs was certainly aware of Duchamp's work and had met Duchamp, albeit fairly briefly, at a party given by Robert Lebel in Paris in 1958. 'Duchamp shot at his paintings,' Burroughs said. 'He said, "It wasn't quite accidental, but I'm a very poor shot" so he didn't know where the bullets were going.' This fitted in perfectly with Burroughs' ideas on introducing random elements, and also acts as precursor to Burroughs' own shotgun paintings of the 80s.

In the mid-50s in both the USA and Europe, young artists began to take objects from everyday life and appropriate them into constructions, collages and paintings. (Picasso and Kurt Schwitters being the two precursors of this trend.) It was the beginning of the consumer society, with its vast accumulations of household goods, industrial junk and discarded objects.

In New York, Robert Rauschenberg used car tyres, beds and actual grass in his paintings, whereas Jasper Johns took on the most everyday images of all, the American flag, numbers and targets, making them new and incorporating boxes with lids, rulers, cutlery and other objects. Abstract Expressionist Willem de Kooning used lips torn from magazines in his ground-breaking 'Women' series.

Three artists from Nice – Yves Klein, Arman and Martial Raysse – also focused on objects. They attempted a 'new sensitivity' where an object would be expressed with 'joyous optimism'. This was not another school of realists; more often or not it was the object itself that was treated: objects were multiplied, divided, broken, exploded into fragments and destroyed in order to realise the artists' 'sensitive intuition' about them. César arrived from Marseille to join the original three and the group became known as Les Nouveaux Réalistes.

Then came Tinguley, Niki de Saint-Phalle, Daniel Spoerri and dozens more; the group began to be referred to as The School of Nice.

César compressed selected parts of cars and bicycles into stackable cubes, using a commercial scrap metal compressor. Arman filled transparent containers with trash, sometimes freezing the contents in place with transparent polyester as if the trash had been set in aspic – like a fly trapped in amber. For one show he filled a whole gallery with trash. In his later work, known as his 'Slices', he took objects – often violins – and sliced them like a hard-boiled egg then separated the pieces and embedded them in quick-setting polyester or cement.

From 1961 onwards, Arman spent a part of each year living at the Hotel Chelsea in New York. The owner, Stanley Bard, encouraged artists of some merit to stay there and pay their rent with art work, so when Burroughs stayed at the Chelsea in 1964, he passed Arman's work in the lobby each day (as well as that of Christo, Larry Rivers and many others).

Burroughs' move to painting was perhaps not as surprising as some critics have thought. After all, Burroughs had never felt himself confined to one genre; in the past he had made films, collages and cut-up tape recordings. Beginning as far back as 1965 with the *Call Me Burroughs* album, recorded in Paris by Ian Sommerville, he produced more than twenty albums of his readings and collaborations. As usual, his pictures are about as far from contemporary abstract painting as his writings are from the American minimal novel or magic realism. As in the cut-ups, Burroughs used his pictures as a means of travel: 'To view these pictures puts the viewer in the position of the creative observer, who creates by observing. There is a distinct sensation when this creation occurs. One is looking at the picture, then a face, a narrow street filled with red mist, a mineshaft, an area of red huts, swim into view ... one can see the surface of the work move and shift and come into focus.' Like flames in a log fire images appear and fade.

Brion Gysin remained a powerful influence on Burroughs' art, his brushwork in particular, and it was not until Gysin's death in 1986 that Burroughs felt able to produce actual paintings or to exhibit his work. 'I didn't start doing paper until after Brion's death, it would have been unthinkable for me to compete with him. I've done a lot better than he did, financially, on painting. Collaborating [on writing] was one thing but as soon as I started painting that would be a matter of competition. Without question Brion would have seen it like that.'

Burroughs' first show was held at the Tony Shafrazi Gallery in New York in December 1987, which sold out. This was quickly followed in 1988 by sell-out shows at the October Gallery in London; the Front Gallery, Vancouver; the Casa Sin Nombre Gallery in Santa Fe; and a number of group shows. 1989 opened with shows in St Louis, Montreal, Basel, Toronto and Rome, by which time his prices had climbed to over $3,000 for each picture and he found that he was able to live as a visual artist. He told *Art News*: 'Painting is a lot easier than writing. A painting can take as little as twenty minutes, where a novel might take a year or more. I'm as deeply into painting as writing now; it occupies practically all my time.' Bill found that he was making so much from painting that, for the first time, he was able to give money to charities: Greenpeace, and animal charities in particular. José Férez, who put on Bill's show at the October Gallery, took over Bill's representation in Europe and began to spend several months of the year working with him in Lawrence.

There was some criticism of Bill's work, suggesting that his shotgun art was a gimmick, but if using a shotgun to achieve desired results is gimmicky, how does one explain painting on broken plates? Yet the same critics took Julian Schnabel's work seriously. Possibly in order to counter the pigeonhole of 'shotgun artist', Burroughs made a formal statement on his art, explaining the importance of random events in his work and showing that there was a serious intent in it. Burroughs did not want to be categorised as a writer who paints in the way that Henry Miller or DH Lawrence had been. Written in January 1989, his statement was printed in the catalogue of his exhibition at Cleto Polcina in Rome, May 1989:

In the Carlos Castaneda books, Don Juan makes a distinction between the tonal universe and the nagual. The tonal universe is the every day cause-and-effect universe, which is predictable because it is pre-recorded. The nagual is the unknown, the unpredictable, the uncontrollable. For the nagual to gain access, the door of chance must be open. There must be a random factor: drips of paint down the canvas, setting the paint on fire, squirting the paint. Perhaps the most basic random factor is the shotgun blast, producing an explosion of colour into unpredictable, uncontrollable patterns and forms. Without this random factor, the painter can only copy the tonal universe, and his painting is as predictable as the universe he copies . . .

What I am attempting then, can be called Nagual Art. The shotgun blast that exploded a can of spray paint, or a tube or other container, is one way of contacting the nagual. There are, of course, many others. The arbitrary order of randomly chosen silhouettes, marbling, blotting . . .

He who would invoke the unpredictable must cultivate accidents and randomness . . . the toss of a coin, or a brush, the blast of a shotgun, the blotting of colour and form to produce new forms and new colour combinations . . .

Since the nagual is unpredictable, there is no formula by which the nagual can be reliably invoked. Of course, magic is replete with spells and rites, but these are only adjuncts of varying effectiveness. A spell that works today may be flat as yesterday's beer tomorrow.

The painter is tied down to the given formulae of form and colour applied to a surface. The writer is more rigidly confined, to words on a page. The nagual must be continually created and re-created.

The bottom line is the creator. Norman Mailer kindly said of me that I may be 'possessed by genius'. Not that I am a genius, or that I possess genius, but that I may be at times possessed by genius. I define 'genius' as the nagual, the unpredictable, the uncontrollable, spontaneous, alive, capricious and arbitrary. An artist is possessed by genius sometimes, when he is so lucky.

15 Conquering the Ugly Spirit

n 1984, Burroughs changed his literary agent from Peter Matson to Andrew Wylie. Bill was 70 years old and, despite the fact that he was translated into more than a dozen languages, as well as his books being available in paperback in Britain and America, he was broke. Wylie proposed that they assemble a multi-book deal, composed mostly of already existing material: *Queer*, *Interzone*, several volumes of correspondence, and essays, as well as *The Western Lands*. Wylie got him a $200,000 deal with Viking Penguin and a £45,000 deal for Britain. It was a great relief; Bill finally had financial security and was able to pay his mounting debts. He no longer felt the pressure to produce, and after handing in *The Western Lands*, he was able to concentrate on his painting and to travel to his art openings in Europe and around the USA.

Burroughs had a lot of material left over after he completed his trilogy, some of which found its way into his next book, *Ghost of Chance*. Bill's lemur-loving eighteenth-century hero Captain Mission, from *Western Lands*, appears but the book is in no way a fourth part of the series. Though *Ghost of Chance* is a very short book by Burroughs' standards, it was a distillation of his current thinking and incorporated some of his most tender and exquisite writing:

> He lay there in the gray light, his arm around his lemur. The animal snuggled closer and put a paw up to his face. Tiny mouse lemurs stole out of the roots and niches and holes in the ancient tree and frisked around the room, falling on insects with little squeals. Their tails twitched

above their heads; their great flaring ears, thin as paper, quivered to every sound as their wide, limpid eyes swept the walls and floors for insects. They had been doing this for millions of years. The twitching tail, the trembling ears mark the passage of centuries.

The book also contained his notorious Jesus text. Bill believed in the historical Jesus, as he explained in a 1988 interview: 'There's a spate of scholars who say that Jesus Christ never existed, that the whole thing was cooked up by the church. I think this is completely erroneous, I don't care what they say; it was either Jesus Christ or somebody else! But just like Shakespeare, it was done by one person. One person is speaking.'

It was the vexed question of miracles that disturbed Burroughs. He was willing to believe that they occurred; he believed in magic and had witnessed weather magic on a number of occasions. 'I mean, any competent magic man can heal the sick sometimes. He can cast out devils, particularly if he installed them in the first place. And of course special effects have come a long way since then.'

It was the motivation that concerned him: 'Well, you know what the Buddhists say about miracles and healing? If you can, don't! In the first place you're setting all sorts of factors into motion and upsetting all sorts of order with incalculable long-range consequences. The healer is often motivated by the most reprehensible self-glorification. I think that he did perform some of the so-called miracles. What he actually did was not all that remarkable but the result was a miracle monopoly by the church, that they can only be performed by authorised personnel, that is, church personnel. And they have to have meticulous verification, they can't have too many saints you see. They've got enough now.'

Bill took the church monopoly on miracle working and combined it with another, typically Burroughsian, concern: 'They are keeping smallpox alive in three locations. It is an extinct disease, and already they're not vaccinating for it. Well there's a nice thriller for you. Terrorists hijack the smallpox virus. And it's one of the most contagious diseases ever known.

251

If that got loose in an unvaccinated population, well . . . I guess they couldn't bear to see the last of it.'

These two themes were combined into a story – what would have earlier been seen as a routine. Burroughs created a museum of extinct species, such as might house the smallpox virus: 'In my story the Christ virus gets loose, so you have hundreds and thousands and millions of people all absolutely convinced "I am the way, none comes to the father except through me!" Well one was more than enough, imagine if you had millions! And all of them gaining adherents, performing miracles, after all, special effects have come a long way since Christ. So there you are. I've just detailed the chaos that would result.'

The first edition of *Ghost of Chance*, illustrated by George Condo, was published in 1991 in a very limited edition by the Whitney Museum of American Art at $1,800. The Whitney was initially concerned about some of the passages about Jesus and asked for their removal, but when told it was all or nothing they decided to brave any complaints from the Friends of the Whitney. The later trade edition had a slightly longer text and Burroughs' own illustrations. This was not the first time that Burroughs collaborated with a noted artist: there were previous fine press books – *Mummies* with Carl Apfelschnitt in 1984; a book on cats with Brion Gysin, called *The Cat Inside*, which was published just before Brion's death in 1986. There were two portfolios with Keith Haring: a 1988 collaboration called *Apocalypse* followed the next year by *The Valley*. The latter reproduced Burroughs' text in facsimile on sixteen etched plates. In 1991, Burroughs had his own limited edition book, called *The Seven Deadly Sins*, in which he provided both text and plates.

Burroughs also produced other, more substantial volumes. He was invited to edit an anthology to be called *The Granta Book of the Extremes of Human Experience*. He agreed to the project but did not like the title. James suggested calling it *The Granta Book of Deathless Prose* – that is, prose with life in it, that has stood the test of time – which Granta accepted. It consisted of Bill's favourite sections from about 40 books including work by Denton Welch, Paul Bowles, Jane Bowles and F Scott Fitzgerald. Grauerholz described the editing process: 'Of course, as you can imagine with William he reads it and says, "We don't need all this, there's just this one paragraph that's good" and I say "Well, okay, but we have to have at least ten pages, to set it up." '

Burroughs wrote an introduction to the whole book and a short introduction and commentary on each selection. 'I have just taken things that I like for different reasons, that I think are very successful, memorable.' He knew which selections he wanted, then his office had to locate the original texts, which in some cases were quite elusive.

Another project completed in 1991 was a 600-page manuscript of a dream book, 'but not confining myself to dreams at all,' he said, 'but things suggested by the dreams and various theories on the meaning of dreams and the use of dreams in painting and in writing. I showed it to Allen [Ginsberg]. He found it quite readable.' Burroughs compared it in structure to Jean Genet's *Prisoner of Love* which had impressed him very much: 'It's very much in that line in that it has no central theme. It goes, just like he goes, off on tangents and this and that. This is the same format, though not the same content.' By the time the editing process was over, the dream book, called *My Education*, had been reduced to a scant 193 pages of text.

As usual it is a map of his ideas at the time of writing. Clearly he was mellowing: 'Last night I was leafing through the *Audubon Book of Animals*; so many beautiful creatures . . . the Flying Fox, exactly like Fletch, and the Black Lemur. Realize how I love animals . . . mammals, that is . . . weasels and skunks and wolverines and seals and bush babies. I am turning into a latter-day Saint Francis. This morning, I rescued a rat from Ginger. It is still in the house somewhere.'

In yet another unexpected departure, in 1989 Burroughs turned to opera, collaborating on Robert Wilson's *The Black Rider: the Casting of the Magic Bullets* for the Thalia Theatre, in Hamburg. Bill wrote the text and Tom Waits composed songs. Described as comic, lively and 'Germanic', *The Black Rider* is a pastiche of operetta, cabaret and rock concerts, based on the tragic tale *Der Freischutz* (the 1810 text that inspired Weber's opera of the same name) by August Apel and Friedrich Laun.

Tom Waits' songs were in English but Bill's text was translated into German. Bill, James and Bill's German translator, Udo Breger, all stayed in the same hotel. Each day Bill would go over to rehearsals where Wilson usually had some changes for him to make: a scene that would have to be rewritten or material that needed to be reorganised. Bill would take it back to the hotel and work on it. He rarely had time to go out to dinner, and just ate his meals at the hotel, working to get the material ready for translation for the next day. 'There was about a ten days [period] when I was in Hamburg working rather intensively,' Burroughs said. 'Then when it came time for the final rehearsal there were all sorts of last-minute changes and things that Bob didn't like and wanted me to do differently, so I was sending faxes back and forth, and anyway it worked out very well.'

The opera opened in Hamburg on 31 March 1990 and Wilson received thirteen standing ovations. By a remarkable coincidence, the applause lasted twenty-three minutes – Bill's magic number. The opera travelled to Vienna in June where it was recorded for Austrian television by ORF, and went on to open in Paris in October. This was a very good trip for Bill because he also attended the March opening of his art show at the Galerie K in Paris, which was very nearly a sell out. His large wooden panel 'Last Chance' was acquired by the Musée des Ecrivains.

At the end of 1991, Burroughs and Wilson began work on another opera. Bill had sent Wilson an idea for a project called *Paradise Lost*, which, in addition to Milton's original poem, was about aliens, UFOs, abductions, and particularly about the 1947 Roswell, New Mexico, UFO crash in which three bodies were supposedly recovered (documented in Kevin D Randle and Donald R Schmitt's *UFO Crash At Roswell*, 1991). In 1989 Burroughs wrote to Whitley Streiber, author of *Communion* and *Transformation*, saying that he would very much like to contact the aliens that Streiber had described. Anne Streiber wrote back saying that they received a lot of crank letters and had to be sure he really was who he said he was. His next letter convinced her, and they invited Bill to spend a weekend at their cabin.

'I had a number of talks with Streiber about his experiences, and I was quite convinced that he was telling the truth,' said Burroughs. 'I was convinced that the aliens, or whatever they are, are a real phenomenon. The abductions, in several accounts, involved sexual contacts. Indeed, that would seem to be their purpose.' To his regret the aliens did not choose to manifest themselves when he was around, but he was openminded about it: 'It may mean that it was not propitious for them to come and pick me up at that particular time. It may mean that they would contact me at a later date, or it may mean that they regard me as the enemy ... We have no way of knowing what their motives are. They may find that my intervention is hostile to their objectives. And their objectives may not be friendly at all.'

Michael Paterniti, in *Driving Mr Albert, a Trip Across America With Einstein's Brain*, reported that Bill's back lawn had been trimmed so that the long grass surrounded the close manicured shape of a huge penis, put there as a landing pad to welcome aliens.

Paradise Lost also connected with some of the ideas in *Ghost of Chance*, and before that, in *Western Lands*, about Burroughs' growing fascination with lemurs. As James Grauerholz described it, 'basically it's a misanthropic concept, an extrapolation of Brion's idea that Man is a bad animal, destroying the globe, just intrinsically full of these seven deadly sins.'

Victor Bockris interviewed Burroughs in Kansas in 1991 and much of their conversation was about invasion by the Ugly Spirit. Bockris was quite agitated about the idea and Bill took on the role of the Old Doctor to calm him. He told Bockris, 'When I go into my psyche, at a certain point I meet a very hostile, very strong force. It's as definite as someone attacking me in a bar. We usually come to a standoff ... As soon as you get close to something important, that's when you feel this invasion, that's the way you know there's something there ... The last thing the invading instance wants to do is confront you directly because that's the end of it. But invasion is the basis of fear; there's no fear like invasion.' Bockris was feeling a strong sense of invasion himself and said that the only way he knew to fight it off was to say 'No, no, no, no.'

But Burroughs laughed. ' "No, no, no, no," doesn't work. You have to let it wash through. This is difficult, difficult, but I'll tell you one thing; you detach yourself and allow this to wash through instead of trying to oppose, which you can't do ... You can't oppose something intellectually that is over-powering you emotionally.' He sympathised with Bockris, 'Listen, baby. I've been coping with this for so many years ...'

In March 1992, during a week that Allen Ginsberg was visiting with Bill, an opportunity arose to evict the Ugly Spirit once and for all. A sweat-lodge purification ceremony was organised for Burroughs' benefit by William Lyon, a professor of anthropology who had been apprenticed for fourteen years to Wallace Black Elk, a Sioux medicine man. Lyon had rented the old Stone House on the hill top outside Lawrence where Burroughs first lived when he moved to Kansas. Next to it Lyon had dug a sweat lodge in order to work with a Navajo Indian shaman named Melvin Betsellie.

The lodge was igloo-shaped, made from a framework of twigs and branches covered with black plastic. In the centre was a fire pit. It was a small gathering: William Burroughs, Allen Ginsberg, James Grauerholz, his boyfriend Michael Emerton, Steven Lowe from William Burroughs Communications, Melvin Betsellie and a Winnebago Sioux woman. Outside a boy tended the fire and food. They were all stripped ready for the smoke and heat: Ginsberg naked, Bill wearing just his shorts.

It was a long, slow ceremony. After lengthy prayers Betsellie used first a feather, then his hands, to waft smoke at each of them, then threw water on the fire, making intense clouds of steam and smoke which filled the enclosed space. Their eyes filled with burning tears and the sweat poured off them.

Bill sat by the entrance feeling weak and uncomfortable, desperate for air but unable to leave the ceremony. Discussing it afterwards with Ginsberg he said, 'I needed air, I needed to get out. I finally lay down near the door and then I felt better ... and ... I had to stick it out and stay there, I couldn't break the spell. As soon as he began using the coals, I immediately felt better.'

The shaman prayed to the coals and blew a shrill bone whistle. Bill Lyon tapped a drum as the shaman waved glowing coals around the room, illuminating the darkness.

After the fourth round of steam heat Betsellie sprinkled water on everyone several times with his feathered fan. He took hot coals in his hand and put them in his mouth, swallowing the bad spirit coal several times and retching it up. Both Michael Emerton and Steve Lowe saw the coal in his mouth, lighting up his gorge. 'It looked quite terrifying, the mask of his face open-mouthed, the inside of his mouth lit up, you could see down to his throat in the red coal light, almost frightening,' said Lowe.

Then the shaman touched Bill with a coal. Bill later told Ginsberg: 'I thought, my God, it's great that he touched me with the coal and I didn't feel any burns or anything. I was very impressed.' Bill couldn't see how the hot coal was moving around in the darkness. The coal seemed to be flying in the air circling around Bill and the fire and back again. The shaman battled with the spirit, caught it and blew it into the fire. Bill was moved by the ceremony and kept thanking them for their prayers until, towards the end, the heat and smoke were too much for him and he begged, 'Please. Please – open the door, some air.'

The traditional long-stemmed pipe of sweet mild tobacco was passed round, and the participants left the lodge for the Stone House where an altar had been set up. There the ceremony continued for a further hour and a half, with Bill seated in a chair, facing the altar fire. The shaman gave him green cedar sprigs to smell and hold in his left hand, and a white eagle feather for his right hand. This was the climax of the long ceremony. On his knees, Betsellie chanted several very long prayers, then repeated a word in his native Navajo tongue while waving smoke at each of them separately. He prayed repeatedly to the bear spirit, the four-legged people, the two-legged people, the crawling people, the insects, the families, the brothers and sisters there and everywhere, the relatives and their own brothers and sisters or relatives. 'Family, all one family, no matter what race we come from. All relatives together in a room.'

The ceremony over at last, they all ate: big servings of pot-roast, baked cheese potato slices, salad, coffee, followed by a home-made, sweet iced cake.

Afterwards Ginsberg asked Bill about his reaction to the exorcism ceremony, and the love and affection shown him by the participants. 'I feel it very deeply,' he said. 'I like the shaman very much ... The way he was crying. Deeply sad, deeply ... That was something ...'

Burroughs told Ginsberg that Melvin Betsellie said it was the toughest case he'd ever handled, and for a moment he thought he was going to lose. He hadn't anticipated the strength and weight and evil intensity of this spirit, or 'entity', as he called it. 'The same way the priest in an exorcism has to take on the spirit,' said Bill. 'Some of them are not strong enough. Some are killed.'

Betsellie told Bill what the spirit looked like. It had a white, skull face but had no eyes, and there were some sort of wings. Allen asked Bill if he had ever seen anything like that. Bill said he had identified it many times in his paintings. He had shown Betsellie some of them and the shaman had recognised the spirit in the swirls of abstract brushwork, pointing to it immediately, saying, 'There it is right there.'

'It's very much related to the American Tycoon,' Bill told him. 'To William Randolph Hearst, Vanderbilt, Rockefeller, that whole stratum of American acquisitive evil. Monopolistic, acquisitive evil. Ugly evil. The ugly American. The ugly American at his ugly worst. That's exactly what it is.'

AG: But then that's the character that has possessed you?
WSB: Yes. That's right.
AG: Did you get anything from the shaman's sweat-lodge ceremony?
WSB: That was much better than anything psychoanalysts have come up with ... something definite there was being touched upon ... This you see is the same notion, Catholic exorcism, psychotherapy, shamanistic practices – getting to the moment when whatever it was gained access. And also to the name of the spirit. Just to know that it's the Ugly Spirit. That's a great step. Because the spirit doesn't want its name to be known.

Burroughs was getting closer and closer to giving the Ugly Spirit a name. He spent 40 years investigating its various guises, systematically revealing and examining its many names and countless methods of operation. The identification of control systems and the devising of means to destroy them always dominated his work. He always fought for complete freedom – freedom from all control, from invasion by alien forces: religion; sexual repression and suppression; the American Way of Life; traditional Family Values; programming by TV, media and the sub-text of language itself; all the big 'isms': nationalism, communism, fascism. He proposed a real naked lunch, when you finally see what is quivering naked on the end of the fork.

When we see the planet as an organism, it is obvious who the enemies of the planet are. Their name is legion. They dominate and populate the planet. 'The deceived and the deceivers who are themselves deceived.' Did Homo Sap think other animals were there just for him to *eat*? Apparently. Bulldozers are destroying the rain forests, the cowering lemurs and flying foxes, the singing Kloss's gibbons which produce the most beautiful and variegated music of any land animal, and the gliding colugo lemurs, which are helpless on the ground. All going, to make way for more and more devalued human stock, with less and less of the wild spark, the priceless ingredient – energy into matter. A vast mudslide of soulless sludge. [*Ghost of Chance*]

He held out little hope for humanity, but reserved his greatest opprobrium for the United States, the country that had held out the greatest promise. In *My Education* he wrote:

The Devil's Bargain applied to a country. If ever a country had the potential to escape the bargain and really fulfil the promises, it was America.
    And what happened?
    'Sell me the American Dream, the American Soul, and I will give you refrigerators groaning with Malvern Spring Water and venison sausage. I will give you remote-controlled color television. I will give you two cars in every garage.'

(At the expense of people starving in remote unimportant Third World areas.)
'You agree?'
An idiot chorus: '*Yes Yes Yes.*'
'And I will give you the POWER to keep what you have.'
Hiroshima.

Bill's sex life, for so long the driving force of his writing, dwindled to a close and from the early 80s he had no regular boyfriend. A decade later he claimed to have lost interest in sex. In *My Education* he wrote: 'My sexual feelings, in human terms, seem to have withered away, or rather, to belong to a body and mind I no longer occupy. But I maintain an intense emotional feeling for animals. Imagine a *big* lemur. Lemur as big as I am, and cuddling up to me – nothing sexual, it's much more intense than that.'

Sometimes a visiting fan stayed over, but his real love was reserved for his six cats: 'I love my cats, I love my cats,' he crooned. 'I love *all* cats.' He spent a great deal of time preparing cat food in individual throwaway silver foil dishes, talking to the large felines who rubbed against his legs. He addressed each one by name and they each had their own dish. He told Victor Bockris that his cats taught him compassion:

They reflect you in a very deep way. They just opened up a whole area of compassion in me. I remember lying in my bed weeping and weeping to think that a nuclear catastrophe would destroy them. I could see people driving by saying, 'Kill your dogs and cats.' I spent hours just crying. Oh, my God. Then there is constantly the feeling that there could be some relationship between me and the cats and that I might have missed it. Some of it is so extreme that I couldn't write it. People think of me as being cold – some woman wrote that I could not admit any feeling at all. My God. I am so emotional that sometimes I can't stand the intensity. Oh, my God. Then they ask me if I ever cry? I say, 'Holy shit, probably two days ago.' I'm very subject to violent fits of weeping, for very good reasons.

Bill became 'an old man with his cats'. He would break off conversations to tend to their needs, constantly jumping up to open cans and empty their litter tray, and rising in the night to let one in, another out. He projected his emotions onto them, and as he aged, so did they. As he outlived his contemporaries, so he outlived his cats, each death a real heartbreak for him.

William Burroughs Communications made Bill financially secure. He no longer had to write another word or do another reading. His life settled into a comfortable routine. He woke around 8 a.m. and took his glass of methadone. Then he would doze in bed until 9 a.m. 'I don't want to get up till the methadone hits because I know I won't be feeling very well.' Then he would get up and shave. By then, one of the young men from William Burroughs Communications would have arrived to make his breakfast: V8 juice, two boiled eggs, toast and three cups of tea. A roster posted over the kitchen counter showed which of four assistants would cook his breakfast and which one would make dinner. After breakfast the methadone would be doing its work. He would do a little reading and plan the day: 'Then I get this terrific rush of energy, rush around and clean up the house. It's a good schedule. The real feeling good lasts for two or three hours, then you're just normal. You're feeling okay. I get the best of both worlds. Taking junk and alcohol. If I was taking it by injection, I wouldn't be able to drink. Times when I had needle habit I couldn't drink a drop, not even a glass of beer, alcohol just turned me sick. I smoke some pot then I work.'

He always had milk and crackers for lunch which he fixed himself. Unless his office had made arrangements for someone to visit, he fed his cats then painted or wrote as the mood took him, with no preset idea or work plan. Three or four times a month he visited his friend Fred Aldrich for some shooting practice, and on Thursdays he and James drove to the methadone clinic in Kansas City. At 4 p.m., sharp, Bill had his first vodka and Coke, both bought in industrial size plastic containers from Dillon's, the local supermarket. As an hors d'oeuvre, Bill indulged in his passion for caviar which was delivered by courier packed in ice. He could not always afford the best and had to make do with American sturgeon eggs but Beluga was what he craved: 'I can imagine someone bankrupting himself buying best Beluga at $28 an ounce . . .' Dinner was early, often with James and other local friends as guests. There was a regular get-together at Bill's house on Thursday nights, but Bill was usually in bed by 9 p.m.

There was no attempt made to kick junk. He had been on it since his return to New York, and intended to stay on it until his death. It meant more to him than just getting high. Junk had made him who he was:

The touch (nudge) of God's Own Medicine led me to *Junky*, [to] *Naked Lunch*, to finding a vacation – I mean, of course, *vocation*. A place in life. *My* place in life – and it opened my eyes to the evil that lurks behind the war against drugs. *Illegal* drugs. Not just any drugs. Once a drug becomes illegal, it acquires a sulfurous glow from the depths of Hell.

So through G. O. M. I gained self-respect – and in so doing, the respect of others.

I am an unabashed cultural Icon. I stand for the truth. I hate liars. [*Last Words*]

His journal entries, published in *Last Words*, recorded his advancing old age:

And what has become of the *New Yorker* cartoons? They are not funny or even comprehensible any more. Where are the cartoons of Charles Adams and Peter Arno?

Yes, where are the snows of yesteryear. And the speedballs I useta know?

Well, I guess it's time for my Ovaltine and a long good night . . .

And the old logo on Old Spice aftershave was an old [etching] of a four-master – now there is an abstract blob, a little boat with outsize sails. Gone all suggestion of spice, and opium and South Sea traders, Conrad. In its place a meaningless smear.

Little things. But they build up into a World I wouldn't want to make, or be a part of.' ...

Arthritis slowly twisting and knobbing my fingers and elbows and shoulders, inexorable as limestone's slow deposit.

Ill-health began to intrude upon his life. In July 1991, he spent three weeks in the hospital in Topeka for a triple bypass operation, following an unsuccessful operation to clear blocked arteries. He fractured his hip falling out of the hospital bed trying to get to the bathroom unaided, but less than six months later Bill was walking around without even a cane. He was soon walking down the flight of steep stone steps that led to the water at his fishing cabin on a lake about fifteen miles from his house, and rowing his boat again.

He developed cataracts on his eyes, but these were successfully removed in routine, same-day surgery at Lawrence Memorial Hospital and he was back home in a few hours. Within days his eyesight had improved substantially and he was once more able to get good scores at target practice.

As he aged, his personality changed; the frosty patrician carapace, which intimidated even Neal Cassady into silence, seemed to thaw. At first he became garrulous: the combination of methadone, marijuana and alcohol meant that he was never sober and tended to talk all the time – his conversation jumping from one subject to another like a grasshopper; often not hearing what the other people in the room said, or disregarding it to follow one of his galloping thoughts. But when he reached his eighties he mellowed, he began listening more to what other people said, and went out of his way to be friendly. Four months before his death he wrote:

I find myself knocking myself out to be charming, and how I love it – to see the subject glow in response. It's a great feeling, that I have only experienced in the last few years. Putting out charm and watching it hit.

This [is] completely different from the fear hit, putting out fear and watching it hit and twist in a cold sore.

I want people to feel better after meeting me, not worse.

He could still be cranky if he wanted, though. Another entry, six months before his death, read:

> January 25, 1997. Saturday:
> I must tell James: Please never conceal from me any nasty letters or reviews. I want the names of these creeps. The addresses, so I can put one of my curses on them. It will give me something to do.

On the afternoon of 1 August 1997, Bill had a coughing fit about twenty minutes after starting on his first drink of the day. He had been having them for about eight months. Minutes later, Tom Peschio, one of the group of Bill's friends who cooked and looked after him, arrived at the house and found Bill in the throes of a heart attack, precipitated by the coughing. He called James, who called in paramedics. Bill's last words, spoken in the ambulance before he lost consciousness, were 'I'll be right back'. He died the next day at 6.45 p.m. at Lawrence Memorial Hospital. James, Tom Peschio and Bill's snake expert friend, Dean Ripa, sat vigil for the twenty-four hours before his death. Bill did not speak. The last entry in his journal was on 30 July. In a scrawling hand, crippled by arthritis, he wrote 'Love? What is it? The most natural painkiller what there is. LOVE.'

The funeral was held on 6 August, at seven in the evening at Liberty Hall, the little theatre at 7th and Massachusetts in downtown Lawrence. Bill had an open casket in the American tradition; cherrywood with a white quilted lining. He wore the thick beige Moroccan singlet given to him in London by his best friend Brion Gysin, and the left lapel of his jacket displayed the insignia of the American Academy of Arts and Letters and that of a Commandeur de l'Ordre des Arts et des Lettres. His famous snap-brim fedora and walking cane were placed at the end of the coffin.

James's mother, Selda, sang 'For All the Saints Who from Their Labours Rest' to a piano accompaniment, and Bill's friend David Ohle read Tennyson's 'Ulysses', one of Bill's favourite poems – one which seemed to describe his own life – and one which he could quote at length. James gave the closing words. People filed past to pay their final respects and several kissed him, including one woman from the October Gallery who kept kissing him full on the mouth, something many of the mourners found offensive. More than 1,000 local people came to view the coffin and to attend the funeral. Huge amounts of flowers were left at Bill's house on Learnard Avenue, and even two weeks later, some anonymous person continued to leave a fresh bouquet each day. Just before the coffin lid was closed at 9.30 p.m., someone placed Bill's favourite gun in his hands and folded his fingers over it. A joint and various other essential items were added to the coffin to assist him in his final journey to the Western Lands.

The next morning a motorcade made the five-hour journey to the Burroughs family mausoleum in the Bellefontaine cemetery in St Louis, where Bill's brother, mother, and grandfather were already interred. Patti Smith arrived to take part, taking a cab to the graveyard straight from the airport. When she reached the gates she insisted on walking to the grave instead of driving. It is a large graveyard and it took the cortège some time to reach the grave even by car, so the burial was delayed while everyone waited for Smith to arrive. She sang an a cappella version of 'Oh Dear, What Can the Matter Be? (Johnny's So Long at the Fair)'. James gave a quiet speech, John Giorno a rousing one, and Anne Waldman read the last three paragraphs from *The Western Lands*. As the grave was filled in by workers using a backhoe, Patti looked furtively from side to side then stooped and pushed a small black bag into the earth. Those who witnessed it assumed it was a bag of heroin. Once the grave was filled and the flowers piled on top, Bill's shooting party, including José Férez and Fred Aldrich, stood and fired a single round over the grave.

Bibliography

BOOKS BY WILLIAM BURROUGHS

Junkie [as 'William Lee'], Ace, New York, 1953

The Naked Lunch [1959 draft version], Olympia, Paris, 1959

Minutes To Go [with Brion Gysin, Sinclair Beiles and Gregory Corso], Two Cities, Paris, 1960

Exterminator [with Brion Gysin], Auerhahn, San Francisco, 1960

The Soft Machine [first draft version], Olympia, Paris, 1961

The Ticket That Exploded [first draft version], Olympia, Paris, 1962

Naked Lunch [1958 draft version], Grove, New York, 1962

Dead Fingers Talk, John Calder, London, 1963

The Yage Letters [with Allen Ginsberg], City Lights, San Francisco, 1963

Nova Express, Grove, New York, 1964

Valentine's Day Reading, American Theater for Poets, New York, 1965 [mimeo]

Roosevelt After Inauguration, Fuck You Press, New York, 1965 [mimeo], reprinted City Lights, 1979

Time, C, New York, 1965 [limited edition]

APO-33, Fuck You, New York, 1965 [mimeo], reprinted Beach Books, San Francisco, 1966

The Soft Machine [second draft version], Grove, New York, 1966

So Who Owns Death TV? [with Claude Pelieu and Carl Weissner], Beach Books, San Francisco, 1967

The Ticket That Exploded [second draft version], Grove, New York, 1967

The Soft Machine [third draft version], John Calder, London, 1968

The Dead Star, Nova Broadcast Press, San Francisco, 1969 [limited edition]

Entretiens avec William Burroughs [WSB interviewed by Daniel Odier, in French], Pierre Belfond, Paris, 1969 [first version of *The Job*]

The Job [revised version, first version in English], Grove, New York, 1970

The Last Words of Dutch Schultz [first version], Cape-Goliard, London, 1970

Jack Kerouac [with Claude Pelieu, in French], L'Herne, Paris, 1971

Ali's Smile, Unicorn, Brighton, 1971 [limited edition]

The Wild Boys, Grove, New York, 1971

Electronic Revolution, Blackmoor Head, Cambridge, 1971 [limited edition]

Brion Gysin Let The Mice In [with Brion Gysin], Something Else Press, West Glover, Vermont, 1973

Exterminator!, Viking, New York, 1973

White Subway, Aloes, London, 1973

Mayfair Academy Series More or Less, Urgency Rip-Off Press, Brighton, 1973 [mimeo]

Port of Saints [first version], Covent Garden, London, 1973 [1975] [limited edition]

The Book of Breething, Ou, Ingatestone, Essex, 1974 [reprinted in *Ah Pook Is Here*]

The Job [second version in English], Grove, New York, 1973

Sidetripping [text to photographs by Charles Gatewood], Strawberry Hill, New York, 1975

Snack, Aloes, London, 1975 [mimeo]

The Last Words of Dutch Schultz [revised version], Viking, New York, 1975

Cobblestone Gardens, Cherry Valley, Cherry Valley, New York, 1976

The Retreat Diaries, City Moon, New York, 1976

Colloque de Tanger [with Brion Gysin; conference papers, in French], Christian Bourgeois, Paris, 1976

Junky [unexpurgated version], Penguin, New York, 1977

Oeuvre Croisée [with Brion Gysin] [*The Third Mind*, in French], Flammarion, Paris, 1977

The Third Mind [with Brion Gysin], Viking, New York, 1978

Letters to Allen Ginsberg, Givaudon/Am Here, Geneva, 1976 [limited edition, reprinted Full Court, New York, 1982]

Naked Scientology [with *Ali's Smile*], Expanded media, Bonn, 1978 [bilingual edition]

Colloque de Tanger, vol 2 [with Brion Gysin and Gerard-Georges Lemaire; conference papers, in French], Christian Bourgeois, Paris, 1979

Blade Runner, a Movie, Blue Wind, Berkeley, 1979

Dr Benway [variant text], Brad Morrow, Santa Barbara, 1979 [limited edition]

Scrapbook 3, Claude Givaudan, Geneva, 1979 [facsimile colour Xerox; limited edition]

Ah Pook Is Here, John Calder, London, 1979

Port of Saints [revised version], Blue Wind, Berkeley, 1980

The Streets of Chance, Red Ozier, New York, 1981 [limited edition]

Early Routines, Cadmus, Santa Barbara, 1981 [limited edition]

Cities of the Red Night, Holt Rinehart, New York, 1981

Sinki's Sauna, Pequod, New York, 1982 [limited edition]

Mummies [with Carl Apfelschnitt], Gunnar Kaldewey, Düsseldorf, 1982

A William Burroughs Reader [edited by John Calder], Picador, London, 1982

The Place of Dead Roads, Holt Rinehart, New York, 1983

Ruski, Hand Job, New York [limited edition], 1984

The Four Horsemen of the Apocalypse, Expanded media, Bonn, 1984 [bilingual edition]

The Burroughs File, City Lights, San Francisco, 1984

The Adding Machine, Collected Essays, John Calder, London, 1985

Queer, Viking, New York, 1985

The Cat Inside [with Brion Gysin], Grenfell, New York, 1986 [limited edition, reprinted Viking, New York, 1992 without the Gysin illustrations]

The Western Lands, Viking, New York, 1987

The Whole Tamale, Horse [nd, np] [mimeo]

Apocalypse [with Keith Haring], George Mulder Fine Arts, New York, 1988 [limited edition]

Interzone, Viking, New York, 1989

The Valley [with Keith Haring], George Mulder Fine Arts, New York, 1988 [limited edition]

Tornado Alley, Cherry Valley, Cherry Valley, New York, 1989

Ghost of Chance [with George Condo], Whitney Museum of American Art, New York, 1991 [limited edition, reprinted without the Condo illustrations, Serpent's Tail, London, 1995]

Seven Deadly Sins, Lococo-Mulder Fine Art, New York, 1992 [limited edition]

Painting and Guns, Hanuman, Madras and New York, 1992

The Letters of William S. Burroughs 1945 to 1959 [edited by Oliver Harris], Viking-Penguin, New York, 1993

My Education, Viking, New York, 1995

Word Virus, the William Burroughs Reader [edited by James Grauer-holz], Grove, New York, 1998

Hibbard, Allen [ed]. *Conversations With William S. Burroughs*. University Press of Mississippi, Jackson, 1999

Last Words, the Final Journals, Grove, New York, 2000

SELECTED DISCOGRAPHY

Call Me Burroughs, English Bookshop, Paris, 1965 [album]; 1995 [CD]

Ali's Smile, Unicorn, 1971 [album accompanying book of the text]

Nothing Here Now But the Recordings, Industrial Records, 1981 [album]

[with Laurie Anderson and John Giorno] *You're the Guy I Want To Share My Money With*. Giorno Poetry Systems, 1981 [album and CD]

Break Through in Grey Room, Sub Rosa [nd] [album and CD]

[with Gus Van Sant] *The Elvis of Letters*, TK Records, 1985 [CD single]

[with Material] *Seven Souls*, Virgin, 1989 [CD and CD single]

Dead City Radio, Island, 1990 [CD]

[with Kurt Cobain] *The 'Priest' They Called Him*, TK Records, 1992 [CD single]

[with Ministry] *Just One Fix*, Sire, 1992 [CD]

Vaudeville Voices, Grey Matter, 1993 [bootleg] [CD]

Spare Ass Annie and Other Tales, Island, 1993 [CD]

Naked Lunch, Warner, 1995 [2-CD]

The Best of William Burroughs From Giorno Poetry Systems, Mercury, 1998 [4 CD box]

[with Material] *The Road to the Western Lands*, Triloka/Mercury, 1998 [CD]

'Burroughs Reading' on [compilation] *OU* Revuedisque 40-41, 1972 [album]

'Burroughs Reading' on [compilation] *OU* Revuedisque 42-43-44, 1973 [album]

'Sharkey's Night' on Laurie Anderson: *Mr Heartbreak*, Warner Bros, 1984 [CD]

'Language Is a Virus' on Laurie Anderson: *Home of the Brave*, 1986 [CD]

'Words of Advice' and 'Kim, Like the Great Gatsby' on [compilation] *Smack My Crack*, Giorno Poetry Systems, 1987 [CD]

'Just Say No To Drug Hysteria' and 'Dead Souls' on [compilation] *Like a Girl, I Want You to Keep Coming*, Giorno Poetry Systems, 1989

'For Here To Go' on [compilation] *10% File Under Burroughs*, Sub Rosa, 1993

'The Do Rights' and 'Naked Lunch' on [compilation] *Cash Cow*, Giorno Poetry Systems, 1993 [CD]

[with Material] 'Words of Advice' on Material: *Hallucination Engine*, Island, 1994 [CD]

'Words of Advice for Young People' on [compilation] *Big Hard Disk Vol 2*, Smash, 1994 [CD]

'Mr Rick Paris' on [compilation] *Cough It Up*, TK Records, 1995

[voice over] *The Dark Eye*, Inscape, 1995 [CD ROM game]

[with R.E.M.] 'Star Me Kitten' on [compilation] *Songs in the Key of X*, Warner, 1996 [CD]

'What Keeps Mankind Alive?' on [compilation] *September Songs*, Sony, 1997 [CD]

[1974 interview with Gerard Malanga] on Gerard Malanga: *Up From the Archives*, Sub Rosa, 1999

ABOUT WILLIAM BURROUGHS

de Loach, Allen [ed]: *Special Burroughs Issue: Intrepid* 14/15, Buffalo, New York, 1969

Mottram, Eric: *William Burroughs: The Algebra of Need*, Beau Fleuve, Coach House, Toronto, 1971

Miles Associates [Barry Miles]: *A Descriptive Catalogue of the William S. Burroughs Archive*, Covent Garden, London, 1973

Mikriammos, Philippe: *William Burroughs, la Vie et l'Oeuvre*, Seghers, Paris, 1975

Goodman, Michael B: *William S. Burroughs: An Annotated Bibliography of His Works and Criticism*, Garland, New York, 1975

Mottram, Eric: *William Burroughs: The Algebra of Need* [revised edition], Marion Boyars, London, 1977

Maynard, Joe and Miles, Barry: *William S. Burroughs. A Bibliography, 1953–73*, Bibliographical Society of the University of Virginia, University Press of Virginia, Charlottesville, 1978

Goodman, Michael Barry: *Contemporary Literary Censorship: The Case History of Burroughs' Naked Lunch*, Scarecrow, Metuchen, N.J., 1981

Bockris, Victor: *With William Burroughs, A Report From the Bunker*, Seaver, New York, 1981

Vale [ed]: *William S. Burroughs, Brion Gysin and Throbbing Gristle. Re/Search 4/5*: A Special Book Issue, San Francisco, 1982

Ely, Roger [ed]: *The Final Academy: Statements of a Kind* [np], London, 1982

O'Brien, John [ed]: *William S. Burroughs Number: The Review of Contemporary Fiction*, v4. No 1. Elmwood Park, Ill. Spring, 1984

Skerl, Jennie: *William Burroughs*, Twayne, Boston, 1985

Ansen, Alan: *William Burroughs*, Water Row, Sudbury, Mass., 1986

Lemaire, Gerard-Georges: *Burroughs*, Editions Artifact, Paris, 1986

Lydenberg, Robin: *Word Cultures, Radical Theory and Practice in William S. Burroughs' Fiction*, University of Illinois Press, Urbana, 1987

Morgan, Ted: *Literary Outlaw, the Life and Times of William S. Burroughs*, Henry Holt, New York, 1988

Grauerholz, James: *On Burroughs' Art*, Suzanne Biederberg Gallery, Amsterdam, 1988

Goodman, Michael B and Coley, Lemuel B: *William S. Burroughs, A Reference Guide*, Garland, New York, 1990

Skerl, Jennie and Lydenberg, Robin [eds]: *William S. Burroughs At the Front, Critical Reception, 1959–1989*, Southern Illinois University Press, Carbondale, 1991

Bockris, Victor: *William Burroughs, Cool Cats, Furry Cats, Aliens, But No Purring* [nd] 1991 [limited edition]

Vilà, Christian: *William S. Burroughs, Le Génie Empoisonné*, Editions du Rocher, Paris, 1992

Miles, Barry: *William Burroughs, El Hombre Invisible*, Virgin, London, 1992

Silverberg, Ira [ed]: *Everything Is Permitted, the Making of Naked Lunch*, Grafton, London, 1992

William Burroughs

Ambrose, Joe; Wilson, Terry and Rynne, Frank [eds]: *Man From Nowhere, Storming the Citadels of Enlightenment with William Burroughs and Brion Gysin*, Gap/Subliminal, Dublin, 1992

Cecil, Paul [ed]: *A William Burroughs Birthday Book*, Temple, London, 1994

Köhler, Michael [ed]: Weissner, Carl: *Burroughs, Eine Bild-Bio-graphie*, Dirk Nishen, Berlin, 1994

García-Robles, Jorge: *La Bala Perdida: William S. Burroughs en México (1949–1952)*, Ediciones del Milenio, Mexico City, 1995

Bockris, Victor: *With William Burroughs, A Report From the Bunker* [revised edition], St Martin's, Griffin, New York, 1996

Sobieszek, Robert A: *Ports of Entry: William S. Burroughs and the Arts*, Los Angeles County Museum of Art, Los Angeles, 1996

Murphy, Timothy S: *Wising Up the Marks, the Amodern William Burroughs*, University of California Press, Berkeley, 1997

Caveney, Graham: *The 'Priest', They Called Him: the Life and Legacy of William S. Burroughs*, Bloomsbury, London, 1997

Loydell, Rupert [ed]: *My Kind of Angel: I.M. William Burroughs*, Stride Conversation, Exeter, Devon, 1998

Mahoney, Denis; Martin, Richard L. and Whitehead, Ron [eds]: *A Burroughs Compendium, Calling the Toads*, Ring Tarigh, Antwerp, 1998

Shoaf, Eric C: *William S. Burroughs: Time. Place. Word*, Brown University, Providence, RI, 2000

Miles, Barry: *The Beat Hotel: Ginsberg, Burroughs & Corso in Paris, 1957–1963*, Grove, New York, 2000

Grauerholz, James W: *The Death of Joan Vollmer Burroughs: What Really Happened?*, American Studies Dept, University of Kansas, Lawrence, 2002

Index

William Burroughs